Hopitutuwutsi
Hopi Tales

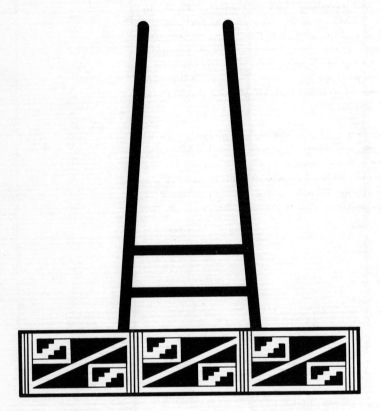

Hopitutuwutsi
Hopi Tales

A Bilingual Collection of Hopi Indian Stories

by Ekkehart Malotki
illustrated by Anne-Marie Malotki

Museum of Northern Arizona Press

Ekkehart Malotki, born in Germany, came to the United States in 1967. He has studied English and Latin philology at the universities of Freiburg and Hamburg and received his Ph.D. in linguistics from the University of Münster for his work on the spatial concepts in the Hopi language. He is now an assistant professor of languages at Northern Arizona University, Flagstaff, where he has taught German, Latin, and Hopi. His main field of research is Hopi linguistics. He is currently engaged in a semantic study of Hopi time expressions and has additional collections of Hopi folklore in the planning.

Anne-Marie Malotki is a native of the French-speaking part of Switzerland. She gained her design experience while working with architects in Switzerland and Germany. She came to the United States with her husband and has assisted him in his Hopi research. She is presently teaching French in the evening division at Northern Arizona University and is pursuing her work in the graphic arts.

Hopisinmuy amungem

To the Hopi people

Contents

vii

List of Illustrations

X

Some years ago I started learning Hopi with the intention of examining the accuracy of Benjamin Lee Whorf's startling observation, that he had discovered in Hopi a language that "contains no reference to 'time', either explicit or implicit." I had at that time no idea that one day a collection of Hopi folklore would be the byproduct of my linguistic research. However, in the course of my fieldwork I realized that traditional folktales were a particularly rich source for expressions of time. While I have now been able to disprove Whorf's thesis, I must confess that, at the start, his science-fiction notion of a people endowed with a timeless language was fascinating both to me and my Hopi teacher, Herschel Talashoma, from the Third Mesa village of Bakavi.

All the tales were narrated to me by Herschel Talashoma. To him as a teacher and storyteller, but also as a friend, I credit the existence of this book. Of all the people who assisted me, my gratitude goes first of all to him.

Thanks are also due to a number of people who helped in the preparation of the manuscript. Michael Lomatewama and Emory Sekaquaptewa checked all or sections of the Hopi text. Barbara Gantt, Arnold Johnson, Margaret Malkind, Frank Bonham, and Debby Park read the English version or portions of it. Karl Luckert added valuable suggestions concerning the introduction and the glossary.

To Hermann K. Bleibtreu, director of the Museum of Northern Arizona, who has given to the Museum's publication program a new direction, I am especially grateful for effecting the bilingual publication of these tales. In addition, I wish to express my admiration and appreciation for the work of Sandra Mahan, Gary McClellan, Rita Arnold, Steve Gustafson, and Ursula Luckert which they did under the direction of Rick Stetter.

The greatest share of my gratitude goes naturally to my wife. Her enthusiasm for learning with me the Hopi language, her help and encouragement in all phases of the editing process were an everpresent source of strength.

Preface

Aliksa'i is the traditional story opener which, in the Hopi dialect area of Third Mesa, serves as a signal to an audience that the storyteller is about to begin his narrative. Its true etymology is not known, but the interjection *ali* 'good, delicious, delightful' may be part of it. Whatever its origin, the utterance has a somewhat magical effect on the expectations of the listener. Now he knows that he is in for some true and original entertainment from one of the hundreds of tales, legends, or myths which make up the extensive body of Hopi oral literature.

The Hopi word for the genre of folklore presented here is *tuuwutsi*. To illuminate the makeup of this word, the Hopi linguist will begin by singling out the adjective *wutsi* which signifies 'false', in the sense of 'make-believe' or 'not real'. It is here fused with the prefix *tuu-* which conveys the idea of 'unspecified, nonhuman objects'. The overall content of *tuuwutsi* thus adds up to something like 'many false or make-believe things'. This notion corresponds, of course, precisely to our intuitive understanding of 'tale' or 'story'.

A good storyteller will be described as a *tuwutsmoki,* literally 'story bag', which implies that he is a 'storehouse of oral tradition'. He will always make it clear to his audience whether a particular story is just a piece of fiction or an actual occurrence from Hopi history, such as a clan migration, the downfall of a former Hopi town, etc. *I' hapi pas qa yaw'i, pas antsa* ('This is not hearsay, this is really true'), will be his closing words.

The purpose for incorporating in this introductory chapter a few in-depth analyses of Hopi words is to make the nonnative reader realize that the linguistic and cultural reality behind these tales is all Hopi. The degree of sophistication of the Hopi language is equal to that of English and of any other language. The unjustified notion of so-called primitive peoples or cultures is frequently accompanied by the proposition that their languages must of necessity be primitive also. The present collection of Hopi tales is presented bilingually to counter this belief, a belief which is largely due to a non-Hopi society which attaches more significance to written language

Introduction

than to spoken language. Many consider the absence of an alphabet and writing sufficient justification to call a language primitive.

For the Hopi reader a portion of his oral tradition is thereby preserved in writing. Once instruction in Hopi reading and writing becomes a curriculum reality at the reservation schools, it will be readily available to him. As for the nonnative reader, the visual impact of Hopi orthography should impress the fact that Hopi is the donor language of these tales and that their English translations are but attempts to approximate the reality of the original in a medium that is widely understood.

Folklore is universal, of course. Every people has responded to its innate imagination and has produced stories around themes of specific needs, desires, goals, frustrations, and taboos which in day-to-day living could not be satisfied or coped with. There exist in folkloristic traditions many motifs and plots which are universally shared and also many restrictions which are prevalent on a worldwide scale. The restrictions concern primarily the time of day and season during which storytelling is permitted.

Hopi custom is no exception. Although a specific day-taboo is absent, and although tale-telling is not limited to nighttime, Hopi tradition is adamant about its summer-taboo. *"Hakiy taala' tuutuwutsqw hakiy tsuu'a kuukingwu,"* explicitly warns a person: "Whoever tells a story in the summertime will be bitten by the rattlesnake." When inquiring about the proper tale-telling time, some Hopi will explain that a storyteller is safe during the cold season and as long as the ground remains frozen. Others specify the month of *Kyaamuya* as storytelling season par excellence and actually refer to that month as *tuwutsmuyaw* or 'storytelling month'.

Kyaamuya corresponds to portions of our December and January. It is considered a very dangerous month and one of the most sacred periods of the Hopi year. The highlight of the religious observances during this season is the *Soyal* or winter solstice ceremony, basically a rite of rebirth. It concentrates efforts to turn back the sun, to initiate a new cycle of life and

xiv

growth. Understandably, there is a multitude of taboos and restrictions which need to be heeded during that month. No animal is to be harmed or killed. No knocking at the door must take place before entering somebody's house. Walking about in public should be soft and subdued. If someone needs to venture outdoors after dark, he should at least smear some ashes on his face—else the moon will drop its blood on him. Any kind of digging is strictly forbidden as the ground is not to be disturbed. Anyone acting contrary to this taboo will ruin his life. Also, one never cuts one's hair during this period, because *Kyaamuya* would build a nest with it. As a result the person would become ill. The only safe place is the inside of the house, a natural place to be during the month of storytelling.

Surprisingly, there are no injunctions on the content of the tales. Anything that will entertain or amuse is appropriate. The Hopi folklore tradition encompasses the full range from simple children's stories to coyote tales, ghost tales, witchcraft narratives, edifying fables, legends, sacred myths, and true historic accounts.

The audience is obliged to answer the narrator in unison. Every complete sentence by him is confirmed with a short expletive *oh* from the listeners. This tells the storyteller that he is still sustaining the interest of the group.

Formerly storytelling happened nearly every evening during *Kyaa-muya*. Whole households came together for the occasion, and everybody, from small children to great-grandparents was present. Occasionally every grown-up member in the audience would contribute his own story. The Hopi language provides a special term for this custom—*tuwuts-qöniwma*—which says 'story turning in a circle'. Today, with the increasing disintegration of Hopi family ties, with color TV, comics, and other mass media entertainment making inroads, Hopi folklore tradition is moribund. With the passing away of the old storytellers, the Hopi folklore tradition now suffers irreparable losses every year.

XV

By presenting this bilingual collection of Hopi tales, an attempt is being made not only to salvage some of the priceless literary heritage of this tribe but also to encourage similar undertakings by the Hopi themselves. Cassette recorders, which are today part of nearly every reservation household, can be used quite effectively in preserving the oral traditions. In addition to Kennard's *Field Mouse Goes to War,* the only Hopi folklore project so far that has led to bilingual publications, was that undertaken by the Northern Arizona Supplementary Education Center.

Hopi tales have been collected by ethnologists, anthropologists, and missionaries as far back as the turn of the century and earlier. However, with the exception of a few interspersed Hopi words, phrases, or songs, they were recorded exclusively in English. Most of these are now tucked away in scholarly journals of folklore and anthropology, old museum notes, master's theses, and other such records. Frequently these recordings feature simply abstracts or plot capsules, which are of interest only to the folklore specialist who happens to compile motif indices.

Other tales which have surfaced in popular magazines or in more accessible publications quite often constitute only derived versions from the above mentioned sources. All too often they have been bowdlerized of all supposedly unprintable words or actions; they have been watered down to make them marketable as children's stories. Thus emasculated and stripped of their authenticity and vigor, they add to the distorted image which surrounds the American Indian today.

While some readers may feel offended by earthy and obscene elements in these tales, these elements are nevertheless an integral part of folk literatures all over the world. Obscenities, whether sexual or excretory, must be seen as a vital ingredient in primal humor. Hopi society manages to cope with so-called obscene matters in a much healthier and a more natural way than its white counterpart. This is so because Hopi children grow up in a linguistic atmosphere where people call a spade a spade. Hopi language

xvi

is not stocked with euphemisms or other erudite borrowings which would be used to cover up certain so-called dirty words or actions. It is also interesting to note that while it is frank and outspoken in its humor, the Hopi language does not even come close to anything that corresponds to a swearword in English. It goes without saying, that ever since the day of contact with Anglo-Americans, borrowing of English four-letter words and swearwords has contributed noticeably to the growth of the Hopi vocabulary. To the reader who is familiar with the stereotypic interpretation of the tribal name *Hopiitu* as 'The Peaceful Ones', the violence which is portrayed in a number of the tales may be more shocking than an occasional obscenity. Ruth Benedict's comparison of Plains and Pueblo Indians, in which she characterized the former as Dionysian and the latter as Apollonian, may indeed have brainwashed many people with false expectations. To be sure, counting coup by touching an enemy in the midst of his camp was never a Hopi ideal. But acts of violence were just as much a part of Hopi society as they were in societies elsewhere in this world. The destruction of the Hopi village of Awatovi, in which most of the inhabitants were murdered, is sufficient proof that the Hopi people have not eliminated violence from their actions. A quick glance at the available corpus of Hopi folk tales reveals that cruelties, atrocities, and death are among the most frequent themes and motifs encountered. And this observation can probably be generalized for most folkloristic traditions of the world.

Folklore shows considerable affinity to dreams. What in reality is shunned, feared, tabooed, or outright impossible may find some sort of fulfillment in folkloristic fantasy. Thus, in a closely knit society, such as Hopi, one of the many functions of folk tales may be to provide an avenue of escape from the social restrictions, much as the antics of Hopi clowns provide comic relief from the pace of a somber ceremony.

Of course, no translation will do full justice to the original in all respects. The well-known Italian proverb, *traduttori tradittori,* which identifies translators with traitors, is valid most certainly in this case. That a translation of anything into another language fails to capture the sounds and intonational patterns of the original is, of course, a truism. More crucial are, however, the various connotations of a given word which are lost in the process of translation. The English versions in this book must, therefore, be taken as approximate equivalents. They are neither totally free translations, nor are they faithful renditions of every word that can be found in the Hopi text. A so-called literal translation has not been intended here. More weight was given to readability. Minor changes, such as replacing a Hopi pronoun with its referent, the occasional insertion of a word for clarification, or the omittance of a redundant phrase, were made intentionally as part of the editor's chores. A good narrator does not only draw from his acoustic repertoire, singing and chanting included, but will also rely heavily on facial mimicry and on physical gestures. These are elements a written record can not capture. A written document, and even more so a written translation, is and will remain a substitute. The present effort is no exception.

The illustrations which accompany the text are derived from several sources. A few decorative elements are of Anasazi provenience. Some are inspired by the mural decorations of historic and prehistoric kivas, such as were excavated at the Pueblo sites of Awatovi, Kawaika-a, and Pottery Mound. Many were drawn from Hopi ceramics, primarily from the finds at the ancient ruin of Sikyatki. A large number of them are near-copies or adaptations of Mimbres figurative bowl designs. Others were created especially for this edition.

The style of the illustrations avoids the current trend toward naturalism. For thousands of years American Indian art has aspired to the principle of abstract and highly geometric representation. Pueblo artists in the Southwest, especially, have always excelled in this stylistic approach. The esthetically successful blend of primitive-simple and stylized-geometric elements is both fascinating and timeless. It is found in petroglyphic and pictographic rock iconography, in basketry ornamentation, ceramic design and woven fabric patterns, sculptured clay and cottonwood carvings, and finally in jewelry and architectural structures. The time span of this art embraces the nameless weaver of a bifurcated burden basket in prehistoric times, the internationally applauded jewelry artistics of the Loloma studio today, and many generations of artists in between.

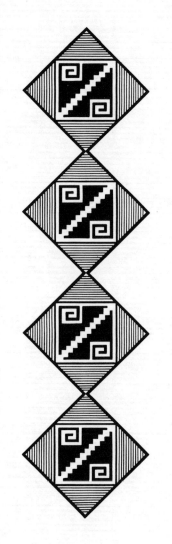

Pöqangwhoyat So'yokot aw Orayvituy amungem Naa'oya

How the So'yoko Monsters Were Killed by the Pöqangwhoyas

Aliksa'i. Yaw Orayve yeesiwa. Yaw pep sinom wukoyesiwa. Noq yaw puma pep Orayvit hisat pay yukyiq kwiniwiq pu' hoopoq komokwisngwu. Pu' pay ima momoyam piw Orayviy kwiniwi paavatnit aw kuywisngwu.

Noq yaw hisat hak komoktot pay yaw pas qa pitu. Noq pay yaw as puma hepyat, pay yaw pas puma qa tutwa. Pu' yaw piw hisat hak maana kuytot, piw pam yaw qa pitu. Noq pay yaw pas kur sinom hin wuuwaya, haqami puma hin hiniwtiqw. Noq pu' yaw oovi aapiy pantaqw, pay yaw himuwa panhaqam haqaminen, pay yaw pas qa ahoy pitungwu. Nungwu yaw wuuhaqniiqam kur haqamiya.

Noq pu' yaw hisat hak mongwit ep pitu. Pu' yaw aw pangqawu, "Pas hapi itam son it hiita as qa hepyani. Pay pi son himu yangqw sinmuy haqami qa hintsakqw oovi pas wuuhaqniiqam kur haqamiya."

Aliksa'i. People were living in Oraibi. There was a large settlement there. And long ago the Oraibi people would go north and east for wood. The women, also, had the habit of going to the water holes north of the village to get water.

One day someone who had gone after firewood failed to return. They searched for him, but could not find him. Then, another time, a girl who had gone to fetch water did not come back. The people simply could not imagine what had happened to these two. And that is how it was from that time on. If a person went somewhere for firewood or water, he did not come home again. A great number of people disappeared during this time.

One day a villager came to the chief and said, "We really have to look for this being, whatever it is. It is quite obvious that someone or something is carrying off the people, because so many have disappeared."

1

"Hep owi," yaw mongwi kita, "pay nu' piw pan wuuwanta, niikyangw pas nu' kur hakiy aw taqa'nangwtini. Pay pi as qa suus yangqw ima put hiita hepmayat, pay pi qa tutwa. Noq oovi pay nu' kur yuk kwiningqöymi Pöövöqangwtuy awni. Puma kya pay as sen put hiita tuwani," kita yaw mongwi. Pu' yaw pay oovi i' hak pangqw nima.

Ep pu' yaw mihikqw i' mongwi Pöövöqangwtuy amungem paas yuwsi. Panis yaw oovi pam pantit pay yaw pam paasatniqwhaqam pangqw aw'i. Pu' yaw pam ep pituuqe amumiq paki, Pöövöqangwtuy aqwa'. Noq yaw naat Pöqangwhoyat tatatsi. Pas pi yaw qa unangwtala. Yaw qa navota pam pakikqö'. So'amsa yaw kur pay navotqe, pu' yaw oovi put qatu'a'awna. Paasat pu' yaw as Pöqangwhoyatuy amumi pangqawu, "Huvam qe'ti'i, hak pakii'," yaw amumi kita. Qa ngas'ew yaw navota. Pu' yaw as pi'epningwu, "Huvam qe'ti'i, hak pakii'." Pay yaw pas kur puma son navotni. Soy yaw e'nang tatatstinuma. Yaw oovi puma pantsakqw, pu' yaw so'am tatsiyamuy atsvewta.

Pas paasat pu' yaw qe'ti. Pu' yaw soy aw pangqawu, "Pew tavi'i, naat itam kwangwa'ewlawu."

Paasat pu' yaw so'am amumi pangqawu, "Hak paki." Pas paasat pu' yaw kur puma put tuwa. Paasat pu' yaw nawus sunyuku.

Noq pu' yaw so'am put tuuvingta, "Ta'a, son pi um qa hiita oovi waynuma," yaw put aw kita.

"Hep owi, pay yep Orayve imuy itimuy sumataq himu haqami hintsakqw, oovi pay pas wuuhaqniiqam kur haqamiya. Pay himuwa komoktot, pay qa pitungwu. Pu' piw himuwa maqte' qa pitungwu. Pu' ima momoyam, mamant, pay himuwa kuyte' pay qa pitungwu. Noq pay pi son himu kya pumuy haqami qa hintsakqw, oovi pas wuukohaqamiya. Paniqw oovi nu' angqö. Pay kya as ima sen itamungem put hiita hepniniqw oovi'o."

"Yes," the chief replied, "I have been worrying about this too, but I can't ask anyone for help. More than once people from here have tried to discover this creature, but were not able to find it. I intend, therefore, to go to the north and pay a visit to the Pöövöqangwt family. I believe they might be successful in finding out something." After listening to these words, the visitor went home.

That same evening the chief carefully prepared all the things that usually appeal to the Pöövöqangwt. As soon as he had accomplished this, he went on his way late at night. When he arrived at the house of the Pöövöqangwt, he entered. As usual, the two Pöqangwhoya boys were playing shinny. Nothing could distract them. They did not even notice that the chief had entered. Only their grandmother heard him and invited him to sit down. Then she turned to the boys and said, "Stop playing, someone has come in." But the twin brothers did not pay any attention to her words. Again and again she appealed to them, "Stop it! Someone has come in." But they just would not listen. They even entangled her and dragged her along in their game. Because they were carrying on in such a manner, the grandmother sat down on their shinny ball.

Now they came to a halt and said to her, "Give us our ball back; we're still having a good time."

But she replied, "Someone has come in." Only then did they notice the visitor and quieted down.

Their grandmother said to the chief, "Well, you must have come for a purpose."

"Yes, of course. In Oraibi where I live, some kind of creature is apparently carrying off our people to an unknown place, because so many of them have disappeared. Whenever a person goes out to gather firewood, he fails to return. Also, if someone goes hunting, he doesn't come back. Someone or something must be responsible for doing this, because so many people have vanished. That's the reason I have come. I was wondering if perhaps the Pöqangwhoyas could find this creature for us."

3

"Antsa'a," yaw so'wuuti kita, "pay pi son ima qa pantini. Pay ason oovi qaavo ima umungem antsa put hiita hepni," kita yaw awi'.

"Kur antsa'ay," yaw pam aw kita, "noq yep nu' it umungem kiva." Pu' yaw pam amumi put hiita yukuutaqay amumi oya. Yaw haalaytoti. Yantit pu' yaw pam pangqaqw nima. Pay yaw nukwangwnavota.

Paasat pu' yaw Pöqangwhoyatuy so'am amumi pangqawu, "Qaavo hapi uma it umuutahay heptoni. Pay pam hapi yep Orayve sinmuy haqami hintsaki. Noq uma hapi oovi qaavo yukyiq kwiniwiq heptoni. Pay pang pam soosovik waynumngwu. Pay uma son haqam aw qa pituni. Niikyangw uma aw pite', uma hapi paasni. Pam hapi pas tokotsi. Noq oovi uma paapu paasni," yanhaqam yaw amumi so'am lavayti.

Noq pay yaw piw puma qa tuptsiwa, niiqe yaw naami pangqawlawu, "Son pi pas hintani. Son pi pas hakiy hintsanni, naamahin pi kya antsa tokotsi," yan yaw hingqawkyangw puma na'uytaya'iwta. Pu' yaw oovi puma qavomi kwangwtoykyangw hisatniqw puuwi.

Pu' yaw antsa taalawva. Yaw puma kwangwtoya hakiy taahay heptoniqe. Pu' yaw oovi puma hisatniqw nakwsu. Kiy angqw kwiniwiq yaw puma nakwsu. Noq pay pi yaw puma pas sutsep tatatsngwuniiqe pay yaw piw puma tatatstima. Pantsakma yaw pumaniiqe pay yaw pas puma qa hoyta. Sun pi yaw a'ni puma tatatstuwiy'taqe oovi pas yaw qa hoyokngwu. Nawis'ew pu' yaw puma haqami hoqlöy'taqat aw pitu. Pep pu' yaw puma hoqlöva tatatstinuma. Pas pi yaw puma kwangwa'ewlawqe, paas yaw kur puma suutoki hiita oovi pansoqniiqe, qa hin yaw puma hiita hepnumniqay anta.

Naat yaw oovi puma pas qa unangwtalqw, yaw kur himu pumuy aw pituqw, puma qa navota. Pas yaw sukwat ngu'aqw, pu' puma navota. Pu' yaw it ngu'aaqat pamwa yaw a'ni itsivuti. "Nuy maatavi'i," yaw aw kita, "taq nu' pas pay pö'ani." Pu' yaw a'ni rohomti. Noq pay yaw sumatavi.

Pu' yaw piw puma tatatsi. Paasat pu' yaw piw ahoy ngu'a. Pas yaw paasat pu' pam aw yori. Uti yaw himu qa soniwa. Pas yaw paasat pu' puma

4

"Of course," replied the old woman, "they can certainly do that. Rest assured that tomorrow they will search for it, whatever it is."

"Good," the chief replied. "Now here is what I have brought for all of you." He then handed them the gifts that he had made especially for them and they were happy. After that he started on his way home again. He had been successful. He had received a favorable response.

Now the grandmother of the two Pöqangwhoyas said to them, "Tomorrow you will set out and look for your uncle. He must be the one who is molesting the Oraibi people. So tomorrow you'll start out from here and go north to look for him. He usually roams around in that area. You are bound to meet him somewhere. But if you find him, you must be very careful. He is a wild beast of a man. So be very, very careful!"

The two, however, did not believe her, and said to each other, "He can't be that bad; he can't harm you that much, even if he's such a monster." They talked like this and secretly laughed. Looking forward then to the next morning, they went to bed early.

Soon after daylight they started out, all excited about their search for this uncle. They headed in a northerly direction, and since they were great shinny fans, they played along the way. They actually did not make much headway. Both of them played equally well and this was the reason that they hardly advanced. Finally, however, they reached a forest and played in it. They were enjoying themselves greatly and completely forgot why they had gone there. It never even occurred to them to search for anything!

They were so absorbed in their game that when a creature approached, they were unaware of it. But the instant it grabbed one of them, they noticed it. The boy that had been caught became furious. "Let me go," he demanded, "I was just about to defeat my brother." He struggled and resisted with all his might until the creature let him loose.

Again the two boys continued with their shinny game and again one of them was seized. Only then did he look at his captor. What a dreadful

u'na kur yaw puma as hiita heptoqay. Paasat pu' yaw pumuy amumi lavayti, "Uma qa hophoyatu. Nu' oovi umuy wikni," yaw amumi kita.

Pay yaw piw puma sunakwha. "Ta'ay," yaw aw kita. Paasat pu' yaw pumuy soma. Pantit pu' yaw pumuy ho'apuy aqw pana. Pu' yaw paasat nakwsu. Pay pi yaw pumuyniqw kur haqami'. Noq pay yaw puma qa tsawiniwma. Pu' yaw pay kur puma piw hin naangaha, niiqe pay yaw puma qa somiwma. Haqam pu' yaw i' himu pumuy wikqa yaw naasungwna. Pu' yaw oovi ho'apuy tavi, nit pu' yaw owat aw kwangwataatsikt pay yaw suupuwva. A'ni yaw herorota. Noq pam hapi yaw kur So'yoko. Pam hapi yaw kur pumuy taaha'am. Pu' pay yaw kur pam piw Orayngaqw sinmuy kiy aw oo'oykyangw pumuy sowanta. Put hapi yaw kur puma hepto.

Pu' yaw oovi So'yoko kwangwavuwqw, yaw puma ho'apuyat angqw yama. Pantit pu' yaw puma aqw owat tangatat, pu' yaw puma na'uyta. Pu' yaw puma na'uyiy'kyangw aw taya'iwta. Hisatniqw pu' yaw taatayi, pu' yaw pangqawu, "Uti, pay kur nu' piw puwva, taq pi nu' ura hakimuy wiknuma, taq pi nu' pituqw itam qaavo naanasnani," kita yawi'. Paasat pu' yaw pam ho'apuy iikwiltat pu' yaw aqwhaqami'.

Paasat pu' yaw Pöqangwhoyat taya'iwkyangw pangqawlawu, "Owatsa iikwiwkyangw pas piw qaavo naasanniqay pangqawu," kitikyangw puma taya'iwta. Paasat pay yaw puma piw tatatstiva.

Pu' yaw So'yoko tuwat haqe'niikyangw yaw kur navota. Pas yaw pam a'ni putut iikwiwta. Pu' yaw pam aqw poota. Pay yaw owasa ho'apuyat angqw tangawta. Paasat pu' yaw a'ni itsivuti. "Pay pi pas nu' puye'em hiita iikwiwta," yaw kita. "Pay puma pas nu'an qa hopitniiqe oovi pay kur piw hin yama. Pay nu' songqa ahoyni," kitat, pu' yaw soosok owat ho'apuy angqw maspat, pu' yaw pam ahoyi.

Naat yaw oovi Pöqangwhoyat pas tsoniy'taqw, pay yaw piw ahoy amumi pitu. Pu' yaw amumi pangqawu, "Pay kur uma piw hin yama," yaw amumi kita. Pay yaw puma pas qa navotqay unangwti. Pu' yaw paasat pumuy piw ngu'a. "Pay nu' pas son umuy qa wikni. Pu' pay son uma waayani," yaw kita. Pu' yaw piw pumuy soma. Pu' yaw ho'apuy aqw pumuy ahoy pana. Paasat pu' yaw piw nakwsu.

monster it was! At that moment the brothers remembered that they had set out to look for something. The monster said to them, "You are bad boys. I will take you along with me."

Surprisingly enough, the two agreed. "All right," they said. With this he tied them up, shoved them in his carrying basket, and started out. They said later that he headed into an area unfamiliar to them. But they were not afraid. They even managed to untie themselves. Finally the creature stopped for a rest. It set the basket down, leaned comfortably against a rock and promptly fell asleep. It snored loudly. This creature was the So'yoko monster. He was their uncle and it was he who had been carrying the people from Oraibi off to his house to devour them. He was the one they had gone to search for.

When So'yoko was sound asleep, they climbed out of the basket. They put some rocks into it and then hid themselves. They laughed at him from their hiding place. After a time he woke up and exclaimed, "Darn it, I dozed off again. I shouldn't have done that. After all, I have these boys with me and we'll have a lavish feast tomorrow after I return home." He shouldered his basket and continued on his journey.

The two Pöqangwhoyas laughed and kept saying, "There he is burdened down with rocks, and he insists that he is going to gorge himself tomorrow." And again they started beating the shinny ball around.

So'yoko noticed somewhere along the way that the burden on his back was awfully heavy. He cast a look into the basket and found only rocks. He became very angry. "I had a hunch I was carrying something odd on my back," he said. "Those two are a pair of good-for-nothings. I will have to go back." Angrily he threw all the rocks out of the basket and started back.

The Pöqangwhoya boys were still having a good time playing ball when he reached them. "So you got out!" he shouted at them, but they acted as if they had not heard. He snatched them up again. "Very well, this time you won't be able to run away." He bound them with ropes and shoved them back in his basket. Then he started out once more.

Pu' yaw pay puma piw hin hintsakkyangw naangaha. Pu' yaw as puma angqw hin yamakniqay naami pangqawma. Pu' yaw suukya pangqawu, "Noq pi songqa navotni itam yamakqö'. Oovi ason haqe' hotskit atpikniqw, pu' itam yamakni," yaw kita.

Pu' yaw oovi panmakyangw pu' yaw haqam wukohotskit atpikniqw, pu' yaw puma hotskit ep tsööpöltit pu' angqw yama. Yaw So'yoko qa navota. Pu' yaw puma put hotskit ang wuuvi. Pas yaw puma oomiq wuuvi. Pepeq pu' yaw puma tsokiwkyangw taya'iwta. Pangqawlawu yawi', "Qa hiita paniy'makyangw, pas piw qavomi kwangwtoyniy'ma," kitalawu yaw puma naami'.

Pu' yaw pay kur piw So'yoko navota, pas yaw ho'apu'at qa putu. Pu' yaw oovi pam ho'apuy piw aqw poota. Noq pay yaw piw sosompi'atsa angqw pakiwta. Paasat pu' yaw piw a'ni itsivuti. "Pay kur piw yamakqw nu' qa navota. Pay pas puye'em oovi nu' qa putut iikwiwta. Pay nu'niikyangw songqa piw ahoyni," kitat, pu' yaw piw ahoy ho'apuy iikwilta. Pu' yaw piw ahoyi. Hisatniqw pu' yaw piw ahoy pumuy amumi pitu. Pu' yaw amumi pangqawu, "Pay kur uma piw hin yama. Uma oovi pangqw hawni," yaw amumi kita.

Pu' yaw puma aw pangqawu, "Um peqw wuuve' itamuy hawnani," yaw puma aw kita.

"Hep uma hawni," yaw amumi kita. Pay yaw puma pas qa nakwha. Paasat pu' yaw So'yoko pangqawu, "Pay nu' son umuy qa hawnani, naamahin pi uma qa naawakna."

Kitat, paasat pu' yaw hiihiita hotskit atpipoq tsovalanta, kohot, pu' piw tuusaqat. Pantit pu' yaw qöqöha. "Pay nu' it uwiknaqw, son uma qa hawni," kitikyangw yaw qöqöha. Hisatniqw pu' yaw kur uwikna. Pu' yaw pangqawu, "Pay pu' songqa hawni. Pu' nu' ahoy ngu'ani." Yan yaw hingqawkyangw amutpikyaqe a'ni hiinuma.

Su'aw yaw oovi qööhi'at pas kwangwa'uwikqw, pu' yaw puma naami pangqawu, "Itam aqw sisiwkukni," yaw kita. Pu' yaw puma oovi qööhiyat aqw sisiwku. Pay yaw puma tookya.

But sure enough, the two brothers again managed to untie themselves. They were discussing their escape and one suggested, "He will surely notice it when we get out. Let's try it when he goes under a tree."

So when he walked under a big tree in a part of the forest, they pulled themselves up on the tree and escaped. So'yoko did not notice it. They climbed the tree, all the way to the top. There they sat, laughing and joking. "Look at him! Carrying an empty basket and looking forward to tomorrow," they kept saying to each other.

But at last So'yoko noticed that his basket was not heavy at all. He looked into it, and when he found only the discarded fetters in it, he was furious. "They made their getaway and I was not aware of it! I had a feeling that my basket was too light." Once more he shouldered his basket and started back. When he reached them, he roared, "Come down from that tree!"

But they replied, "Climb up here and try to get us down!"

"You come down," he yelled. But they refused. Thereupon So'yoko said, "Just wait. One way or another, I'll get you down."

He now started amassing all sorts of things like sticks and grass under the tree. After that he built a fire. "Once I have this burning, they are bound to come down." Mumbling like this, he built his fire. Finally, as he lit it, he said, "Now they will definitely come down. And when they do I'll get hold of them again." Confidently, he strode around right under them.

Just when his fire was flaming up nicely, the boys said to each other, "Let's piss down on it!" So they pissed down on his fire and extinguished it.

Paasat pu' yaw So'yoko piw itsivuti. "Puye'em, songqa yanhaqam hintini. Pay puma pas hiitu qa hophoyatu, pay niikyangw nu' songqa hawnani, naamahin pi qa naawakna." Kitat pu' yaw pikyay'ngway horokna. Paasat pu' yaw hotskit saavutiva. Pu' yaw pam pephaqam a'ni itsivu'iwkyangw hotskit tutku, saavulawu. Pay yaw oovi hiisavotiqw pay yaw hotski wayayayku. Oovi yaw pavan a'ni wayayaykuqw, pu' yaw So'yoko hotskit na'atsqökna. Paasat pu' yaw pay hotski pumuy enang wa'ö.

Yan pu' yaw pam pumuy piw ahoy ngu'a. Paasat pu' yaw piw ahoy pumuy soma. Pu' piw ahoy ho'apuy aqw pumuy pana. Pantit pu' yaw ho'apuy aqw huur soma. "Pu' pay son yamakni," yaw kitikyangw. Paasat pu' yaw piw ahoy pumuy iikwiltat pu' piw nakwsu. Paasat pu' yaw pay puma kur hin yamakni.

Pay yaw oovi wuuyavotiqw yaw kur puma haqami öki. Pephaqam yaw kur i' So'yoko kiy'ta. Pu' yaw kiy aw pituuqe, aqwhaqami pangqawu, "Pu' hapi nu' pas lööqmuy wikva. Uma oovi koysömiq qööyani. Itam qaavo pas naanasnani," kita yaw aqwhaqami'.

Pu' yaw hak angqaqw hingqawu, "Antsa'a, pay nu' aqw qööni. Noq antsa panis mukiitiqw, itam aqw pumuy amyani. Is ali, kur itam qaavo pas naanasnani," kita yawi'. Pam hapi yaw kur it So'yokot nööma'at.

Pu' yaw puma piw kur lööqmuy tiy'ta, So'yoknawuutim. Paasat pu' yaw oovi So'yokwuuti timuy ayata, "Uma koysömiq wuuhaq kohot oyani. Itam pas pavan mukinayat pu' aqw imuy amyani," kita yaw timuy awi'. Pu' yaw oovi So'yokhoyat koysömiq kohot oo'oya. Paasat pu' yu'am yaw aqw qööha.

Pu' yaw pumuy So'yoko kivaapeq pay haqami pösömiq tavi, ho'aput angqw pakiwtaqamuy. Pangqw pu' yaw puma naami pangqawlawu, "Itamuy kur tuupeni, noq oovi itam pay aapiy itaangahuy mömtsani. Pay songqa sumukiitini koysö'amu," kita yaw pumaniiqe, pu' yaw puma pay ngahuy mömtsa.

Pu' yaw So'yokwuuti koysömiq qööqe pu' yaw a'ni aqw qööna. Pavan yaw uuwingw koysöngaqw wupa'leleta. Paasat pu' yaw pangqawu, "Pay it

So'yoko's anger soared up again. "I knew that something of this sort would happen! But I'll get them down from there, despite everything." He pulled out his stone axe and started chopping down the tree. He was extremely irate while hacking away at the tree and cutting it into pieces. When he had toiled for a long time, the tree started to sway. As it began to topple, So'yoko pushed it over. The tree crashed to the ground, carrying both of the boys with it.

So once more So'yoko had caught them. He tied them up again and threw them in his basket. But this time he tied the lid shut. "They won't get away anymore," he said, putting them back on his shoulder and departing. Now there was no way for them to escape.

Many hours later they finally arrived at his destination. Apparently it was the place where the monster lived. Upon reaching his house, he shouted into it, "I have brought two, so fire up the ground oven! Tomorrow we will gorge ourselves."

A voice answered from inside, "Very well, I'll start the fire right now. As soon as the pit is hot, we'll throw them in. Will we have a delicious feast tomorrow!" The voice that answered him was that of So'yoko's wife.

The couple also had two children and it was to them that the So'yoko woman now said, "Put a lot of wood into the oven. Once it's good and hot, we'll bury these two in it." So the So'yoko children filled the oven with firewood and their mother lit the fire.

Meanwhile So'yoko deposited the two boys, who were still in the carrying basket, in a corner of the house. They said to each other, "They intend to roast us! Let's chew our medicine ahead of time. It'll be very hot, that pit." Hastily they chewed their medicine.

When the So'yoko woman had the fire soaring, she added a lot of fuel. The fire was shooting up in big flames out of the ground pit. "When this

11

panis tsootso'q, pay itam aqw pumuy amyani. Noq pay qaavo su'aw songqa paas mowa'iwtani," kita yawi'.

Paasat pu' yaw puma kivay epeq qööhiy aw maqaptsiy'kyaakyangw pay kwangwayese, So'yoknanatim. Pi'ep yaw taaqa pangqawngwu, "Kur haqawa qööhit aw poota'a, sen naat qa tsootso'a."

Pu' yaw himuwa piw aw kuyvatongwu. Hisatniqw pu' yaw kur tsootso'a. "Ta'ay, pay itam aqw amyani," yaw kitota. Pu' yaw paasat pumuy angqw koysömi iikiwma. Pep pu' yaw pumuy ho'apuy angqw horokna. Yaw oovi pumuy horoknaqw, yaw puma koysömiq yori. Pavan yaw paalakoro'ta, a'ni yaw muki, a'ni yaw töövu'iwta.

Paasat pu' yaw So'yoktaqa pangqawu, "Ta'ay, aqw tuvaa'." Pu' yaw oovi So'yokwuuti pumuy aqw tuuva. Paasat pu' yaw pumuy amumiq uuta.

Noq pumuy yaw panis aqw tuuvaqw, pu' yaw puma ngahuy pavoya. Pay yaw paasat koysö ahoy hukya. Pay yaw qa muki. Yan pay yaw puma piw qa hinti. Pu' yaw pay puma pangqaqw naami hiita kwangwayu'a'ata. So'yoknanatimuy yaw puma amumiq taya'iwta. "Pas piw kya wuuwantotaqw itam pay kwasiwma." Pay ii'it yaw puma pangqw naami yu'a'atakyangw taya'iwta. "Pay itam haak yangqwni," yaw naami kita. "Ason itam pay pas mihikqw pu' yamakni, pumuy tokvaqö'." Yan yaw puma naami pasiwna. Pu' yaw pay oovi puma pangqaqw pakiwta. Hisatniqw pu' yaw suukyawa pangqawu, "Pay kya tokvay, itam yamakni." Pu' yaw oovi puma pangqw as hin yamakni. Oomiq pi yaw puma qa pitungwu. Pu' yaw oovi paasat suukyawa sukwat oomiq tsöpaata. Paasat pu' yaw puma höta. Pu' yaw suukyawa angqw yama. Paasat pu' yaw pam angqw mitwat langakna. Yan yaw puma pangqw yama.

Pay yaw kur antsa paasat So'yoknanatim tookya. Paasat pu' yaw puma amumiq paki. Kwangwatokya yawi'. Paasat pu' yaw puma So'yoknawuutimuy timuyatuy tsöpaata, pu' yaw puma pumuy angqw koysömiq tsöpma. Pu' yaw puma pumuy pansoq tuuva. Pantit pu' yaw puma piw aqw ngahuy pavoya. Paasat pu' yaw koysö piw ahoy a'ni mukiiti. Paysoq yaw

12

burns down, we'll put them in and cover them up. By this time tomorrow they should be well done."

After that, the So'yokos sat down and made themselves comfortable in their house while waiting for the fire. Every so often the man would growl, "Someone check on the fire."

One of them would go and look in. Finally the fire was out. "Well, let's put them in," they said. So'yoko himself carried the boys on his back to the fire pit. There he pulled them out of his basket. Now that the brothers were out they were able to cast a glance into the pit. It was a red hole, exceedingly hot and glowing with smoldering embers.

Eagerly, the So'yoko man said, "Well, throw them in!" The So'yoko woman cast them in and closed the opening.

No sooner had she thrown them in than the boys spat their medicine out. Immediately the hot fire pit cooled down and it was not hot any more. Thus they remained unharmed. They talked and laughed at the So'yoko family. "They probably think we're turning into nice brown roasts in here." They talked like this and laughed heartily till one of them suggested, "Let's stay here for now. Later, when it's dark and they're asleep, we'll climb out." They decided to do this and stayed there until one of them said, "They should be asleep now. Let's get out." But when they tried to get out of the oven, they couldn't reach the ceiling. Therefore, one of them lifted the other up so that he could make an opening. Then he climbed out and pulled the other up.

The So'yokos slept all through this and were still asleep when the Pöqangwhoyas entered the house. They picked up both the So'yoko children, carried them to the fire pit and threw them in. Then they spat some of their medicine into the pit. Instantly it was red hot again. The So'yoko children were sizzling nicely after the opening was shut. "That's more like it," they said to each other. "That will be some feast the couple has tomorrow!"

13

So'yokhoyat kwangwatsiririta. Yantit pu' yaw puma pumuy aqw uuta. "Yantani," yaw naami kita, "pay qaavo naawuutim songqa naasanni."

Yantit pu' yaw puma piw angqw ahoy kiiyamuy aw'i. Paasat pu' yaw as puma haqami na'uytani. Noq pay pi yaw So'yoknawuutim pas kwangwavuwqe qa navota, puma amuqle' waynumqw. Pu' yaw puma wukosisivut tuwa. Haqe' yaw oovaqe kwap'iwta. "Pay itam put hiitawat aqw pakini," yaw naami kita. Paasat pu' yaw puma aqw wuuvi, haqe' siivu oyiiqat, pansoqa. Pu' yaw puma pas suswukosivut aqw paki. Pangqaqw pu' yaw puma puuwi.

Naat yaw oovi puma puwqw, pay yaw kur naawuutim taatayi. Su'its yaw tayta. Pu' yaw So'yoktaqa nöömay aw pangqawu, "Um qatupte' aw wukohurusuktani. Pay son itaasikwitpe qa paas mowati. Oovi um panis hurusukyukuqw, pay itam tuumoytani. Noq nu' pay uusavo oovi itaasikwitpey yaahani," kita yaw nöömay awi'. "Pay pi haak tsaayom puwni. Pay pi ason hisatniqw puma taataye', tuwat nösni," kita yawnit pu' yaw yamakma.

Paasat pu' yaw So'yokwuuti tuwat tuupataqe pu' yaw wukohurusuklawu. Su'aw yaw oovi pam hurusukyukuqw, pu' yaw koongya'at sikwitpet inkyangw paki. Pay yaw kur piw sukwat angqw kyatkuqe yaw put tuumoykyangw paki. Pu' yaw paasat pangqawu, "Is ali, pas kur itam naasanni," yaw kita.

14

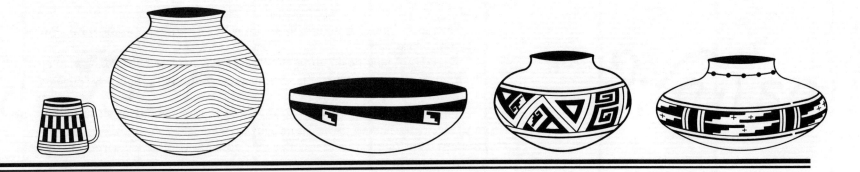

They went back to the house and looked for a place to hide. So'yoko and his wife were fast asleep and didn't even hear the boys when they walked past them. Then the Pöqangwhoyas spotted some large pots up on a shelf, all in a row. "Why don't we get into one of them?" they said at the same time. So they climbed up to the pots, crawled into the largest and fell asleep.

They were still sleeping when the So'yoko couple woke up, early for them. The So'yoko man said to his wife, "When you get up make a lot of *hurusuki*. Our roast should be well-done by now. As soon as you've prepared the pudding, we'll eat. I'll go ahead in the meantime and take the roast out of the pit. Let the children sleep for a while. They can eat later."

The So'yoko woman boiled some hot water and made a large amount of *hurusuki*. She had just finished when her husband came in with the roast. He had already bitten off a chunk from one and was chewing as he entered. "What a feast we're going to have!" he exclaimed.

15

"Hep owi," pu' yaw nööma'at aw kita. "Pay itam pay tuumoytani. Pay nu' yuku," kita yawi'.

Paasat pu' yaw oovi puma tuumoyta. Pavan yaw alilitikyangw pi'ep yaw himuwa pangqawngwu, "Is ali, pas paas mowa'iwta. Son puye'em ima qa yantani," pi'ep yaw kitangwu.

Pu' yaw puma pangqw siivut angqw amumi na'uykuyta. Amumi yaw na'uytaya'iwta. "Naap timuy tuumoykyangw qa nanvota," kitikyangw yaw puma pangqw pumuy aw tayta. Pay yaw oovi pas wuuhaq sikwitpey angqw sowaqw, pu' yaw puma amumi pangqawu, "Uti, hakim naap timuy tuumoyta," kita yaw amumi'.

Pu' yaw taaqa pangqawu, "Son pini, puma naat puuwi. Itam Pöqangwhoyatuy tuumoyta," kita yawi'.

Pu' yaw puma piw amumi pangqawu, "Uti, hakim naap timuy tuumoyta." Pu' yaw pay puma pi'epningwu.

Hisatniqw pu' yaw kur taaqa itsivuti. "Ya himu pas panis haqaqw hingqawlawu? Son pi itam naap itaatimuy tuumoytaniqö'. Puma naat puuwi," kita yawi'. "Niikyangw itam hepni. Himu piniiqe oovi pas qa qe'ti?" kitat pu' yaw wunuptu. Pu' yaw ep hiihiita ang pumuy hepnuma. Pay yaw qa hiita tuwa. Pu' yaw piw ahoy aw qatuptu.

Naat yaw oovi pu' piw kwangwatumoyvaqw, pu' yaw puma piw amumi pangqawu, "Uti, hakim naap timuy tuumoyta."

Paasat pu' yaw sungnuptu. Pu' yaw angqw timuy aw'i. "Son pi itam pumuy tuumoytaniqw, pas hak panis pangqawlawu. Nu' oovi tsaakmuy qatuptsinani," kita yawi'. Pu' yaw timuy aapayamuy suwlöknaqw, pay yaw qa hakim ang puuwi. Paasat pu' yaw ahoy sunamtö. "Pay kur kya pas qa atsata. Pay kya pas itam antsa naap itaatimuy tuumoyta. Oovi pi qa hak aapayamuy ang puuwi. Noq yangqaqw hak hingqawu," yaw kita. Kitat pu' yaw angqw oovaqe siisivut kwap'iwtaqat aw'i. Pu' yaw sukwat wuvaata. Pay yaw qa himu angqö. Paasat pu' yaw piw sukwat, pu' yaw pay pam pangqe put siisivut wuvaatima. Hisatniqw pu' yaw puma angqw pakiwtaqat suuput wuvaata. Pu' yaw puma piw sukwat aqw supki.

"Yes," answered his wife, "we can eat any minute; I'm ready."

So then they started eating. They were full of praise for the meat and every so often one of them would say, "How delicious, they're really tender. I knew they would be just like this."

Meanwhile, the Pöqangwhoya brothers were peeking at them and laughing to themselves. "They are feasting on their own children and don't know it!" they kept saying while they watched them. When the couple had already devoured a large part of their roast, the two boys spoke up, "How awful and disgusting! There are two people eating their own children."

The man replied, "Oh no, our kids are still asleep. We're eating the Pöqangwhoya boys."

Again the boys said, "How awful, those two people are feasting on their own children." They repeated these words again and again.

After a while So'yoko became angry. "Who is it that keeps talking there all the time? We can't be eating our own children; they are still in bed. Why don't we look for these voices. Who on earth is it that won't quit talking?" he asked and got up. The couple was searching through all sorts of things, but could not find anybody. So they sat back down again.

They were still enjoying their meal when the voices started up again, "How disgusting, those people are feasting on their own children!"

This time So'yoko leaped up and stormed toward the bed of his children. "It's impossible that we are eating them as someone keeps insisting. So let me get the kids out of bed." He yanked the children's blanket, but there was no one under it. He swung around. "I suppose it's true. I guess we are actually eating our own children, since they're not in their beds. And by the way, I believe, these voices are coming from somewhere around here," he roared, heading for the place where the pots were lined up. He struck one but there was no one in it. Then another, and another. Then he simply smashed them as he went along. Finally, he hit the very one in which the brothers were hiding. They swiftly climbed out and into the next.

17

Pantsakma yaw puma pangqe. Yaw siivuyamuy wuvaataqw, pu' puma piw sukwat aqw supkingwu. Hisatniqw pu' yaw puma kur hiita aqw pakini. Pu' yaw paasat puma angqw tso'o. Paasat pu' yaw pepeq pumuy amungk So'yoknawuutim savinuma. Hiihiita yaw puma atsvaqe tso'tinuma. Hisatniqw pu' yaw suukyawa So'yokot hotngayat sukwsu. Pantit pu' yaw pam sukwat mu'a. Pantit pu' yaw piw sukwat. Yantiqe pu' yaw naat pumuy qa wuvaataqw, pay yaw pam pumuy niina.

Pu' yaw puma naami pangqawu, "Is ali, pas kwangwa'ewti," yaw kita. "Noq itam sen imuy hintsanni?" yaw kita. "Pay pi itam qötöyamuy ayo' tukye', ngas'ew put itaasoy aqw yawmani," yaw puma kita.

Paasat pu' yaw oovi puma pumuy qötötku. Paasat pu' yaw puma pangqaqw pumuy yawkyangw nima. Pu' yaw puma kiy aw haykyala. Pu' yaw pay puma piw hin wuuwa. Yaw puma naami pangqawu, "Itam as itaasoy tsawinaniy," yaw kita. Pay yaw piw sun unangwti. Paasat pu' yaw puma put nan'ik ang paki. Pankyangw pu' yaw puma kiy aw'i. Uti, yaw a'ni soniwa. Pankyangw puma yaw soy aqw paki. Pu' yaw puma pepehaq soy ngöynuma. Pu' yaw okiw so'am pepehaq waytiwnuma. Pas yaw puma qa qe'ti. Nungwu yaw paapu okiw so'am sisiwkukutinuma, pu' piw siisisitinuma. Pantsakkyangw pu' yaw pas kya pi maangu'iqe pu' yaw angqe' wa'ökma.

Pas yaw pumuy no'a. Pas yaw paasat pu' puma qe'tiqe pu' qötöy tsoopa. Pas yaw puma soy aw taya'iwta. Paasat pu' yaw so'am pumuy maamatsi. "Is uti, ya pay piw uma'?" yaw amumi kita.

"Owi. Ya itam ung tsaawina?"

Paasat pu' yaw so'am qatuptu. "Is uti, kur pi pas uma hiitu qa hopiit. Suupan as pas qa atsat uma So'yokotu," yaw amumi kita, "noq pay kur piw uma'a." Paasat pu' yaw piw yanwata. "Askwali." Paasat pu' yaw amumi haalayti. "Askwali, pay kur uma su'an yuku. Itam oovi qaavo taalawvaqw yuk kiimi imuy maataknawisni," yaw amumi kita.

Paasat pu' yaw oovi puma qavomi it maqaptsiy'kyangw kwangwtoya. Pu' yaw oovi talöngva. Pay yaw oovi taawansap'iwmaqw, pu' yaw imuy

They continued in this manner. Whenever he struck their pot, they quickly jumped into another. After a while there wasn't a pot left for them to hide in. So they leaped down. The two So'yokos took after them and lashed out at everything in their path. The Pöqangwhoyas kept jumping over all sorts of things. After a while one of them suddenly picked up So'yoko's quiver and first shot one of them dead and then the other. Thus it happened that they killed the So'yokos before they were able to get at them.

Thereupon the brothers said to each other, "Boy, that was a lot of fun. I wonder what we should do with them? Well, if we cut off their heads, we can at least show them to our grandmother."

So they cut off the heads and started home with them. They were close to their house when they hit upon another wild idea. "Why don't we scare our grandmother?" they said to each other. Both were for it. So each of them slipped one head over his own, and disguised in this outfit they entered the house. What a dreadful sight they made! They walked up to their grandmother and started chasing her around. The poor woman ran away from them, but they simply would not let up. Soon, their old grandmother was urinating and defecating from fear all over the house while on the run. By and by she got so exhausted that she finally collapsed.

That really amused the boys. They stopped and took off the heads. They laughed loudly at their grandmother. Now she recognized them. "Oh dear, is that the two of you again?" she asked.

"Yes, did we frighten you?"

With this their grandmother got up from the floor. "You're really a couple of ill-behaved boys. I actually thought you were the two So'yokos," she reproached them, "but as it turns out, it's just you two again." Then her attitude changed again. "Thank you." She was grateful to them for what they had done. "Thank you, you have completed your task just right. Tomorrow, when it's daylight, we'll go to Oraibi and present these heads."

Now the boys started looking forward to the next day. The new day came and when it was getting on toward noontime their grandmother said,

so'am amumi pangqawu, "Uma yuwsini," yaw amumi kita. "Uma pumuy hiita aqw söngnani. Nen pu' itam yangqw Oraymiyaqw, uma pumuy nan'ik söngniy'mani."

Pu' yaw oovi puma nan'ik pumuy awtay aqw sööngönta. Paasat pu' yaw puma yukuqw, pu' yaw puma pangqaqw nankwusa. Oovi yaw puma Orayviy kwingyaqw aw kuukuyvaqw, pay yaw kur pumuy sinom tutwa. Pu' yaw naa'awinta kwiningyaqw yaw hiitu amumiq hoyoyotaqat. Pu' yaw sinom amumiq taayungwa. Noq so'am yaw mootiy'ma. Pu' puma naatupkom angk. Nan'ik So'yokotuy qötöyamuy sööngönma. Pu' yaw puma pangqw kiimi yungya. Pu' yaw angqw yuumosa kiisonmiya. Kiisonmi yaw puma yungt, pu' pep poniwwiskyaakyangw pu' pay yaw piw ahoyya. Oovi yaw ahoyyaqw, pu' paasat yaw mongwi amumi nakwsu. Pep pu' yaw pam pumuy amumi haalayti. Pu' yaw soosoyam sinom piw amumi haalaytoti. Pu' yaw puma pangqaqw ahoy ninma.

Hal owi, kur mongwi pumuy amumi haalaytit, pu' pumuy naatupkomuy So'yokotuy qötöyamuy kwusuna. Yanti yaw pami'.

Yanhaqam yaw puma Orayvituy amungem pumuy niina. Paapiy pu' yaw pay qa hisat hak haqami'. Naat oovi Orayvehaqam sinom yeese. Pay pi hiisa' peeti. Pay yuk pölö.

20

"You get dressed now and stick these heads on something. When we march to Oraibi, each of you can carry one."

So each of them stuck a head on his bow. After that they started out. When they appeared north of Oraibi, some people discovered them approaching the village from the north. All the people stared at them. Grandmother walked in front, followed by the two brothers, each of them with an impaled So'yoko head. They entered the village and walked straight to the plaza. When they reached it, they went around it in a circle and then started back again. As they passed the village chief, he went up to them. He thanked them. And all the people, too, expressed their gratitude. Then the three Pöövöqangwt started back home.

After the chief had thanked them, he took the two So'yoko heads away from the brothers. This is what he did.

And this is the way the Pöqangwhoya brothers destroyed those monsters for the Oraibi people. And this, I suppose, is the reason there are still people living in Oraibi today. And here the story ends.

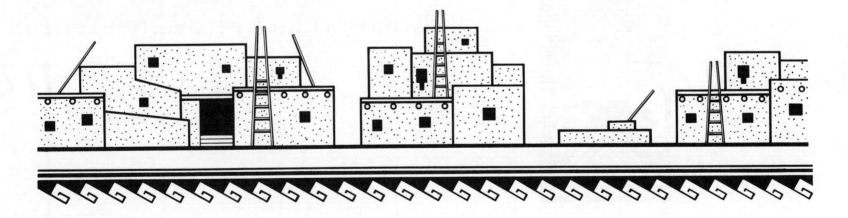

Kokosori

Kokosori and His Witch Wife

Aliksa'i. Yaw Orayve yeesiwa. Noq yaw pep qa an'ewakw sinom yeese. Noq yaw pep hakim puhunawuutim nuutum kiy'ta. Pay yaw puma naat qa hiita tiy'ta. Noq pay yaw i' taaqa pas qa na'öna, sutsep yaw pasminingwu. Taala' pi yawi', noq oovi pang yaw pam qa ööna. Noq yaw pam hisat piw pasvenit ahoy pituqw, pas yaw kiiyamuy ep nöqkwivi kwangwahovaqtu. Noq pam yaw oovi kwangwtoya nösniqe. Pi'ep yaw nöömay tuuvingtangwu, "Ya itam hisatniqw tuumoytani?"

"Pay hiisavoniqw'ö," yaw aw kitangwu. Noq pu' yaw kur hisatniqw pu' tunösvongyaataqe pu' yaw put tuutsamta, "Um pewni, itam tuumoytani," yaw kita.

Pu' yaw pam angqw aw'i. Noq pay yaw puma qa nöqkwivita, pay yaw puma hiita nöösa. Noq pay yaw pam piw nöömay qa tuuvingta sen pam nöqkwiviy'taqö'.

Noq pu' yaw pay aapiy pantaqw, pay yaw pam ephaqam as navotngwu

Aliksa'i. People were living in Oraibi. A great number were living there. Among them was a newly-married couple that had no children. The man was very industrious. He always went to the field. It was summertime and he worked hard. One day when he came from the field there was a smell of stew in his house. His mouth watered and he asked his wife several times, "When are we going to eat?"

"In a little while," she would answer. At last she laid out the food and called him. "Come, we are going to eat," she said.

He went, but they had no stew! They ate something less tasty; but he didn't ask his wife if she had some stew.

From then on it was like that. Sometimes when he came home from the field he would smell something good, but they never had it to eat. Then one

23

pasngaqw pite', kiiyamuy ep yaw himu kwangwahovaqtungwu. Pay yaw puma piw qa put nösngwu. Noq pam yaw hisat piw pasngaqw pituqw, piw yaw an nöqkwiphovaqtu. Noq nööma'at pi yaw qa epe'. Naat yaw pam piktaqe qa yuku. Noq pu' yaw pay oovi pam kiy ep maqaptsiy'ta. Pu' yaw kur yukuqw, pu' puma nöösa. Ep pu' yaw pam pan wuuwa, "Ya sen itam hintoq oovi pas qa nöqkwivit nösngwu?" yan yaw pam wuuwa. "Paapu nu' kur pas hin navotni."

Niiqe pu' yaw oovi pam piw pasmi haawi. Pay yaw pam qa kwangwa-tumalay'ta, niiqe pu' yaw pay pam iits angqw nima, pay naat qa pas tapkiqö'. Yaw pam pituqw nööma'at qa qatu. Paasat pu' yaw pam kiy ep yuumoq paki. Yaw pam aqw pakiqw, ali yaw nöqkwivi kwangwahovaqtu. Pu' yaw piw puhuviki. Pepeq yaw kur put nööma'at oyiy'ta. Yan yaw pam pepeq yori niiqe pu' yaw pam wuuwanta, "Haqami pa pam put hin-tsanngwuniqw oovi itam qa put nösngwu?" yan yaw pam wuuwa. "Paapu kur nu' pu' mihikqw qa puwni," kita pam naami'.

Paasat yaw nööma'at haqaqw pitu. Noq pay yaw pam piw qa tuu-vingta. Paasat pu' yaw puma tapkiqw piw nöösa. Pu' yaw pay pam pas qa hin puwniqay anta. Pay yaw as pi'ep nööma'at pangqawngwu, "Pay pi itam wa'ökni," yaw kitangwu.

Noq pay pam yaw pas qa pan unangwti. Pankyangw pu' pay yaw pas nungwu mihi. Paasat pu' yaw pam nöömay aw pangqawu, "Pay pi itam puwni," yaw kita. Pu' yaw antsa oovi puma wa'ö. Paasat pu' yaw pam pay atsavuwva. Pay yaw pam as taykyangw navuwiy'ta, noq aqle' yaw nööma'at supninita, noq pay pam yaw pas sun yanta.

Oovi yaw naat pam pantaqw, yaw hötsiwayamuy angqaqw hak kuyva. Pay yaw na'uykuyva. Paasat pu' yaw nööma'at paas put aqle' qatuptu. Paasat pu' yaw hötsiwngaqw kuyvaqa angqaqw na'uyhingqawu, "Um sööwu'uy," yaw kita. "Ya pay puuwi?"

"Piiyi," pu' yaw nööma'at aqw kita.

Paasat pu' yaw piw angqw pangqawu, "Kur um aw pootani. Wuko-

day when he returned from the field, there was again that same smell of stew. However, his wife was not there. She had not finished making piki yet. So he waited in the house. When she was done they ate. It was then that he thought, "Why is it that we don't eat any stew? This time I will make a point to find out."

Thereupon he went down to the field again, but he did not enjoy his work and came home when it was not yet evening. His wife was not at home. He went into the backroom of the house. Again there was stew there, and its good smell was in the air. There was also new piki. So here his wife had put these things, and this is how he found them. And then he thought, "What on earth does she do with this food that we never eat? Tonight I will not sleep," he said to himself. "I will find out."

Then his wife returned, but again he did not ask her any questions. When it was early evening they had supper. Afterwards he felt no real desire to go to bed. His wife kept saying, "Well, shall we lie down?"

But he shook his head. As soon as night had fallen, he said to his wife, "All right, I'm ready for bed." They lay down and he pretended to fall asleep. But he was actually awake, and only appeared to be asleep, while his wife tossed and turned next to him. He, however, kept quiet and didn't move.

While this was going on, suddenly someone appeared at their door and peeked in. His wife rose carefully, and the one who had peeked in at the door whispered, "You are late! Is he asleep?"

"I don't know," the wife replied.

Then the visitor said, "Why don't you check. Pull a hair on his big toe. If he sleeps tight he won't notice anything."

25

kukvosiyat epeq um höömiyat kur langaknani. Sumats pi huur puuwe' son navotni," aw yaw kita.

Paasat pu' yaw oovi pam wuuti koongyay kukvosiyat epeq höömiyat langakna. A'ni yaw as tuyva. Noq pay yaw pam pas qa poniniyku. Paasat pu' yaw nööma'at aqw pangqawu, "Pay kur huur puuwi, pay oovi qa navota," kitat pu' yaw qatuptu.

Paasat pu' yaw iipaqniiqa angqaqw pangqawu, "Um pisoqtini, pay mihi."

Paasat pu' i' wuuti yaw aapamiqhaqami pakima. Pu' yaw angqaqw ahoy hiita tsöpkyangw yama. Pu' yaw iipoqhaqami horokna. Paasat pu' yaw piw ahoy aqwhaqami pakima. Paasat pu' yaw piw hiita yawkyangw yama. Pu' yaw angqw put aw'i, pu' yaw put aqlavaqe hiita tavi. "Yantani," yaw kita. Paasat pu' yaw yamakma.

Panis yaw·oovi yamakmaqw pu' yaw pam qatuptu. Pu' yaw pam put aw poota hiita put nööma'at aqlavaqe taviiqat. Noq yaw kur tiposhoyat pam put aqlavaqe tavi. Paas yaw okiw laakiwta. Maslakvut hapi kur put aqlavaqe tavi. Pu' yaw pam put ayo'haqami tuuva. Pantit pu' yaw pam tuwat yama. Yaw pam yamakqw naat yaw pu' kiiyamuy hoopo nangk. Taaqa yaw wuutit mookiyat engem tsöpma.

Oovi yaw tuuwayamaqw, pu' yaw pam amungki. Pangqaqw pu' yaw pam pumuy amungk nana'uytima. "Haqami pa ima hoyta?" yan yaw pam wuuwankyangw. Pay yaw pas yuumosa hoopoq. Pas yaw oovi puma haqtoti, noq nawis'ew yaw puma kur haqami öki. Yaw haqami puma kivami öki. Pu' yaw aqwhaqami puma nangk pakima.

Paasat pu' yaw pam amungk aw'i. Pu' yaw pam kivats'omi wupqe, pu' yaw pam nguutat ang paki. Pang yaw pam pakiwkyangw amumiq tayta. Yaw wukotsovawta sinomu. Noq put nööma'at puma yaw aqw pakiqw, amumi yaw pangqaqwa, "Pas uma qa pituy, itam teevep umuy nuutay-yungwa," kitota yaw amumi'.

Paasat pu' yaw wuuti pangqawu, "Hep owi, pas ipuwsungwa qa iits

So the woman pulled a hair on her husband's toe. It hurt, but he did not stir. "Yes, he is sound asleep," the wife said. "He didn't notice a thing."

She got up, and the one who was outside said, "Hurry up, it's already late!"

The wife disappeared into the next room and came back with something in her arms and carried it outside. She returned and went again into the backroom. Once more she carried an object out, but this time she came up to her husband and laid it down beside him. "That'll do it," she said, and then she was gone.

She had hardly left when her husband got up to take a closer look at what his wife had placed beside him. It was a baby, all dried up, a human mummy! He hurled it away from him in disgust and went out. He saw that his wife and her friend were just east of his house, one behind the other. The man was carrying the woman's bundle.

When they were out of sight, he went after them. He followed, making sure that he was hidden while going along. "Where could they be going?" he wondered. They were heading due east. When they had walked quite a distance they arrived at a kiva unknown to him and disappeared into it, one after the other.

He followed them there, climbed onto the roof and crawled into the matting cover of the kiva opening. From there he watched. A crowd of people was gathered below. When his wife and the man entered, people called to them, "You did not show up! We have been waiting here for you all this time."

The woman replied, "My husband would not go to bed early. This is why we came so late. Well, let's not waste any more time—let's get to it."

27

puwnakwhaqw, oovi itam qa iits pitu," kita yaw amumi'. "Ta'a, noq pay oovi qa sööwuni, pay itam aw pitsinayani," yaw kita.

Put hapi yaw kur nööma'at pas pepeq mongwi. Pu' yaw oovi paasat sukwat aw pangqawu, "Ta'a, pay um wunuptsinani," yaw aw kita. Paasat pu' put hakiy ayataqat pam yaw angqw kwiniwiq, niiqe pangqaqw yaw hiita horoknat, pu' angqw kivat naasami yawma. Pu' yaw pep put wunuptsina. Yaw himu ngöla. Pantit pu' yaw pangqawu, "Ta'a, pay aw pituni."

Paasat pu' yaw suukya hak angqw aw nakwsu, ngölat awi'. Aw yaw pitut pu' yaw angqe kopangtsööqö. Nit pay yaw qa hinti. Paasat pu' yaw mongwi pangqawu, put nööma'at, "Pay hapi hak haqaqw tayta, oovi qa aniwti," yaw kita. "Uma nöngakye' hepyani."

Paasat pu' yaw tootim, taataqt nöngakqe pu' yaw as hakiy hepya. Noq pay yaw qa hak haqamo. Pu' yaw pay ahoy piw yungya. "Qa hak haqamoy," yaw kitota.

"Ta'a, haqawa kur piwni," yaw kita. Paasat pu' yaw suukyawa tuwati. Ngölat atsvaqe yaw kopangtsööqö. Pay yaw piw qa hinti. Paasat pu' yaw piw mongwi pangqawu, "Pay hak pas haqaqw tayta, oovi qa aniwti," yaw kita. "Uma nöngakye', pas paapu paas hepyani."

Paasat pu' yaw piw nönga. Paasat pu' yaw pas puma paas hepya. Noq pay yaw kur haqawa put tuwa. Pu' yaw aw pangqawu, "Um qa yangqaqw yantat aqw pakini," yaw aw kita. Pay yaw pam sunakwha. Pu' yaw oovi pam amum aqw paki.

Paasat pu' yaw piw soosoyam ahoy yungqw, pu' yaw piw pangqawu, "Ta'a, itam kur piwyani." Paasat pu' yaw piw suukyawa angqw aw'i. Pu' yaw angqe kopangtsööqö. Pantikyangw pay yaw wukomongwuniwti. Panis yaw oovi qatuptut pay iipoqhaqami yamakma. Pu' yaw puma pepehaq put angqe naanangk pantsatskya. Pay yaw pas hak naap himuniwtingwu. Peetu yaw ii'istniwtoti, pu' peetu saasawyam. Pay yaw pas hak naap himuniwtingwu. Pantsakkyaakyangw pu' yaw puma pangqw nöönganta.

The man was surprised to realize that his wife was the leader there. She commanded one of the people, "Go ahead, set it up!" The person she had given the order to went to the north side of the kiva, got something out and carried it to the center of the kiva. There he put it in an upright position. It was some kind of hoop. When he had done that, she said, "All right, let's begin!"

One started for the hoop. When he reached it, he did a somersault over it. But nothing happened. Now the leader, the man's wife, said, "Someone must be peeping in. That's why it didn't work. Go out and search."

Several boys and men went out and looked, but there was no one. They came back in. "There is no one," they reported.

"Well, then someone else try," she said. So another one took his turn and did a somersault over the hoop. Again nothing happened! The leader said, "Someone must be watching, or it would work. Go out and search more carefully!"

Again they went out, and searched everywhere. This time a man discovered the husband. "Don't stay up here—come in," the man said, and the husband promptly agreed and entered.

When all of them were inside, she said, "All right, let's try it again." One of the men stepped up to the hoop and somersaulted over it. And as he did so, he changed into a huge owl! No sooner had he landed on his feet than he rushed outside. Suddenly they were all vaulting over the hoop, one after the other. As they did so, they were transformed into all sorts of

Hisatniqw pu' yaw soosoyam nöngakma.

Pay yaw pam epeq nal'akwsingwa. Paasat pu' yaw pam pan wuuwa, "Kur peqw pam it noovay'mangwuniqw, oovi itam qa hisat it itaakiy epeq nösngwu."

Pu' pay yaw oovi pas nawutstiqw pu' yaw piw ahoy ökiwta. Pay yaw himuwa pakye', pu' piw ngölat atsvaqe kopangtsööqökngwu. Paasat pay yaw piw ahoy yan sinoniwtingwu. Hisatniqw pu' yaw piw ahoy soosoyam tsovalti. Paasat pu' yaw mongwi pangqawu, "Ta'a, uma mamant, momoyam aw o'yaqw itam noonovani."

Paasat pu' yaw oovi antsa mamant, momoyam tunösvongyaatota. Paasat pu' yaw puma noonova. Is ali, yaw puma naanasna, pas pi yaw himu nunukngwasa'. Pas yaw puma naanasna. Pu' yaw soosoyam öö'öyaqw, paasat pu' yaw piw mongwi pangqawu, "Uma ang ayo' qenitotaqw, itam aw pitsinayani. Pay suutalawvangwu, pay itam oovi qa sööwuyani," yaw kita.

Pu' yaw oovi piw ang ayo' suuqenitota. Paasat pu' yaw kur puma tiivani. Paasat pu' yaw oovi hiita wukomokiwtaqat kivat sunasave tavi. Pantit pu' yaw pangqawu, "Ta'a, pay pi hak himuy tuwiy'tangwu. Uma angqw umuumuy ömaatotaqw, itam aw pitsinayani."

Paasat pu' yaw suukyawa purukna. Yaw kur pep mas'ö'öqa mookiwta. Pu' yaw himuwa angqw aw nakwse', pu' angqw himuy kwusungwu. Hisatniqw pu' yaw soosoyam himuy angqw ömaatota. Paasat pu' yaw put nööma'at angqw aw'i, niiqe pu' yaw aw lööqmuy tavi. "Imuy um akwni," yaw aw kita.

Pu' yaw paasat aw pitsinaya. Yaw puma pepehaq tiilalwa. Put hapi puma ööqat akw maasantotaqw, pam hapi yaw pumuy tuunimuyatuy ööqa'am. Puma hapi yaw pepeq kur pas tuunimuy ööqayamuy akw maasantotangwu.

Pay yaw oovi naat qa pas wuuyavo tiivaqw, pay yaw kur pam puwva. Hisatniqw pu' yaw pam taatayi, niikyangw pay yaw pam haqe' taatayi. Yaw

creatures! Some became coyotes, others bats. They could change into al-most anything. Soon the kiva was empty.

The husband alone remained. Then he thought, "So this is the place where she has been bringing the food, and that is the reason we never ate it at our house."

After some time had passed, they started coming back. The minute one of them came in, he somersaulted back over the hoop and in this way was transformed back into his human shape. Soon they were all gathered· again. The leader said, "Well, you girls and women, bring out the food. It's time to eat."

The girls and women set up the meal and they began eating. What a feast it was! They ate to their hearts' content. Everything was delicious and they stuffed themselves. When all were satiated, the wife spoke again. "After you have cleared everything away, we will get started. The morning light comes quickly. Let's not waste our time."

They hurried to put everything out of the way, as if preparing to dance. The wife placed a big bundle in the center of the kiva and said, "Well, you know what's yours. Pick out your own and then we'll begin."

One of them untied the bundle. Skeleton bones were wrapped up in it! Each of them would go up and pick out his own. After a little while all of them had selected their bones. Then his wife came up to him and handed him two. "You use these," she ordered him.

Then they started dancing. The bones they used were, of course, the bones of people that had fallen prey to them. So they actually carried out their hand gestures with the bones of their own victims!

They had not been dancing long when the man fell asleep. After a long time he woke up. He was in a strange place. He seemed to be lying on a narrow ledge. When he looked up, he was amazed to see a sheer wall towering above him. Downward, too, there was a vertical drop. Because he

31

haqe' hiisaq putsiwyat ang yaw pam wa'ökiwta. Yaw pam oomiq taatayqw, is tathihiya yaw oomiqhaqami a'ni tuupela. Pu' yaw piw atkyamiqhaqami piw an a'ni tuupela. Pay pi yaw pam pas hiisaq putsiwyat ang wa'ökiwtaqe, kur hin yaw pam namtökni. Pay yaw oovi pam nawus pang nakwhaniy'ta. Paasat pu' yaw pam qa haalayti. "Naapi pas kur nu' piw inömay angki," yan yaw pam wuuwa. "Pay pi kur nu' hin yangqw wupni. Piw nu' kur hin yangqw hawni," yan yaw pam wuuwaqe qa haalayi.

Naat yaw oovi pam yan wuuwantaqw, yaw put himu atsmi tsokilti. Noq pay pi yaw kur pam hin aw hintiniqe pay nawus sun yanta. Naat yaw oovi pam pantaqw, piw yaw himu aw lavayti. "Okiway," yaw aw kita, "okiw um yangqe okiwhinta. Noq nu' ung ookwatuwqe oovi angqöy," yaw aw kita. Yaw kur tutsvo. "Pay um haak yang yantani. Naat hakim son hisatniqw qa pituni. Puma hapi ung tuuvatoqam songqa pituni. Noq oovi uumiq hapi hiita wahitaqw, um hapi qa aw yootokmantani. Pay ason himuwa pas utsmi huurtiqw, put ason um sowani. Naap hapi um aw yootokye' son hapi um qa posni. Pay puma hapi paniqw uumiq put wahitani. Son oovi uumi qa pangqawkyangwni um aw yootokniqat, noq um hapi qa uunatini. Pay nu' ason son piw ahoy qa pituni," aw yaw kitat pu' yaw waaya.

Pu' yaw pam antsa hakimuy nuutaykyangw pu' piw wuuwanta, "Hakim pa angqaqwniniqw oovi pangqawu?" Yan yaw pam wuuwantaqw, yaw haqaqw antsa hiitu hingqawma. Pas yaw hiitu kupisvekiwma. Suutsep-ngwat yaw sumataq put aqw pituto. Panmakyangw yaw put aqw oongaqw hiitu kuyva. Yaw pam amumiq tayta, niqw yaw kur Sikyaqöqlötu. Pas yaw hiitu qa lavayqe'tingwu. Pu' yaw pay angqw put aqw kukuytikyangw, pu' pay aw piw hingqawkyangw yaw epeq ooveq hiihintsaki. Pay yaw hinte', pas wunimat pu' piwningwu. Niiqe it yaw hiita taawiy'ta:

was lying on this extremely narrow ledge, it was impossible for him to turn around. He was forced to hold that position. He became unhappy. "Why did I have to follow my wife?" he thought. "I can't climb up from here, nor is there a way down from here."

As he worried about his situation, something landed on him. Because he couldn't do anything about it, he had to hold still. While he was lying there, to his surprise the creature addressed him. "Oh you poor man!" it said. "What a sorry state you are in. I have come because I felt pity for you." It seemed to be a wren. "Remain here for the time being, for there are two who will yet come and try to throw you off. They will cast things at you, but you must not grab them. Later, if one of these things sticks to you, you can eat it. But if you grab for it yourself, you are bound to fall off. That is the reason that they will be throwing those things at you. They will surely ask you to grab for them, but stand firm. I will be back later." After these words, the wren left.

While the man was waiting for the two, he asked himself, "What on earth was he warning me about?" While he wondered this, he heard the voices of two creatures approaching. They talked incessantly, and with every step they came closer. All at once they appeared above him, and he looked up at them. They were evidently two Yellow Qöqlös. Yellow Qöqlös are ones that never cease talking. Off and on they looked down at him, and while they were talking to him, they kept doing all sorts of things up there. From time to time they danced and sang.

33

Kokosori, Kokosori
Yangqaqw vi nu' umuy tuwaviy'ta.
Kokosori, Kokosori
Yangqaqw vi nu' umuy tuwaviy'ta.
Naayaya naap nöömay unangwyatniqö'ö
Suutupelnasave taataviwa.
Meeyeye ayahay ayaha'ay'a
Meeyeye ayahay ayaha'ay'a.
Nuy kur oomi tsokya'a,
Nuy kur atkyami tavi'i.
Kokosori, Kokosori sori
Ayaha, iyihiyihi.
Kokosori.

Kitat pu' yaw epeq Kokosori kitangwu. Pan pi yaw pam taaqa
maatsiwa, Kokosori. Paasat pu' yaw tiitso'qe pu' yaw it aqw pangqawu,
"Um hapi itamuy it uumiq maspitaqw, um hapi aw yootokmantani," yaw
aqw kita. Pu' yaw antsa put aqw tuupevut wahita. Noq pay pi pam yaw
tutavotniiqe pay pas qa aw yootokngwu. Pu' yaw as pi'ep aw pangqawngwu
aw yootokniqat. Noq pay yaw pam qa hiitawat aw yootokq, pay yaw kur
sulawti. Yan pay yaw puma pangqw put qa tuuvat, pu' pay ahoy yaw
haqami'.

Paasat pu' yaw pay antsa qa wuuyavotiqw pu' yaw tutsvo ahoy put aw
pitu. Yaw put aw haalayti. "Pay um su'antiy," yaw aw kita, "pay um hapi as
naap uunate', pay son um pi as qa posni. Noq pay um su'antiqe oovi qa
uunati. Niikyangw pay son naat piw yantani. Pu' hapi pay pas suyan ung
tuuvatoqa pu' angqwni. Noq pay um hapi qa tsawnani. Pay um qa tsawne'
songqa piw ayo' yamakni. Noq yep it nu' oovi ungem yanva," kitat pu' yaw
aw hiita tavi. "Ason pituqw pu' um it mömtsani. Pu' pay um it mötstaqw,
pu' hapi son uumiq qa hawni. Oovi ason pay pas uumi pituniqw, pu' um it

34

Kokosori, Kokosori
From here I see you.
Kokosori, Kokosori
From here I see you.
Naayaya. It was my own wife's wish
That I was placed there in the middle of the cliff.
Meeyeye ayahay ayaha'ay'a
Meeyeye ayahay ayaha'ay'a.
Put me up,
Put me down.
Kokosori, Kokosori sori
Ayaha, iyihiyihi.
Kokosori.

They seemed to know his name—Kokosori. When they had finished
their dance, they shouted down to him, "We will throw these things to you.
Be sure to catch them!" First they hurled ears of baked sweet corn at him.
But the man followed the wren's advice and did not try to catch them.
Again and again they told him to grab for the corn, but he did not move his
hand until there were no more cobs left. So, without having thrown him off
the cliff, they departed.

Before long the wren returned to him, happy to see the man. "You did
the right thing," the wren said to him. "If you had given in, you would have
fallen off for sure! You did right when you stayed firm. But this isn't the
end. Another creature will come that will most certainly throw you off
unless you do what I tell you. Do not be afraid, for if you don't panic you
will come through all right. Here," he said, and handed him something.
"You must chew this when the creature arrives. While you are chewing the
medicine, the monster will come down to you. When it is about to reach

aw pavoyani. Pay paasat son um qa hin ayo' yamakni. Um hapi oovi it qa suutokni. Pay kur um su'an yukuqw, pay nu' son naat piw qa ahoy pituni." Kita yaw awnit pu' piw aapiyo'.

Paasat pu' yaw pam piw wuuwanta, "Himu pa pu' angqaqwniniqw oovi pangqawu?" Yan yaw pam wuuwa. Nit pas yaw pam paasat pu' u'na suukya yaw tuupevu put atsmi huurti. Paasat pu' yaw oovi pam put kwusuuqe pu' put sowa. Su'aw yaw pam oovi put sowat pu' yaw piw hiita navota. Suupan yaw himu tu'mumutima. Paasat pu' yaw pam piw oomiq tayta. Hisatniqw yaw angqw atsngaqw himu aqw kuyva. Yaw himu nuutsel'ewayo'. Pu' yaw pay epeq naanahoy yortinuma. Pantsakkyangw pu' yaw angqw put aqw haayiwma. Pas paasat pu' yaw pam maamatsi, yaw kur wukolölöqangw'u. Paysoq yaw angqw aqw hahayiltima. Pas pi yaw hoskaya. Yaw oovi angqw put aqw haayiwmaqw, pu' yaw pam ngahuy su'u'naqe pu' yaw pam put suumötsitsiyku. Pu' yaw pam pangqw lölöqangw oongaqw aqw suusus hoyta. Panmakyangw pu' yaw pay put pas aqw haykyala. Oovi pay yaw pas put aw paapu tongokniniqw, pu' yaw pam aw ngahuy pavoya. Pay yaw paasat put qa aw tongokt, pay yaw atsva atkyamiqhaqami se'elhaq posto. Pu' yaw posq, yaw epehaq sinom tsaykikita. Put hapi yaw lölöqangwuy ang kur sinom mookiwyungwa, popwaqt. Puma hapi kur put pang taviyaqe pu' as piw tuuvawisqw, pay pamwa pumuy maspa. Yan yaw pam put wukolölöqangwuy tuuva.

Pu' yaw pay qa wuuyavotiqw pu' yaw piw tutsvo ahoy pitu. Pu' yaw aw haalayti, "Pay um su'an yuku," yaw aw kita, "pay um oovi haak yang yantani. Ason nu ahoy pite' pu' nu' ung hawnani," yaw aw kita. Paasat pu' yaw piw ahoy atkyamiqhaqami'.

Pu' yaw kur pam pepeq tuwat piw ngahuy tuupelmo pavoyaqw, pu' yaw tuupela atkyaqw oomiqhaqami tsi'a. Pang yaw pu' pam masay, pöhöy tsuruminmakyangw oomiq wupto. Hisatniqw pu' yaw put taaqat ahoy aqw

you, you must spit your medicine on it. If you carry everything out right, I will come back to you." After these words the wren departed.

The man wondered fearfully, "What can it be that is coming?" Then he remembered the one baked ear of corn that had landed on him. He picked it up and ate it. He had just eaten it when he heard something— a dull, thundering noise. He strained his eyes looking up. Suddenly something looked down at him from above where he lay. It was a most horrible-looking creature! It kept glancing from side to side, and now it began letting itself down toward him. At last he recognized what it was: it was a gigantic snake. Its dimensions were tremendous. While it came dangling toward him he remembered his medicine just in time and chewed it hastily. The snake slowly inched its way down. Closer and closer it came. Then, as it was about to touch him, he spat at it. The snake writhed. Without touching the man, it fell past him, down and down, until finally it crashed to the bottom. To his astonishment, a swarm of people appeared down there, crying. For the snake had contained people, sorcerers and witches! They were the ones who had put him in that place and had come to throw him off the ledge! Instead, he had now thrown them off.

Soon after this the wren came back. He was beside himself with joy. "You have finished this up right," he said, "so stay here for the time being. When I return, I will help you down." Then he disappeared again.

The wren now sprayed his medicine against the wall, whereupon the wall cracked from top to bottom. He inserted his wing and breast feathers into this crack as he climbed up. A little while later he reached the top

wuuvi. Yaw himu qa soniwa, paalavölangpuhoya yawi'. Ngasta yaw pöhöy'ta, piw ngasta yaw masay'ta. Paasat pu' yaw put aw pangqawu, "Ta'ay, nu' ung hawnani. Um oovi namtökye' inutsva tsooraltini. Pay um pu' son posni."

Paasat pu' yaw oovi pam namtökiwma. Pay yaw pam antsa qa hin posniqay unangwti. Oovi yaw pam namtökiwmaqw, pu' yaw tutsvo put atpikyaqe paki. Paasat pu' yaw atpipahaqw pangqawu, "Um hapi huur uvimani. Ason pas nu' pangqawqw pu' um uuvosiy puruknani. Naap hapi um naat nuy qa pangqawqw, puruknaqw, pay itam hapi naama songqa posni. Um hapi oovi qa uuvosiy puruknani," kita yaw awi'.

Paasat pu' yaw pam huur uviiti, noq pay yaw antsa puma hawto. Pay yaw susmataq puma atkyami hoyta. Panmakyangw hisatniqw pu' yaw piw put atpipahaqw hingqawu, "Ta'ay, puruknaa'," yaw aw kita. Paasat pu' yaw pam poosiy purukna. Pay yaw kur puma haawi. Paasat pu' yaw put aw tutsvo pangqawu, "Ta'ay, kur aw taatayii'," yaw aw kita. Paasat pu' yaw pam tuupelat aw taatayqw, is uru yaw oomiqhaqami'. Aqwhaqami yaw tutsvot masa'at, pöhö'at tsurum'iwta. Put hapi yaw kur puma ang haawi.

"Ta'ay," pu' yaw aw kita, "kur um amumi yorikni. Ima hapi as ung tuuvawisa, noq pay um su'an yukuuqe, pay umsa imuy maspa. Noq pay naat songqa piw hin naapowatotaniqw, oovi pay pi um yaapiy pay nimani," yaw aw kita. "Pay pi niikyangw um hapi pituqw, pay uunöma songqa qatuni. Son hapi uumi qa haalaytini. Pu' pay um piw an aw haalaytini. Pay um qa hin aw unangway'tani. Pay ason pi son hin naami tuwat qa navotni."

Yanhaqam yaw put aw tutaptaqw, pu' yaw pam pangqaqw nakwsu. Panmakyangw pu' yaw pam antsa pitu. Noq antsa yaw nööma'at put pitsinaqe yaw aw haalayti. Pu' yaw pam piw an aw haalayti. Pu' yaw antsa puma ep mihikqw puuwi.

Qavongvaqw yaw pam iits taatayqw, pay yaw kur nööma'at qatuptu niikyangw yaw qa haqam. Pu' yaw pam angqw iipo yamakqw, aw yaw kiiyamuy taatö yaw nööma'at hintsakma. Hiihin yaw wunimantima, pu'

where the man was. What an unsightly appearance the wren presented! He was a little red creature of a roundish shape. He had no more feathers and no more wings. But he said to the man, "Well now, I will get you down to the ground. So turn around and lie face down on top of me. You can't fall now. Just lie flat on me."

So the man turned over. He had no sensation whatsoever that he might fall. While he was turning around, the wren got under him and spoke to him from underneath, "Keep your eyes closed tightly on the way until I tell you to open them again. If you open them before I command you to do so, we will both fall. So be sure not to look."

The man shut his eyes tightly and they started their descent. He could feel them moving downward. After a period the wren said, "Now, open your eyes." So the man opened his eyes and saw that they had reached the bottom. The wren said to him, "Now, take a look at that!" He looked at the wall and was startled that it was so high! And all the way up the wren's wing and breast feathers were stuck into it. They had evidently climbed down on them.

"Now," the wren said to him, "look at all those people! They are the ones who set out to throw you off, but by doing the right thing it was you who destroyed them instead. Somehow they will manage to heal themselves again, so go home and leave this place. When you get back, your wife will be there. She will certainly be happy to see you, so be as happy as she. Don't hold a grudge against her. She'll learn her lesson later."

Obediently, the man left that place, and after a long time reached his home. And indeed, his wife seemed glad to get him back again. He also showed his happiness, and they actually slept well that night.

The following morning, he woke up early, but his wife had evidently already gotten up. She was nowhere in sight. When he stepped outside, his wife was on her way to the area south of their house and was acting

39

yaw piw hiihin maasanma. Pantsakmakyangw pu' yaw pas piw ngasta yuwsiy'ma. Pantsakmakyangw yaw taatöq tumpoq hoyoyotima. Oovi yaw naat pan wunimantimakyangw yaw aqw tatkyaqöymiqhaqami tso'okma. Yan yaw pam nöömay ngastati.

Paasat pu' yaw aapiy mimawat popwaqt tuwat pay yaw pas himuwa hihin hintit pay yaw piw mokngwu. Pantsakkyaakyangw yaw puma pas sulawti. Puma hapi yaw kur lölöqangwuy ang mookiwyungwa. Noq pam hapi pumuy soosokmuy oovi qöya. Yanhaqam pay yaw pamsa ayo' yama. Pay yuk pölö.

strangely. She was going along, dancing in a strange way and making all kinds of crazy gestures. What's more, she was stark naked! In this way she slowly approached the edge of the southern mesa. Dancing along like this, she stepped over the edge and fell down the south side. This is how the man lost his wife.

Thereupon the other witches and sorcerers perished in turn from the slightest of causes. In this way they were all wiped out. They had all been in that snake, of course. So it was he who had caused all of their deaths. And he was the only one who survived. And here the story ends.

41

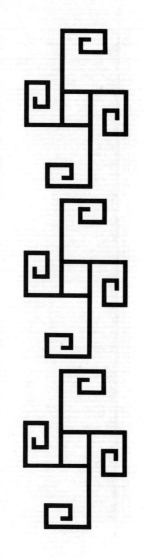

Palöngawhoya Soy Niina

How Palöngawhoya Killed
His Grandmother

Aliksa'i. Yaw Pöqangwwawarpive yeesiwa. Noq pep yaw Pöqangwhoyat kiy'ta. Puma naatupkom tiyooyat. Wuuyoqwa yaw Pöqangwhoya yan maatsiwa, pu' tsaywa tupko'at pamwa yaw Palöngawhoya. Pay puma yaw panis soy'ta. Pas yaw puma qa navotngwu. Naamahin yaw so'am hiita meewantangwu, pay yaw pas puma qa navotngwu. Sutsep yaw puma tatatsngwu, putsa yaw puma apit.

Qavongvaqw piw yaw tatatsngwu, noq yaw kur tömö'ti niiqe yaw hisat nuva'iwkyangw talöngva. Noq pay kya pi yaw son puma nuvat ang kwangwatatatsniqe, pu' yaw puma wuuwanta hintsakniqay, noq pu' yaw suukyawa pangqawu, "Itam as maqtoni," yaw kita, noq pu' pay puma yaw sun unangwti.

Niiqe pu' yaw oovi puma makyuyuwsi. Awtay, hoohuy, puuvut yaw

Aliksa'i. They were living at Pöqangwwawarpi. The Pöqangwhoya twins had their house there. The brothers were little boys. Pöqangwhoya was the older's name; the younger was called Palöngawhoya. They had only their grandmother to live with and as a rule they never obeyed her. Although she would forbid them to do certain things, they simply would not listen. The boys played shinny ball all the time; that was the only thing they were good for.

They played day after day and then winter came, and one day when it was daylight, there was snow on the ground. And, I guess, because they could not drive their ball through the snow very well, they began wondering what to do, when one of them suggested, "Why don't we go hunting?" They were both for it.

They put on their hunting clothes and got their gear, such as bows and

puma himuy tsovala. Pu' yaw puma soy aa'awna, "Itaasoy, itam maqtoy. Pay pi itam sen suukwhaqam tuwe', hiita kwusivaniy," yaw puma soy aw kita.

"Ta'a," yaw amumi kita, "paapu hakim qa pas hisatniqw pay angqaqw ahoy nimangwu," yaw amumi kita. "Taq iyoho'tingwu, pu' naap hisat hak piw toknamuse', qa su'aqw nimangwu," yaw amumi kita.

"Ta'ay, pay itam son pas tapkiqw pay pituni." Kitat pu' yaw puma pangqw yama, kiy angqw. Pangqw pu' yaw puma kwiniwiqwat nakwsu. Pay pi yaw hisat pang pay owatpelpa taatapt kyaastangwu. Panmakyangw pu' yaw puma sukw kuktuwa. Pu' yaw puma put angk. Hisatniqw pu' yaw puma warikna. Wariknaqe pu' yaw puma put ngöyva. Pay yaw qa wuuyavonit pay paki, wuko'owat yaw atpipoq.

Piw yaw pam kur pep owat atpikyaqe naahoy hötsi. Pu' yaw i' wuuyoqwa, Pöqangwhoya, tupkoy aw pangqawu, "Um kwiningqöyngaq- watni, pu' nu' yangqwatni. Itam nan'ivaqw aqw yantaqw, pay haqawa songqa ngu'ani."

Pu' yaw oovi tupko'at kwiningqöyngaqwat aqw qatuptu, aqw tamötswunuptu. Pu' yaw awtay ang hoohuy tumostsokya. Pu' yaw pam pangqwat aqw tumostsokiy'kyangw aqw tunatyawta. Noq pangqwat yaw iyoho'o, kwiningqöyngaqw.

Pu' wuuyoqwa tatkyaqöyngaqw yaw aqw yaahanta. Pu' yaw hiisa- voniqw Pöqangwhoya yaw tupkoy aqwhaqami töqtingwu, "Naat qa yama?" yaw aqwhaqami kitangwu.

"Qa'ey," yaw angqaqw ahoy kitangwu.

Pu' yaw pay puma nungwu wuuyavo pep put aqw hintsaki. Pu' yaw hisatniqw Pöqangwhoya tupkoy aqwhaqami piw töqti, "Um qa tuwa? Naat qa yama?" Pay yaw qa angqaqw hingqawu. Pu' yaw piw, "Qa yama? Qa tuwa?" Pay yaw pas qa angqaqw hingqawqw, pu' yaw paasat pam Pöqangwhoya kur hin wuuwa, "Sen pam haqami'?" pam yaw yan wuuwaqe, pu' yaw pam aqwa'.

arrows and other things, together. Then they told their grandmother, "Grandmother, we're going on a hunting trip. Maybe if we find one or two rabbits we'll bring something home."

"All right," she replied, "but don't come back too late. It gets cold now; also one might start for home in the wrong direction and end up getting lost."

"Good, we'll be back before evening." Saying this they left the house. They started north. In the olden times there were lots of rabbits there on that rocky slope. Eventually they discovered the tracks of one. They followed the tracks and soon startled the rabbit. They chased it, but before long it vanished under a big boulder.

By chance the hole under the rock was open on both ends, so the older of the two, Pöqangwhoya, said to his brother, "You go over to the north side while I stay here. By covering both sides, one of us should certainly catch it."

So his younger brother positioned himself on the north side and knelt facing the hole. Then he fitted his bow with an arrow and, having it ready, watched the opening. It was bitter cold on that northern side.

On the south side Pöqangwhoya began to dig into the hole. After a while he shouted to his brother, "Hasn't it come out yet?"

"No," the answer came back.

They had been at work for a long time, when Pöqangwhoya yelled to his brother on the other side, "Don't you see it? Isn't it out yet?" But there was no reply. He repeated, "Isn't it out? Can't you see it?" When the other did not answer, Pöqangwhoya was at a loss. "Where on earth did he go?" he wondered going over to him.

Pu' yaw pam aqw toni, tupkoy aqwa'. Naat yaw aqw tumostso-kiy'kyangw tamötswunuwta. "Ya um hintiqw pas qa hingqawu?" yaw pam tupkoy aw kita. Qa aw yaw hingqawu, piw yaw qa ngas'ew aw yori. Pu' yaw pam awniiqe pu' yaw pay qötöveq hihin wuvikna. Pu' yaw aw pangqawu, "Ya um hintiqw pas qa hingqawu?" Pay yaw pas qa aw hingqawu.

Pu' yaw pam aw pas taatayi, pu' yaw pam wiiwila. Huur yaw patu-sungw'iwta. Kur yaw pam pansoq tumostsokiy'kyangw patusungwti. Pu' yaw pam paasat pay qa taavot angk yaahantat, pu' yaw pam tupkoywat iikwilta pay pantaqat. Iikwiltat pu' yaw pam pangqw put iikwiwkyangw nima.

Pu' yaw pam pitu. "Askwali, uma pitu," yaw so'am amumi kita.

"Hep owi," yaw pam aqw kita, Pöqangwhoya, "itam tapyahantaqw i' kur patusungwti," yaw pam soy aw kita.

"Is uti, pas̀ pi uma hiitu hintsakngwu," yaw kita Pöqangwhoyat awi'.

"Pay nu' haak oovi yuk taviqw, pay kya hisatniqw möötsatini," yaw soy aw kita, niiqe pu' yaw qöpqöt aqlavo tupkoy tavi. Pu' yaw pam paasat pavan piw aqw qööna. Paasat pu' yaw so'am pay ep hiita hintsaknuma. Noq pam pi yaw Palöngawhoya naat tumostsokiy'kyangw patusungw'iwta. Pu' yaw oovi naat pumuy so'am ep hiita hintsaknumqw, pu' yaw kur pam möötsati. Möötsatiqe pu' yaw pam hoohuy maatavi. Hoohuy maatapqw, yaw ang hoohu'at suyma awtayat angniikyangw yaw okiw pam soysa mu'a.

Pas yaw pumuy no'a. Pu' yaw puma naami pangqawu, "Ya itam itaasoy hintsanni?" yaw puma naami kitalawu. "Sen itam itaasoy hin-tsanni?"

"Pay pi itam son nawus qa amtoni," yaw puma kita. Pu' yaw oovi puma put mokyaata. Pu' yaw haqawa pi iikwilta. Pu' yaw puma soy amto. Yaw puma angqw pay kiy taavangqöymi Pisatvelmo'. "Pay itam yep taavang-qöyve Pisatvelpe amni," yaw puma kita.

Pu' yaw oovi puma panso put iikwiwta. Pu' yaw puma ep pituuqe, pay yaw put mookiwtaqat tavi, nit pu' yaw puma qölötiva. Naat yaw oovi puma

He stepped around the rock and walked up to him. His brother was still kneeling and holding the arrow in place on his bow. "Why didn't you answer me?" he scolded. But there was no reply. His brother did not even so much as look at him. So Pöqangwhoya went to him and tapped him on the head. "Why didn't you answer me?" he asked. But again he got no answer.

He took a closer look at Palöngawhoya and then he shook him. His brother was frozen stiff. He had evidently frozen while aiming his arrow into the hole. So instead of pursuing the rabbit further, Pöqangwhoya flung his younger brother on his back the way he was and carried him home from there.

When they got there, grandmother greeted them, "Thank you, you are home."

"That's right," Pöqangwhoya replied. "We started digging out a rabbit and my brother froze."

"Oh dear, you two do the darnedest things!" she exclaimed.

"I'll leave him here for the time being. He should thaw before long," he said to his grandmother. Then he placed his younger brother next to the fire and piled a lot of wood on it. Grandmother busied herself while Palöngawhoya, frozen solid, still knelt and held his arrow on the bow. She was working away when Palöngawhoya suddenly thawed. This made him release his arrow. It crossed the bow and shot grandmother right through the heart.

Now that really tickled the boys. "What are we going to do with her now?" they kept asking each other. "I wonder what we should do with her?"

"Obviously we'll have to go and bury her," they said. So they bundled her up; one of them loaded her on his back, and they went to bury her. They started from their house towards the west side, to Pisatvela. "We'll bury her here on the west side," they said.

So the boys carried her to Pisatvela and when they got there they placed her, bundled up as she was, on the ground. They began to dig a hole

47

qölölawqw, pay yaw so'am hintiqe atkyamiq mumamayku. Pu' yaw pay pas nungwu a'ni mumamaykuqe pay yaw tsawi. Yaw soyamuy torikuyi'at angqw yama, mookiwtaqat angqw, pu' yaw so'am mumamataqw yaw torikuyi'at kwangwawipipitima. Pas yaw pumuy no'a. Pas yaw pumuy no'aqw yaw puma taya'iwta, niiqe pu' yaw puma naami pangqawu, "As tum kur piw aqw kwistoy."

Pu' yaw oovi puma aqw put soy kwisto. Pu' yaw puma put soy ahoy oomiq yawma. Pu' yaw paasat puma pay put pas naap muuma. Pu' yaw piw anti. Yaw torikuyi'at kwangwawipipitima. Pas yaw pumuy no'iy'ta. Pu' yaw pay puma put qa amt, pay teevep pep put mumunlawu. Pas pi yaw pumuy no'iy'ta. Pu' hapi yaw aqw mumamataqw, pu' yaw torikuyi'at wipipitimaqw, pu' yaw puma aw taya'iwtangwu.

Naat yaw oovi puma put pantsakqw, pay yaw so'am taatayi pay pi a'ni himuniiqe'. Pu' yaw amumi a'ni itsivuti. "Uma hiitu qa hophoyatu," yaw kitat, pu' yaw murikot kwusut pu' yaw pumuy pangqw ngöyta ahoy kiy aqwa'. Pu' yaw puma a'ni waaya. Pu' yaw so'am pituuqe pay yaw pöhikiw-va. Pay yaw pumuy qa hintsana.

Yan yaw naat puma soy qa amqw, pay yaw ahoy taatayi. Naat kya oovi songqe haqam soosoyam yeese. Pay yuk pölö.

and while they were still busy digging, something happened and the old woman started rolling downhill. As she rolled faster and faster she began to unwrap. Her braid slipped out of the bundle and flipped from side to side while she rolled down the slope. That really amused them, so much so, that they started laughing and then said to each other, "Let's go get her again."

So they went down the hill, picked her up, and carried her back up to the top. This time they were going to roll her off themselves. So they did it again and her braid once more flipped along nicely. They really got a bang out of that. So instead of burying her, they rolled her downhill all day long. It was great fun for them, because whenever she rolled down, her braid would flip back and forth and they laughed their heads off at that.

They were still doing that when their grandmother came to life again. After all, she was a woman with supernatural powers. Now she really scolded them. "You rotten misfits," she shouted, and she picked up a stick and chased them all the way back to the house. The two brothers ran away as fast as they could. By the time grandmother got to the house she had calmed down and did not punish them.

This is how grandmother came to life before they buried her. I suppose all of them are still living somewhere. And here the story ends.

Maana niqw Tiyo
Qatsiy oovi Naahepnuma

Hide and Seek with Life at Stake

Aliksa'i. Yaw Orayve yeesiwa. Noq pep kiive taavang qalaveq yaw hak tiyo kiy'ta. Pu' yaw hoopaqwat qalaveq piw hak maana kiy'ta. Noq put maanat yaw as pay aw tootim tunglay'yungwa. Noq pay yaw pas qa hakiy naawakna.

Noq i' tiyo yaw yumuy'ta. Noq yaw pam hisat nay engem paasayat aw tuuwalatoniqe pu' yaw oovi pam panso'. Niikyangw pam yaw it maanat kiiyat iikye'. Noq piw yaw kiy angqaqw put aw hingqawu. Noq pas yaw pam qa tuptsiwa, qa hisat pi yaw pam maana hakiy tiyot aw naap hingqawu, niqw oovi pas yaw pam qa tuptsiwa. Niqw yaw put tuuvingta, "Um haqami'?"

"Pay nu' itanay engem paasayat aw tuuwalato," yaw aw kita.

Pu' yaw paasat maana pangqawu, "Ya sen nu' son umumni?" yaw aw kita.

"Pi um pi. Pay pi um inumumninik inumumni," yaw pam aw kitat pu' pay aapiyo'.

Aliksa'i. They were living in Oraibi. There at the western edge of the village lived a certain boy. And at the eastern edge, a girl had her home. The young men craved the love of that girl, but she did not want any of them.

The boy still had his parents and one day he went to watch his father's field and guard it against animals. On his way he passed the house of this girl. To his surprise she called out to him. He could hardly believe his ears, for never had that girl spoken on her own to any boy. "Where are you going?" she asked him.

"I'm going to watch my father's field," he replied.

The girl suggested, "Why don't I accompany you?"

"That's up to you. If you want to, you can come along with me," he said and went on his way.

51

Paasat pu' yaw maana kiy aw pakiiqe pu' yaw piikit mokyaata. Pantit pu' yaw pam pangqw angki. Pu' yaw oovi tiyo pasve pituuqe, pay ep nay uuyiyat ang pootiy'numqw, pu' yaw maana angk pitu.

"Um pitu?" yaw pam aw kita.

"Owi," yaw kitat pu' yaw nitkyay horokna. "Itam mooti nösni," yaw kita. Kitat pu' yaw pikmokiy tsawikna. Pu' yaw tutskwave usimniy puhukna. Pu' yaw puma oovi naama pep put nöösa. Yaw oovi puma paas nösq, pu' yaw maana pangqawu, "Pas itam as hintsakni," yaw kita.

"Ta'ay, hintsakni?"

"Itam as naahepnumni, niikyangw hak hakiy naalös tuwe', hak hakiy niinamantani," yaw kita.

Pu' yaw pay pam nakwha. "Ta'ay," yaw kita, "hak mooti na'uytatoni?" yaw kita.

Pu' yaw maana tiyot aw pangqawu, "Um mooti na'uytatoni."

"Qa'e," yaw tiyo kita, "um pi pan naawaknaqe, oovi um mooti na'uytatoni."

Pu' yaw pay puma pep naamisa'a. Hisatniqw pu' yaw pay maana mooti na'uytatoni. Paasat pu' yaw pangqawu maana, "Yang um tutskwava tsooraltini," yaw aw kita. Pu' yaw oovi pam ang tsooralti. Pantiqw pu' yaw put usimniy akw naakwapna nit pu' yaw aw pangqawu, "Um hapi qa inungk taytani. Ason nu' pas na'uyte', ung aa'awnaqw, pu' um nuy heptoni," yaw aw kita. Pantit pu' yaw maana na'uytato. Uysonaq yaw pam haqami na'uytaniqay hepnuma. Hisatniqw pu' yaw pam uuyit atpipoq paki. Pantit pu' yaw pam "taw" kita.

Paasat pu' yaw tiyo qatuptut pu' maanat hepto. Pu' yaw pam pephaqam put hepnuma. Pu' yaw pam kukyat as anga'. Pay yaw haqami uuyit as aw kuk'at so'taqw, pay yaw qa haqamo. Pas yaw pam as soosovik hept qa tuwa. Pu' yaw pam paasat piw haqami kuk'at so'taqw panso ahoyi. Nit pay yaw piw qa tuwa. Paasat pu' yaw pam pangqawu, "Um pewni. Pay pi nu' ung qa tuwa, um oovi pewni," kita yawi'.

The girl went in her house, wrapped up some piki and ran after him. So the boy arrived at the field and, while he was checking his father's corn plants, the girl caught up with him.

"So you have come?" he said to her.

"Yes," she answered and then she took out the journey food. "Let's eat first," she said and unfastened the bundle of piki. She spread her shawl on the ground and they ate together. When they had eaten their fill, the girl said, "Why don't we do something?"

"Very well, what?"

"Let's play hide and seek. And whoever finds the other four times shall kill him," she said.

"All right," the boy agreed, "who is going to hide first?"

The girl replied, "You."

"No," the boy protested, "this was your idea so you hide first!"

They argued back and forth like this till the girl finally gave in. She said to him, "Lie flat on the ground here." So he lay down. She covered him with her shawl and warned him, "Don't watch me. And don't come looking for me until I let you know that I am hidden." Then the girl went to hide herself. She started looking for a hiding place in the middle of the corn plants. After a while she crawled under a plant. Then she shouted, "Now!"

So the boy got up and went to look for the girl. He searched all over for her. Then he followed her tracks. They ended at a corn plant but she was not there. Although he looked all over, he could not find her. He returned to where her tracks had stopped and again he couldn't discover her. So he shouted, "Come here, I can't find you."

53

Paasat pu' yaw paysoq put aqlap uuyit atpipahaqw yaw maana yama. Pu' yaw aw pangqawu, "Yangqw nu'niqw, um nuy qa tuwa."

Paasat pu' yaw piw puma angqw ahoy maanat usimniyat aw'i. Paasat pu' yaw pam tuwat maanat naakwapna. Pu' yaw tuwat aw pangqawu, "Um hapi qa inungk taytani. Ason nu' pas pangqawqw, pu' um nuy heptoni." Kitat pu' yaw tuwat na'uytato.

"Ya sen nu' haqami na'uytani?" yaw kitikyangw angqw paasat qalavoq pam wari. Pepeq pu' yaw pam suwaptsokit atpipoq na'uyta. Pantit pu' yaw tuwat "taw" kita.

Paasat pu' yaw maana tuwat put hepto. Pay yaw kukyat angniiqe yaw paasat qalavoq kuk'at so'ta. Paasat pu' yaw maana pangqawu, "Um pangqw yamakni. Pay nu' ung tuwa, um oovi yamakni."

Pu' yaw nawus i' tiyo angqw yama. Paasat pu' yaw puma piw ahoy haqaqw yaynaqay panso'. Paasat pu' yaw maana piw tiyot naakwapna. "Um hapi qa inungk taytani." Kitat pu' yaw piw na'uytato. Pu' yaw pam pep pasve haqami na'uytaniqay piw hepnuma. "Ya sen nu' haqami pu' na'uytani? Haqami sen nu' na'uytaqw nuy qa tuwani?" yaw kitikyangw pam pep pasve naahoy wawartinuma. Hisatniqw pu' yaw pam sukw uuyit aw pituuqe, pu' yaw pam put angqw talayat tsoopat pu' aqw paki. Pantit pu' yaw pam ahoy naamiq put tsurukna. Pantit pu' yaw pam "taw" kita.

Paasat pu' yaw tiyo piw put hepto. Pu' yaw pam pep put pasve hepnuma. Pu' paasat qalava piw yaw enang heeva. Pay yaw pam pas qa tuwa. Pu' yaw pam kukyat piw as anga'. Noq pay yaw mootiwat piw an uuyit aqlavo so'ta. Noq pay yaw pas qa haqamo. Paasat pu' yaw pay pam nawus piw pangqawu, "Um inumi naamataqtani, pay pi nu' ung qa tuwa."

Naat yaw oovi pu' kitaqw, paysoq yaw aqlap uuyit talayat yaw angqaqw yama. Pu' yaw aw pangqawu, "Yangqw nu'niqw, um nuy qa tuwa," yaw aw kita.

Paasat pu' yaw i' tiyo qa pas haalayti. Nungwu pay yaw pam löös maanat qa tuwaqw, pay pam put suus tuwa. Paasat pu' yaw puma piw ahoy

54

Thereupon the girl came out from under a plant right next to him. "Here I am," she said. "You didn't find me."

They returned to the girl's shawl. Now it was his turn to cover up the girl. He said to her, "Don't watch me. And don't come looking for me till I tell you." With that he left to hide.

"Now, where am I going to hide myself?" he said as he ran to the edge of the field. He hid under a saltbush. Then he, too, called, "Ready!"

Now it was the girl's turn to search for him. She followed his tracks that ended at the edge of the field. Then she said, "Come out from there, I have found you."

The boy had to crawl out and they went back to the place where they had started. Now the girl covered the boy again. "Be sure you don't watch me," she said and went to hide. Again she looked in the field for a place to hide. "I wonder where I should hide myself this time? Where would be a good hiding place?" Saying this, she ran back and forth in the field. Finally she came to a corn plant and after pulling out its tassel she climbed in. Then she reached out and replaced the tassel and signaled that she was ready.

Again the boy went to find her. He searched for her in the field and along its edge but could not find her. Once more he followed her footprints. Just as they had the first time, they stopped near a corn plant. But the girl was nowhere in sight. Again, he had to say, "Reveal yourself, I can't find you."

No sooner had he spoken than she came out of the corn tassel of the plant next to him. "Here I am. You didn't find me," she said.

Now the boy was not at all happy. Up to now he had failed to find her two times and she had found him once. So they went back to their starting place and the girl said to him, "Well then, go hide again. I have found you once and so far you haven't found me."

qeniy aw'i. Paasat pu' yaw maana put aw pangqawu, "Ta'a, pay pu' um piw na'uytatoni. Pay pi nu' ung suus tuwa, noq um naat nuy qa hisatniqw tuwa," kita yaw awi'.

Paasat pu' yaw i' tiyo maanat piw naakwapna. Paasat pu' yaw tiyo na'uytato. "Ya sen nu' haqami na'uytaqw nuy qa tuwani?" yaw kita.

Pu' yaw pam oovi pep haqami na'uytaniqay hepnumkyangw yaw qalavoq pituqw, piw yaw hak aw hingqawu, "Pew umni," yaw aw kita, "pay ung suus tuwa, noq um oovi pewniqw, nu' ung tupkyani," yaw aw kita. Noq yaw kur taawa. Paasat pu' yaw oovi taawa put aqlavo tangaqwunut tsööqökna. "Put um ang peqw wupni. Um peqw wuuve', inuukwayngyangaqw na'uytaqw, pay son ung tuwani," kita yaw awi'.

Pu' yaw oovi pam tangaqwunut ang taawat aqw wuuvi. Pu' yaw pam put aakwayngyavoq na'uyta. Pantit pu' yaw "taw" kita.

Paasat pu' yaw maana put hepto. Pu' yaw pam pasve put soosovik heeva. Pu' paasat qalava piw. Pu' yaw pam as kukyat ang piw. Noq pay yaw haqami tsomooyat aw kuk'at so'ta. Noq pay yaw pas put qa tuwa. Pu' yaw piw ang ahoy. Nungwu yaw paapu maanat poli'ini'at naanap hinti, teevep yaw pam naarikyangw a'ni wuuwankyangwniqw ooviyo'. "Ya sen pam haqami na'uytaqw, oovi pas nu' qa tuwa?" Pu' yaw pam piw kukyat anga', nit pay piw yaw tsomooyat aw kuk'at so'ta. Paasat pep pu' yaw maana wuuwanta, "Ya sen pam haqami na'uyta?" Paasat pu' yaw piihuy horokna, pu' yaw mapqölmiq piihuy hiisaq kuuya. Pantit pu' yaw put aqw tayta. Pantit pu' yaw kur pay put tuwa. Susmataq yaw piihuyat angqw taawat aakwayngyangaqw pam na'uyiy'ta. Paasat pu' yaw pangqawu maana, "Um hawni, pay nu' ung tuwa. Taawat um aakwayngyangaqw na'uyiy'ta."

Paasat pu' yaw taawa put aw pangqawu, "Ta'ay, yupa, nawus haawii', pay pi ung tuwa."

Kitat pu' yaw pam put ahoy hawna. Pangqw pu' yaw piw puma ahoyi. "Pay nu' ung pu' löös tuwa, noq löös peeti," yaw kita.

Yaw tiyo qa haalayti. Paasat pu' yaw maana piw it naakwapna, nit pu'

So the boy put the shawl back over the girl and went to hide. "I wonder where I can hide so she won't find me?" he said.

Looking for a hiding place, he reached the edge of the field, when a voice surprised him. "Come here to me," it said. "She has found you once already. I will hide you." It was evidently the sun that had spoken to him. The sun drove a rainbow into the ground next to him. "You can climb up on that and come here to me. When you are up you can hide behind me and she won't be able to find you."

So the boy climbed up to the sun along the rainbow. He hid behind it and then shouted, "Now!"

Thereupon the girl went searching for him. She searched everywhere in the field including the part along the edge. She also went along his tracks. They ended at a little hill, but since she couldn't find a trace of him there, she went back. In the meantime the girl's butterfly hairdo had become all disarrayed because she was thinking so hard all the time that she kept scratching her head. "Where, I wonder, did he hide that I can't find him at all?" She followed his tracks anew and again they stopped at the little hill. She was puzzled. "I wonder where he hid?" She took her breast out of her dress and let a little bit of milk flow into her open hand. She looked into it and now she saw him. It was quite plain in the milk that he was hidden behind the sun. So she called, "Come down, I've found you. You are hiding behind the sun."

Thereupon the sun said to the boy, "All right, go on, you have to climb down, whether you want to or not. She has discovered you."

After these words the sun helped him down, and the two headed back again. "I have found you twice; only two more times are left," she said.

The boy was not happy about this. The girl covered him again and

piw na'uytato. Paasat pu' yaw i' tiyo usimniy qalangaqw hölöknaqe pu' angk tayta. Noq yaw kaway'uyit aqwat wari. Paasat pu' yaw oovi put aa'awnaqw, pu' yaw pam piw hepto. Pu' yaw as pam piw pep put hepnuma, kaway'uyit anga'. Panso pi yaw kuk'at so'ta. Noq pas pi yaw kaway'uyi a'ni hootakiwyungqw, pas yaw kur haqami na'uyta. Pu' yaw pam as paas put heeva nit pay yaw pas qa tuwa. Paasat pu' yaw pam nawus piw pangqawu, "Pay pi nu' ung qa tuwa, um oovi haqaqw na'uyiy'te', yamakni," kita yaw pami'.

Paysoq yaw put aqlap kawayvatngat angqaqw yama. "Yangqw nu'niqw, um nuy qa tuwa," yaw aw kita.

Pu' paasat yaw puma piwni. "Pu' um piw tuwat na'uytatoni."

Pu' yaw oovi maana piw naakwava. Paasat pu' yaw i' tiyo piw na'uytato. Pay yaw pam paasat qa haalay'iwkyangw, "Is ohi, pay nuy löös tuwaqw, naat nu' pas qa hisatniqw tuwa. Ya sen nu' haqami na'uytaqw nuy qa tuwani?"

Naat yaw pam yan wuuwankyangw haqami na'uytaniqay heptoq, yaw hak piw put aw hingqawu, "Pew umni," yaw aw kita, "nu' ung ookwatuwqe oovi nu' ung tupkyani," yaw aw kita. Paasat pu' yaw pam tuwa. Paysoq yaw uuyit aqlap tutskwamiqhaqami hiisayhoya hötsi. Noq pangqw yaw kur kookyangwso'wuuti put wangwayi. Pu' yaw pam oovi aqw paki.

"Nu' ung ookwatuwqe oovi ung tupkyani. Pay nungwu ung löös tuwa, noq yangqw pay son ung tuwani," aw yaw kitat, pu' yaw kiy atsva wishöviy laanata.

Pantiqw pu' yaw pam "taw" kita. Paasat pu' yaw maana piw it hepto. Pasve yaw wawartinuma. Soosok hiita yaw aa'atpikyaqe kukuytinuma, nit pay yaw put qa tuwa. Pay yaw oovi pas su'awwuyavo put hepnumt pay yaw put qa tuwa. Paasat pu' yaw piihuy angqaqw piw hiita horokna, kur yaw ruupita. Paasat pu' yaw put aqw taatayi. Oova yaw mooti taatayi, noq pay yaw qa haqamo. Paasat pu' yaw piw namtökna. Paasat pu' yaw atkyamiwat taatayi. Paasat pu' yaw pay kur piw tuwa. Susmataq yaw ruupiyat angqw

went to hide herself. This time the boy lifted the edge of the shawl and followed her with his eyes. She was running toward the watermelon plants. She gave her signal and he went looking. He tried to find her among the watermelon plants, because that was where her footprints ended. But because the watermelon plants had a great many vines, he did not know where she was hidden. He searched very carefully, but did not find her. Finally he had to call again, "I can't find you, so come out from where you are hiding."

Then she emerged from a watermelon right next to him. "Here I am, but you didn't see me," she said.

So they decided to do it again. "Now it's your turn to hide."

The girl covered herself and the boy left to hide. He was very discouraged now. "Poor me, she has found me twice, while I haven't found her even once. Where, I wonder, can I hide so she won't find me?"

While he was still thinking and looking for a hiding place, someone spoke to him again. "Come here," the voice said. "I pity you, so I will hide you." Then he spotted the place the voice had come from. Right next to a corn plant there was a tiny hole that led into the ground. It was Spider Woman who had called him from there. So then he crawled in.

"I took pity on you; therefore, I am going to hide you. She has already found you twice, but she won't discover you in here," Spider Woman said to him and then she spun a web over her house.

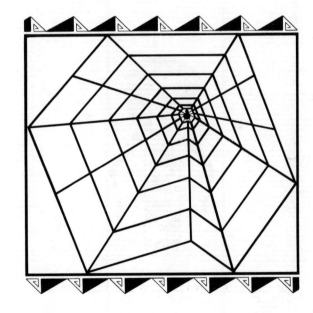

The boy shouted, "Now!" and the girl started out to look for him. She ran all over the field. She looked under everything, but did not find him. By now she had looked around for a long time and yet had failed to find him. So she pulled something out of her breast again. It was a crystal. She looked into it and at first scanned the sky above, but he was not there. Then she turned the crystal over and looked downward. She discovered him again. The crystal showed quite clearly that he was in Spider Woman's house. "Come out of there," she said, "I found you."

kookyangwso'wuutit kiiyat angqw pakiwta. "Um yamakni," yaw aw kita, "pay nu' ung tuwa."

Pu' yaw pam nawus angqw yama. Paasat pu' yaw i' tiyo pas qa haalayti. "Is ohi, pu' pay suus peeti. Suus piw nuy tuwaqw, pay nu' pö'ini," kita.

Pu' yaw puma piw angqw ahoy usimnit aw'i. Paasat pu' yaw maana put naakwapna. Pantit pu' yaw piw na'uytato. Pu' yaw pam piw angk tayta. Pay yaw piw hoopoq wari. Noq kaway'uyit pi yaw kwiningqöyva pövawya, noq ep tokinen pi yaw yokvaqw, pangqe pövawyat angqe yaw paa'iwta. Noq pangqw yaw pavatyam tangawta. Panso yaw i' maana. Pu' yaw pansoq pam paki. Pay yaw pam paasat pavatyaniwti.

Paasat pu' yaw tiyo piw as put hepnuma. Pay yaw pas qa tuwa. Pas pi yaw pam pi'ep as ahoy ang hepngwu haqe' hepqay. Naat yaw oovi pam put qa tuwat, pas yaw pam paanaqmoki. Pu' yaw pam put paahut u'na. "Ura pi pövavaqe paahu. Nu' mooti pansonen, hikwt, pu' ason piw hepni," kita yaw pam naaminiiqe pu' yaw pam angqw panso'. Pu' yaw pam aw pituuqe angqw hiiko. Pantit pu' yaw pam pangqawu, "Pay pu' nu' ung qa tuway, um oovi haqamnen pewniy," kita yawi'.

Paysoq yaw aqlangaqw paahut angqaqw yama. "Yangqw nu'niqw, um nuy qa tuwa," yaw aw kita. "Um hiihikqw nu' uumi taytaqw, um nuy qa tuwa." Noq antsa pi yaw i' tiyo hiihikqw, yaw antsa put aw paangaqw pavatya kuyvat pu' ahoy piw aqwhaqami pakima. Pam yaw kur maana put aw kuyva asa', noq qa hin pi yaw pam maananiiqat pam wuuwa.

Pu' yaw puma piw angqw ahoy haqaqw yaynaqay awi'. Paasat pu' yaw maana pangqawu, "Suus hapi peeti," yaw kita. "Pu' hapi nu' ung tuwe', pu' ung pö'ani."

Paasat pu' yaw pas i' tiyo qa haalayti tisa'. Paasat pu' yaw oovi pam maanat naakwapnat pu' piw na'uytato. Pay yaw pam paasat kur haqami na'uytani. Naat yaw oovi pam pep wuuwanta haqami na'uytaniqay, niqw yaw kookyangwso'wuuti it aw pangqawu, "Taatöq um qalavoq taqatskimi

So he had to come out. Now the boy really grew despondent. "Dear me, only one time left. If she finds me once more I am beaten," he said.

They then returned to the shawl. The girl covered him up and went to hide. Once again he watched her. She started running east. On the northern side of the watermelon plants there was a little wash. The night before it had rained, so there was some water in it now and tadpoles were swimming around. That was the girl's destination. She dived in and changed into a tadpole.

The boy went in search of her, but he simply could not find her. Again and again he searched back along the places where he had already looked. He still had not discovered her when he got thirsty. He remembered the wash. "There is water in the wash. I'll go there first to drink and then I will continue looking for her," he said to himself. When he arrived, he drank. Then he shouted, "I haven't been able to find you. So if you are somewhere, come here."

Right next to him, she came out of the water. "Here I am, but you didn't find me," she said in reply. "While you were drinking, I was staring at you, but you didn't see me." And, indeed, while the boy had been drinking, a tadpole had looked at him from the water and had disappeared again. Evidently it was the girl who had been looking at him, but it had never occurred to him that it was she.

Hereupon they returned to their starting place and the girl said, "One more time is left. If I find you, I will have beaten you."

Now the boy was desperate. He covered the girl up and went to hide. He didn't know where to hide anymore. He was still thinking about a hiding place when Spider Woman spoke to him. "Go south to the edge of the field where your uncle lives in a shed," she said. "When you get to him, he will hide you and she won't be able to find you."

uutahay awni," yaw aw kita. "Put um awniqw pam ung tupkyani. Pam ung tupkyaqw pay son ung tuwani," yaw aw kita.

Pangqw pu' yaw oovi pam taqatskimiq wari. Yaw pam aqw pituqw qa hak haqamo. Pu' yaw pam pangqawu, "Itahay, um nuy tupkyaniy."

Yaw pam kitaqw, yaw sukw taqatskit hokyayat angqaqw ho'aya yama. "Peqw um pakini," yaw aw kita niiqe pu' yaw put taqatskit hokyayat ep poosiyat horokna. Pu' yaw pam aqw paki. Put yaw kur aasonaq hötsi. Paasat pu' yaw ho'aya piw aqw paki, pu' yaw naamiq uuta.

Paasat pu' yaw "taw" kita. Paasat pu' yaw maana put hepto. Paas yaw pam put pasve heeva, pu' oova, pu' atkye'. Pay yaw pas qa tuwa. Paasat pu' yaw kukyat anga'. Noq taqatskit yaw aqw kuk'at so'ta. Noq pay yaw qa haqamo. Paasat pu' yaw maana wuuwanta, "Ya sen haqami na'uytaqw oovi nu' qa tuwa?" Paasat pu' yaw mamlatsiy lengiy akw mowanata. Pantit pu' yaw wupamlatsiy naqvumiq tsurukna nit pu' yaw tuqayvaasiy'ta. Susmataq yaw taqatskit sukw hokyayat ang pakiwta. Pu' yaw paasat pangqawu, "Um yamakni, pay nu' ung tuwa. Taqatskit hokyayat um ang pakiwta."

Pu' yaw pam nawus piw angqw yama. Pangqw pu' yaw puma piw ahoy uysonmi'. Paasat pu' yaw put aw maana pangqawu, "Ta'a, pay pi nu' ung naalös tuwa, noq oovi nu' ung nawus niinani," kita yaw awi'. "Itam oovi peqwni." Pangqw pu' yaw puma taqatskimiqa'. Pu' yaw puma epeq pituqw, pu' yaw maana taqatskit akwningqöyve qölöta. Pantit pu' yaw put aw pangqawu, "Ta'a, um uunapnay tavini, pu' uutukwaviy piiwu. Noq pu' nu' ung niinani. Pay pi nu' ung pö'a."

Kitat pu' yaw kweeway angqaqw poyot horokna. Oovi yaw pam napnay nit pu' tuukwaviy taviqw, pu' yaw put höömiyat tsöqö. Pantit pu' yaw put qölömi lölökinta. Pantit pu' yaw qölömiq put kwaptuku. Pu' yaw qölömiq put ungwayat kuuya. Pantit pu' yaw aqw aama. Pantit pu' yaw piw angqw hihin kwiniwi'. Pep pu' yaw piw sukw qölötaqe pansoq pu' yaw put aama. "Yantani," yaw kita, "pay pi nuwupi nu' ung pö'a," kita yawnit

He ran to the field shelter, but when he reached it, he did not see anybody. So he called, "My uncle, hide me!"

Thereupon a wood worm came out of one of the poles that held up the shed. "Come in here," he said. The worm removed a knot from the post and the boy crawled in. Inside it was hollow. Then the worm followed and closed the opening after him.

The boy yelled, "Now!" and the girl went searching for him. She searched carefully on the ground, then above, and then below. She simply could not find a trace of him. So she followed his tracks. They ended at the field shed. But he was not in sight. The girl thought, "I wonder where he keeps himself hidden that I can't find him?" She moistened her fingers with her tongue, stuck her forefinger in her ear and listened with great concentration. It was quite obvious that he was in one of the shed posts. So she called, "You can come out, I have found you. You are inside the pole of the shed."

So he was forced to come out again. When they walked back to the area where the corn plants were, the girl said to him, "Well then, I have found you four times and will have to kill you. So let's go here." They went toward the shed and when they arrived, the girl dug a hole on its northern side. Then she ordered him, "All right, take off both your shirt and your necklace. Then I will kill you. After all, I have won!"

Saying this, she pulled a knife out of her belt. After he had taken off his shirt and necklace, she grabbed his hair and dragged him to the hole. There she cut his throat so that the blood poured into the hole. She covered it up with sand and then went a little further northward. There she made another hole and buried him in it. "So now," she said, "it can't be helped; I beat you." Thereupon the girl went home with the blue shirt and the necklace of the boy.

pu' pam maana pangqaqw put tiyot sakwanapnayat nit pu' tuukwaviyat yawkyangw nima.

Noq pay yaw tapkiqw it tiyot yumat qa pitsina. "Ya sen pam haqaminiiqe oovi qa pitu? Noq ura pi pam hoopaq maana kiy'taqa amum pasmihaqaminiqw, pam kya as hin navotiy'tani. Kur nu' aqw tuuvingtatoni."

Pu' yaw oovi put tiyot yu'at maanat kiiyat aqw'a, niiqe pu' yaw tuuvingta, "Ya um qa navotiy'ta Kwavöhö haqaminiqö'? Um pi ura amum se'el pasmihaqami'. Pas pam qa pitu."

Paasat pu' yaw maana pangqawu, "Hep owi, antsa nu' se'el yangqw put angk panso'o. Noq pay pam nuy angqw ahoy hoonaqw, oovi nu' pay se'elhaq ahoy naala pitu. Haqami pi oovi pam'i. Pay nu' qa navotiy'ta," kita yawi'.

Yaw put tiyot yu'at qa haalay'iwkyangw pitu. Puma pi yaw ep tavoknen kanelninayaqe put yaw puma tuupey'yungwa, niiqe pay yaw puma qa pas put kwangwanönösa, pay yaw put pas angqw hihin yukuya. Noq yaw pay puma tunösvongyay pas qa ayo' piw qenitotaqw, yaw sikwiyamuy aw tootopt homimita. Paasat pu' yaw put tiyot yu'at tootoptuy ayo' hoonanta. Naat yaw oovi pam pumuy ayo' hoonantaqw, piw yaw suukya tootovi put aw lavayti, "Um hintoq nuy ayo' hoonanta? Taq pi nu' put angqw nööse', umungem Kwavöhöt heptoni. Um oovi qa nuy ayo' hoonantani. Noq nu' ööye' umuutiy heptoni."

Pu' yaw pay pam oovi put qa aw hintsaki, noq pu' yaw sikwit angqw pas öyqe pu' yaw pangqawu, "Pay nu' songqa tuwani." Kitat pu' yaw pam tootovi pangqw pasmi'. Pu' yaw pam pep pumuy kukyamuy ang yannumkyangw hisatniqw pu' taqatskimiq pitu. Pepeq pu' yaw pam tutskwava ungwat tsölöm'iwtaqat tuwa. Pantit pu' yaw pam haqam maana qölöt aqw amqw, put yaw piw tuwa. Pu' yaw pam put aqw yaaha. Pu' yaw pam angqw tiyot ungwayat tsootsona. Pu' yaw pam angqw kwiniwi haqam tiyo aamiwtaqw panso'. Pep pu' yaw pam piw put aqw yaaha. Pantit pu' yaw

When it became evening, the boy had not come home to his parents. His mother said, "I wonder where he went that he is not back yet? Let's see, this girl that lives in the east was going to accompany him to the field. She might know something. Let me go ask her."

So the boy's mother went to her house and asked her, "Haven't you any idea where Kwavöhö is? You went this morning to the field with him. He is not home yet."

The girl replied, "Yes, I actually followed him there this morning, but he sent me back again, so I came home all by myself quite a while ago. I don't know where he is."

The boy's mother was sad when she returned. The day before they had slaughtered a sheep and had roasted it, but now they didn't enjoy their meal and ate only very little. They had not yet cleared the floor area on which the food was spread when the flies began to swarm around it. So the boy's mother shooed the flies away. While she was busy doing that, one fly, to her great surprise, spoke to her, "Why are you driving me away? Let me eat and I will search for Kwavöhö for you. Please don't chase me away. When I'm full, I will go and look for your child."

The mother did not harm the fly. When he was full, he said, "I am sure I will find him," and then he flew off to the field. While flying along the footprints of the boy and girl, he came to the field shelter. There he saw blood spattered on the ground. And not long after, he discovered the spot where the girl had covered the blood. He dug a hole in the ground and sucked out the boy's blood. Then he flew north to the place where the boy was buried. He dug out another opening and inserted the blood back into his body. It did not take long till his heart started beating again.

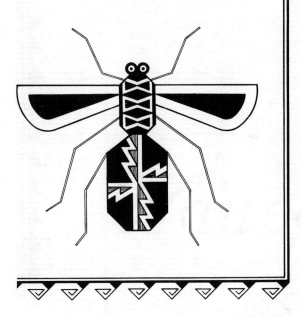

pam put ahoy aw ungwayat tangata. Pantiqw pu' yaw pay qa wuuyavotiqw pay yaw ahoy unangwa'at tsotso'tiva.

Pu' yaw tiyo pangqawu, "Ya um hakniiqe oovi nuy ahoy taatayna?"

"Pay nuu'uy," yaw aw kita, "nu' ung ookwatuwqe oovi angqö. Noq ungum ung nuutayyungway. Itam oovi nimani," kita yawi'.

Paasat pu' yaw puma pangqaqw nima. Pu' yaw puma pituqw, yaw yumat haalayti. Paasat pu' yaw tootovi amumi pangqawu, "Qaavo hapi um put maanat kiiyat aqwni. Hingqawni pi uumi'. Pay hapi son uumi qa haalaytini. Pu' pay um piw qa aw hin unangway'tani. Pu' hapi son uumi qa tunösvongyaatani, noq um hapi pay put angqw qa nösni. Pu' pay um panis aw uunapnay nit pu' uutukwaviy tuuvingtani. Pu' uumi hapi taviqw, pu' um aw pumuy wiiwilat pu' ason angqw yamakni." Yan yaw tootovi tiyot aw tutapta.

Pu' yaw oovi pam qavongvaqw hisatniqw pu' maanat kiiyat aqw'a. Antsa yaw pam aw pakiqw, yaw sumataq as qa tuptsiwa. Nit pu' yaw pay antsa aw haalayti. "Ya um ahoy pitu?" yaw aw kita. Paasat pu' yaw antsa engem suutunösvongyaata. "Yep um nösni," yaw aw kita.

Noq pay yaw pam qa nakwha, "Nu' pay qa tsöngmokiwta. Nu' pay inapnay nit pu' itukwaviy oovi angqö. Um oovi taviy'te', inumi ahoy put tavini."

Pu' yaw oovi aapamiqhaqami pakima. Pu' yaw angqaqw ahoy napnayat nit pu' tuukwaviyat yawkyangw yama. Noq yaw aapamiq hötaqw pam aqw yori. Pas yaw epeq hiihiimu wukotangawta, kyahakhiimu. Put hapi yaw kur pam tootimuy qöyankyangw nawkilawqe, oovi pas puuvut niitiy'ta. Pu' yaw oovi put aw napnayat nit tuukwaviyat ahoy taviqw, pu' yaw pam aw wiiwilat pu' aw pangqawu, "Pay nu' it oovi angqö."

Noq i' tiyo yaw maanat kiiyat aqwniqw, pu' yaw aakwayngyap tootovi put yumuyatuy aw pangqawu, "Uma mit maanat kiiyat aqwni, nen uma kiiyat iip umuutiy nuutaytani." Yan yaw pam pumuy tutapta.

Pu' yaw oovi puma pangqw maanat kiiyat aqw'a. Pay yaw oovi puma

66

Now the boy said, "Who are you that you brought me back to life?"

"It's me," the fly said. "I came because I pitied you. But your parents are waiting for you, so let's go home."

So they went home and when they arrived his parents were glad. The fly said to them, "Be sure and go to that girl's house tomorrow. I don't know what she will say to you. She will probably greet you nicely. Also, don't show that you have a grudge against her. She will most likely spread food on the floor for you, but do not eat of it. Only ask for your shirt and necklace. When she hands them to you, shake them at her and then leave." Those were the fly's instructions to the boy.

On the following day he went to the girl's house. When he entered, she didn't quite believe it, but then she greeted him happily. "Are you back again?" she asked. Thereupon she brought food for him. "Here, eat," she said.

But he declined. "I'm not hungry. I came for my shirt and necklace. If you have them, give them back to me."

She disappeared in the back room and returned with his shirt and necklace. As she opened the door, he cast a glance inside. All sorts of valuable things were gathered there. She had evidently taken them from the boys she had killed, because she had so many. When she handed him back his shirt and necklace, he shook them at her and said, "These are the things I came for."

Now after the boy had left for the girl's house, the fly told his parents, "You, too, go to the girl's house and wait in front for your son." This is what he instructed them to do.

So they went there and waited outside for their son to come out. The

put iipaq nuutaytaqw, pu' yaw ti'am yama. Su'aw yaw oovi put yamakqw, pu' yaw maanat kiiyat ephaqam himu paroskikita. Pu' yaw puma aw yorikyaqe pangqaqwa, "Ya himu'uy? Ya himu pas aapavehaqam paroskikita?" Pu' yaw pay kur aqle' sinom kiy'yungqam nanaptaqe aw wukotsovalti.

Noq pam hapi kur maanat aw napnay nit pu' tuukwaviy wiiwilat pu' angqw yamakqw, pay yaw pam maana paasat tiikuywuutiniwti. Pay yaw paasat qa lomamana. Yaw wuutit an torikuy'ta, pu' yaw qöötsat usta. Nit pu' yaw pam kur kiy aapamiq kyaahakiway aqw höta. Noq pu' pepeq pam hiihiimu tangawtaqa, pay yaw pam soosoy ahoy hiituy puukyayamuy angqw yukiwyungqay, pay yaw pam soosoy ahoy puma hiituniwti. Sowi'ngwam, sowiit, taatapt pangqw yaw puma iipoq yuyutya. Kur puma yaw pangqw yuyutyaqw, oovi pas paroskikita.

Paasat pu' yaw Tiikuywuuti pangqawu, "Pay pi uma nawus kyaananvotyakyaakyangw imuy tuutuvosiptuy noonovani. Pay as qa yanhaqamniqw son ima as sinmuy mamqasyani," kita yawi'. Nit pu' yaw paasat sukw sowi'ngwat aqle' yamaktoqat pu' yaw ngu'a. Paasat pu' yaw pam put löway angqw hovalangwuyat akw pu' motsovuyat maamapri. Pantit pu' yaw maatavi. "Yantani," yaw kita, "pay nawus yaapiy ima sinom kyaananvotyakyaakyangw umuy noonovani." Pam hapi yaw put sowi'ngwat pas naap hovalangwuy akw maamapriqw, oovi yaw paniqw ima tuutuvosipt pas sinot yaavoqhaqami pay hova'ikwyangwu.

Yanti yawnit pu' yaw pam pangqw yamakt, pu' yaw pangqw tuwat teevenge pumuy amungki. Niiqe yaw pam Payutmovehaq qatu. Pay yaw qa suukya aw yori. Yanti yaw pamniiqe oovi pam yaw pumuy tuutuvosiptuy pokmuy'ta. Noq oovi yaw antsa himuwa pumuy maqtoniqw, it Tiikuywuutit engem paas yuwsingwu, piw pas taqvahot yaw naawaknangwu. Pu' yaw paniqw oovi yaw hak piw put engem paahote', put mihikqw hom'oyngwu.

Naat kya haqam pumuy pokmuy'ta. Pay yuk pölö.

instant he emerged, they heard something like a clattering and rattling noise in the front room of the house. They looked at the house and said, "What is that? What are those clattering sounds in the front room?" The people living in the vicinity also became aware of the noise and gathered in a large crowd.

The boy had, of course, shaken his shirt and necklace toward the girl when he left. That very moment, the girl was changed into Tiikuywuuti. Now she no longer looked pretty. Her hair was done in a plait like a married woman's and she wore a white cape. She had evidently opened the door to the room with all the valuables. All the things that were stored in there— no matter what skin they were made of—were transformed back into what they had originally been. The deer, jackrabbits, and cottontails ran out to the front of the house making this clattering noise.

Then Tiikuywuuti said, "I will make it difficult for you to eat these game animals. If you had not done this to me, they wouldn't have been afraid of people." She grabbed one deer that was coming out past her and rubbed its snout against her vulva so it would pick up the smell. Then she released it. "That's the way," she said to the animals. "From now on these people will be able to eat you only with great hardship." Because she had rubbed that deer with her own scent, these game animals can smell a person over a great distance.

Then she in turn went out and followed the animals in a westerly direction. She now lives somewhere at the Little Colorado River, but no one has ever seen her. And because of this she owns all the game animals. Therefore, if someone wants to go hunting, he prepares prayer feathers for Tiikuywuuti. She also wants upright prayer sticks. So if someone has made a prayer stick for her, he offers it to her at night.

She probably still rules all those animals. And here the story ends.

Popwaqt Maanat Uu'uyaya

How the Old Wizard Plotted to Seduce a Beautiful Girl

Aliksa'i. Yaw Orayve yeesiwa. Noq pep yaw hakim naawuutim kiy'ta, niikyangw yaw puma lööqmuy tiy'ta, maanat nit pu' tiyot. Tiyowa yaw wuuyoqa. Pas yaw put siwa'at lomamana. Tootim yaw aw tunglay'yungwa, noq pay yaw pas qa hakiy naawakna. Pay yaw as sutsep aw tutumayman-taqw, pay yaw pas qa hisat hakiy aw unangwtavi.

Noq yaw kivanawit tootim, taataqt putsa yu'a'atotangwu hin as yaw sen haqawa put aptuniqay. Noq yep Kwitave kivay'yungqam yaw piw hisat put yu'a'atota. Noq pu' yaw kivamongwi'am amumi pangqawu, "Pas nu' umungem aw wuuwantaqe, pay kya as itam hin put maanat hakiywat engem angwutotani," tootimuy yaw amumi kita.

Paasat pu' yaw tootim tuuvingtota, "Ya himu'uy?"

"Hep owi, nu' wuuwantaqw qaavohaqam, umuy piw hisatniqw soosoyam tsovaltiqw, pu' nu' umuy aa'awnani," yaw amumi kita.

Aliksa'i. People were living in Oraibi. A couple lived there that had two children, a girl and a boy. The boy was the older one, and the younger child was a beautiful girl. Many young men wanted her love, but she didn't care for any of them. They kept coming to her house at night trying to sleep with her, but she never gave in to any of them.

In the kivas the main topic of discussion was how one of the boys or men might seduce her. Those who had their kiva at Kwitavi, the Excrement Place, were also talking about this matter one day. Their kiva chief said to them, "I have been racking my brains to figure out how we might win that girl's love for one of you."

Thereupon the boys asked him, "Do you have an idea?"

"Yes, I was thinking that I would reveal my plans to you some time tomorrow when all of you are gathered again."

"Antsa'ay," yaw aw kitota. Pay yaw kur naat pam qa paasat pumuy aa'awnani hin wuuwantaqay. Yan yaw oovi puma it navotiy'kyaakyangw pangqaqw kiikiy ang tokwisa.

Paasat pu' yaw antsa qavongvaqw hisatniqw yaw soosoyam Kwitave kivay'yungqam tsovalti, pay yaw hihin taawansaproyakiwtaqö'. Paasat pu' yaw kivamongwi pangqawu, "Ura nu' tooki umumi hingqawu, ura nu' hiita wuuwantaqay umumi pangqawu. Noq pay kya uma soosoyam tsovalti, niqw oovi nu' umuy aa'awnani hin wuuwantaqayu. Pay pi uma navotiy'yungwa pam maana pay su'awtapkiwmaqw kwayngyavoningwu. Sutsep pam paasatsa kwayngyavoqningwu. Noq oovi uma nöngakye' uma hiita hepyani, hiita angqw uma mötöptotaniqay put uma tsovalayani. Paasat pu' haqawa it ngölat yukuni, silaqapngölat. Put ura hakim mötövuy akw mumu'yangwuniqw, put ngölat haqawa yukuni," kita yaw amumi'.

Paasat pu' yaw tootim, taataqt haalay'unangway kivangaqw nöönganta, hiita angqw mötöptotaniqay hepwisniqe oovi. Pu' yaw antsa puma put hiita tsovalayaqe, yaw kivaape kwangwtoyniy'kyaakyangw mötöplalwa.

Paasat pu' yaw piw mongwi'am amumi pangqawu, "Pay kya uma haykyalayay. Pay qa wuuyavo aqw peeti maana kwayngyavoqniqata. Noq oovi nu' umuy aa'awnani hintotini umaniqat. Uma hapi yangqw nöngakye', pu' uma put maanat kiiyat a'iip it akw nanavö'yani. Noq pu' paasat uma pep pantsatskyaqw, pu' hapi songqa yamakni kwayngyavoninik. Pu' oovi hapi yamakye', umuqle'niqw, pu' haqawa, pay naap haqawa, it ngölat aqle' muumani. Paasat pu' uma soosoyam son pi qa aw umuumötövuy wahitotani. Pu' hapi oovi maanat aqle' ngölaniqw, pu' haqawa it mötövut akw put maanat kukyat mu'ani, pay naap haqawa."

Paasat pu' yaw suukya tiyo naatavi, "Nu'awuy," yaw kita.

"Antsa'ay," yaw kivamongwi kita, "pew umni."

Paasat pu' yaw i' tiyo naataviiqa angqw aw'i. Pu' yaw put aw mötövut tavi. Yaw hiisayhoya mötövu. Put hapi yaw kur i' kivamongwi pay pas paniqw naap yuku, put hapi yaw akw maanat hak mu'aniqat oovi. Yaw

72

"Very well," they replied. Evidently he was not going to tell them yet exactly what he had in mind. Knowing this, they went home to sleep.

On the following day, just a little after noon, when all the kiva members had gathered at Kwitavi, the kiva chief said, "As you remember, last night I mentioned that I was going to share my thoughts with you. Now that you are all assembled I will reveal my plan to you. You are, of course, aware that the girl you dote on has the habit of going to the toilet toward mid-evening. She always leaves at the same time for the dump at the village edge. Now, to begin with, I want you to go out and search for some things. Gather materials from which you can make corncob darts. Then one of you, just anyone, make a cornhusk wheel. You know, the kind that children throw feathered darts at. That is the wheel someone should make," he said to them.

The boys and men left the kiva in a happy mood in order to look for the material to fashion the darts. When they had gathered everything, they began working on the darts with great anticipation.

Then their chief spoke to them again, "I suppose you are almost done. There is not much time left till the girl goes to relieve herself. I will, therefore, outline to you what you are to do. Go out and play this game in front of the girl's house. She will certainly come out when she wants to relieve herself. When she walks past you, any one of you is to roll this wheel past her. All of you will then hurl your darts at it. As the wheel is rolling past her, one of you is then to hit the girl's foot with this dart. Any of you will do."

One of the young men volunteered, "I'll do it."

"Very well," said the chief, "come here to me."

The young man who had volunteered went over to the old chief, who handed him the dart. It was tiny. The kiva chief had fashioned it himself so that someone would injure the girl with it. That was the reason it was so tiny, but it had a very sharp point. Some wren feathers were attached to it.

73

oovi hiisayhoya, niikyangw piw yaw a'ni tsukuy'ta. Pankyangw pu' yaw piw tutsvot masayat masay'ta. Pam hapi tutsvo pay tuskyaptsiro, noq put yaw masayat masay'ta. Pu' hiita pi yaw akw pam put mötöphoyat tsukuyat lelwi.

Paas yaw oovi yan amumi tutaptat, pu' yaw amumi pangqawu, "Ta'ay, yupave, pay aqw haykyalti. Pay pi itam sakinaye' su'an yukuyani," kita yaw amuminiqw, pu' yaw puma nönga.

Pangqw pu' yaw puma maanat kiiyat aqwya. Pu' yaw puma aw ökiiqe, pep iip aw pitsinaya. Yaw puma kwanonotikyaakyangw pep nanavö'ya. Pay yaw oovi puma su'awsavo pep pantsatskyaqw, pas yaw qa yama. Okiw yaw as puma kiiyat aw suyortikyaakyangwyaqw, pay yaw pas qa ngas'ew piw amumi kuyva.

Su'aw yaw oovi pay puma qe'totiniqay u'nangwyaqw, yaw kiy angqw maana yama. Paasat pu' yaw puma pas paapuya. Pu' yaw oovi puma aw tunatyawkyaakyangwyaqe yaw oovi pumuy amumi haykyalaqw, pu' yaw haqawa maanat su'aqwat ngölat muuma. Paasat pu' yaw puma mötövuy aw wahitota. Pantsatskyaqw, pu' i' tiyo mötöphoyat himuy'taqa nuutum aw tuuva, niikyangw pam pay pi tutavotniiqe pay maanat kukyat mavasta. Piw yaw pam su'an yuku, maanat yaw suukuktönsiveq yaw mu'a.

Pu' yaw pay okiw maana naavakhuruuta, nit pu' pay pep suqtuptu. Pep yaw pam qatuwkyangw a'ni pakmumuya. Pu' yaw tootim angqw awyaqe pu' yaw as aw pangqaqwa, sen haqawa angqw engem mötövut tsoopaniqay. Noq pay yaw qa hakiywat nakwhana, niiqe pay yaw naap angqw ayo' tsoopa.

Pu' yaw kur yu'at puma navota pam pakmumuyqw, niiqe pu' yaw angqw aw'i. Pu' yaw aw pituuqe yaw tuuvingta, "Ya um hinti?" yaw aw kita.

Noq pas yaw peep qa hu'wana. Pas yaw ason pu' lavayti, "Pay nu' yep imuy mötövut akw nanavö'yaqamuy amuqle'niqw, pay suukya mötövu sumataq inumi wukumtiqe su'ikuktönsiy aqw tsööqö. Niikyangw pay nu'

As is well known, the wren is a crazy bird and it was with its plumes that the dart was feathered. In addition the chief had smeared something on the tip of the tiny dart that they were not familiar with.

When he had given them these careful instructions, he said, "O.K., go on, it's nearly time. If we're lucky, everything will go as planned."

Thereupon they left and went to the girl's house. When they arrived, they started playing in front of the house. They did a lot of yelling and shouting as they played. They played for a long time, but she did not come out. It was pitiful how they would look at her house every so often and she did not even peek out at them.

Just when they were about to quit, the girl came out. Now they really went at it again. They kept an eye on her and as she approached, one of them rolled the wheel in her direction. They hurled their darts at it and while they were doing this, the boy who had the tiny dart threw his along with the others. Following instructions, however, he aimed at the girl's foot. He executed his throw just as planned and hit the girl right in the heel.

The poor girl burst into tears and, crying loudly, sat down right where she was. The boys ran up to her and asked if one of them should pull the dart out for her. But she did not let anyone help her and pulled it out herself.

Then evidently her parents heard her crying and came out to her. When they reached her, they asked, "What happened to you?"

She could hardly answer. But after a pause she was able to speak. "I was passing these boys playing their dart game when one dart bounced off toward me and drove right into my heel. But I managed to pull it out," she said to her parents.

angqw tsoopa," kita yaw yumuy awi'.

"Ta'ay, itam tur ung pay itaakiy aw ahoy wikniy." Kitat pu' yaw puma put mantiy wunuptsina. Pantit pu' yaw puma put kiy aw nan'ivaqw nguy'ma. Pu' yaw puma put kiy aw panaaqe, aapat ang wa'ökna. Pu' yaw aw pangqawu, "Pay um haak pang sun wa'ökiwtaqw, pay songqa qalaptuni," kita yaw puma awi'.

Paasat pu' ima tootim put maanat mu'ayaqe pay yaw puma paasat qe'toti. Yaw qa kwangwa'ewti. Pu' yaw oovi pay puma pangqw ahoy kivay aqwya. Paasat pu' yaw pumuy mongwi'am tuuvingta, "Ya uma hin yukuyay?"

Paasat pu' yaw aa'awnaya, "Pay itam su'an yukuyay, pay itam mu'ayay."

Paasat pu' yaw mongwi'am haalayti. "Kur antsa'ay, kwakwhay, uma su'an yukuyay. Yan pi nu' naawakna. Pay itam son oovi hakiywat engem qa tuutuyqawvani," kita yaw amumi'.

Is, paasat yaw tootim kwangwtapnaya. Haqawa pi yaw aptuni. Yan yaw puma wuuwankyaakyangw kwangwtotoya.

Paasat pu' yaw i' maana kiy ep wa'ökiwta, noq pas yaw kuk'at qa qalaptsiwmat, suutsepngwat yaw wukovös'iwma. Pantsakkyangw yaw nungwu oomiq hoyoyoyku. Pu' yaw as paava'at tuuhikyat wiktama. Pu' yaw pam as aw hintsanqw, pay yaw pas qa alöngti. Pantsakkyangw pu' yaw pay pöösangw pas put unangwmiq pitu. Pay yaw ep tapkimi pam mooki.

Paasat pu' yaw ima yumat, paava'at, pu' taahamat, yaw okiw puma pephaqam put aw tsaykita. Hisatniqw pu' yaw puma yan unangwtoti. Paasat pu' yaw na'at pangqawu, "Ta'ay, pay pi nuwupiy, pay pi itam kur hintsatsnani. Noq oovi nu' engem yuwsiqw, itam nawus tavitoniy," yaw tiy aw kita, tiyot awi'.

Pu' yaw oovi pam yuwsi. Paasat pu' yaw puma naatim put tavito. Orayviy taatöq hoopoq tumpoq yaw puma pitut, pu' yaw puma aqw haawi. Pang pi Orayviy taatöq hopqöyva tu'amqölö. Pephaqam pu' yaw puma put

76

"All right, why don't we take you back into the house," they replied and helped their daughter onto her feet. Then, holding her on both sides, they led her into the house. They had her lie down and told her, "Lie there quietly for a while and you'll be all right."

The boys that had wounded the girl stopped playing. The fun was gone. They returned to their kiva and there they were asked by their chief, "How did you make out?"

They told him, "We did just as planned; we hit her."

Now the chief was happy. "Well all right, thank you, you've done fine. That's the way I wanted it. Now we will definitely get her for one of you."

Great then was the joy among the boys. Anyone might win her now. Their minds were full of anticipation.

Meanwhile the girl was lying in the house and her foot, instead of getting better, swelled more and more. Not only that, the swelling was moving upward. Her brother had gone to fetch a medicine man, but although he treated her, she didn't improve. By and by the swelling reached her heart. That day toward evening she died.

Her parents, her brother, and her uncles all wept over her. It was heartrending. Finally they came to themselves again and her father said to his son, "Well, it can't be helped, there is nothing we can do. When I have made prayer feathers and all the other things that are proper for her now, we must go bury her."

Thus he made everything ready for the burial. Then father and son started for the burial place. When they reached the southeastern mesa edge of Oraibi they descended to where the graveyard was. There they buried her and went back home.

oovi tavi. Yantit pu' yaw puma pangqaqw ahoy nima.

Pu' yaw oovi puma yaasathaqam yesqw, pu' yaw tiyo lavayti, "Pas nu' itsivuti," yaw kita, "pas nu' itsivutiqe, oovi nu' pay pas kur hin mihikqw qa aqw puwtoni. Nu' pay pas aqw puwte', pas suyan hin navotni. Pay pi songqa hintiqw, oovi pam pas suyukilti. It nu' pas naap hin navotni," yaw pam yumuy aw kita.

Pu' yaw na'at aw pangqawu, "Antsa'ay," yaw aw kita, "pay pi antsa um pantininik, pay pi um pantini."

"Hep owi," pu' yaw kita, "pas nu' itsivutiqe oovi'o." Paasat pu' yaw oovi pam pösaalay kwusu, pu' yaw hotngay piw iikwilta. Pantit pu' yaw pam pangqw kiy angqw yama.

Pu' yaw pam angqw Orayviy taatöq. Taatöq yaw pam pitut pu' hoopoq. Pu' yaw pam hoopoq tumpoq pituuqe, pu' yaw naami pangqawu, "Pay pi nu' yangqw aqw puwni," kita yaw pam naami'. Pay pi yaw pangqw susmataq haqam puma siwayat amqö'. Suyan pi yaw muytala. Pu' yaw oovi pam pangqw tsoorawta. Pankyangw pay yaw kur pam hisatniqw puwva.

Noq pas kya yaw oovi suutokihaqtiqw, yaw pam taatayi. Yaw pam siway tuu'amiyat aw yorikqw, pay yaw naat susmataq ep anta. Pay yaw kur qa himu aw hinti. Naat yaw oovi pam yantaqw, yaw himu haqam paklawu. Nawayvösöt hoopaqw, tuukwit ahopqöyngahaqaqw, yaw himu paklawu. Pay yaw pas piw suus paklawu. Pu' yaw pam as tuqayvaasiy'taqw, pay yaw pas qa piiwu. Noq pas yaw nawutstiqw pu' yaw piiwu. Paasat pu' yaw pay pas Nawayvösöt aatavang oovehaqam yaw piw paklawu. Pantit pu' yaw pay piw qe'ti. Panmakyangw pu' yaw piw. Paasat pu' yaw Orayviy suhopqöyngaqw tuphaqam yaw piw paklawu.

Pu' yaw i' tiyo pang tupkye' as aqwhaqami kwiniwiq taytaqw, pay yaw pas qa himu haqamo. Yaw oovi pam pantaqw piw paklawu. Paasat pu' yaw pay pas hayp kwiningya atpiphaqam. Pu' yaw pam oovi aqw taytaqw, yaw himu angqaqw kuyva. Uti, yaw himu a'ni soniwa. Paysoq yaw hiihiita naahoy kwetsma. Paasat pu' yaw pam maamatsi himuniqö'. Yaw kur

Somewhat later when they were sitting together at night, the boy said, "I'm furious, and because I am so mad I can't help going to her grave to sleep. By spending the night there I will certainly find some kind of answer. There must be something wrong for her to have died so suddenly. This is what I would like to find out for myself."

Then his father replied. "All right," he said, "if you truly want to do that, then go ahead."

"Yes," the boy replied, "I am beside myself with rage." With that he picked up his blanket, shouldered his quiver, and walked out of the house.

He headed in the direction south of Oraibi. When he had gotten there, he went east. Upon reaching the east, he said to himself, "I will sleep up there with the grave in sight." He had an unobstructed view of the place where they had buried his younger sister. It was clear moonlight. So he lay down flat on his stomach and soon fell asleep.

He woke up at about midnight and looked over at his sister's grave. It was still clearly visible and was the way it had been. Nothing had happened to it. Suddenly something started crying. East of Nawayvösö, on the east side of the butte, some creature was crying. He heard it just once. He held his breath and listened closely, but it did not reoccur. Then, finally, after a long pause, there it was again. Sounds of crying, west of Nawayvösö, somewhere high up. Then the sounds stopped again, in due time starting anew. The crying was on the east side of Oraibi at the foot of the mesa.

The boy strained his eyes to look along the base line of the mesa all the way to the north, but there was no one in sight. Then he heard the crying again. This time it was quite close in the north, somewhere below him. While he was looking in that direction, something came into view. It was a terrible looking creature, hurling to left and right the obstacles that were

kwewu. Naat yaw oovi pam put aw taytaqw, piw yaw angqaqw himu angk kuyva. Niikyangw paasat pu' pay yaw hak taaqa. Pu' yaw piw suukyawa, pu' piw. Paayom yaw taataqt kwewut laywisa.

Paasat pu' yaw pam pas itsivuti. "Son puye'em qa yanhaqam hinta-niqw, oovi nu' pay pas yepeq puwniqay itsivuti," kita yaw pam naami'. Pam yaw oovi itsivu'iwkyangw amumiq tayta. Yuumosa angqw siwayat awya. Pu' yaw aw öki. Pu' yaw kwewu ep naahoy owat maspiva. Soosok yaw oovi owat ayo' maspat, pu' yaw yaahanva.

Paasat pu' i' tiyo yaw awtay kwusu, nit pu' hoohuy piw sukwat. Pantit pu' yaw pam paas oovi tumostsokya kwewut mu'aniqay. Yanti yaw pamnit, pu' yaw pam wuuwa, "Hintsatsnani pa puma isiwayniiqe oovi aqw yaahantota?" Yan yaw pam wuuwaqe, pu' pay kwewut qa mu'a. "Nu' kur pas hin navotniy. Hintsatsnani pi puma isiwayuy."

Paasat pu' yaw kur kwewu aqw haykyalaqw, paasat pu' yaw taataqt tuwatya. Hisatniqw pu' yaw horoknaya. Horoknayat, pu' yaw paas hiita ep mokyaatota. Paasat pu' yaw suukyawa iikwilta. Pu' yaw pay ahoy haqaqw ökiiqay, piw ahoy aqwat nankwusa. Iikwiwtaqa yaw mootiy'maqw, pu' mimawat yaw angkya. Paasat pu' kwewu pumuy layma.

Oovi yaw kwiniwi tupo tuutuwayamaqw, pu' yaw pam amungk tumkyaqe wari. Pangqe yaw pam pumuy amungk nana'uytima. Pay yaw pas yuumosa Orayviy hopqöyvaqe tupkye' kwiniwiqya. Pu' yaw kwiniwiq tupoq ökiiqe, pepeq pu' yaw oomi yayva. Paapiy pu' yaw hoopoq, noq pay yaw kur pep Orayviy kwiningya hoophaqam yaw kur kiva. Panso yaw kur puma put wikya. Pu' yaw antsa aw ökiiqe yaw aqwhaqami yungma.

Pu' yaw pam pangqw aw'i, haqami yungmaqat awi'. Put yaw pam pep kivat aw qa hisat yori. Pu' yaw pam aw pituuqe pu' aqw kuyva. Pas yaw epeq kyaasta. Taataqt, tootim, pu' pay hikiyom momoyam piw. Noq pam yaw aqw kuyvaqw, qöpqöt kwiningyaqw yaw siwayat taviy'yungwa. Noq yaw oovi pam aqw kuytaqw, pu' yaw siwayat oovat akw naakwapnaya. Pantotit pu' yaw aw tsootsongya. Pantotit pu' yaw pay hiita pi yaw

in its path. Then the boy recognized it. It was a gray wolf. He was still staring at it when another being appeared behind it. It was a man. Then another and then one more. Three men were following the wolf.

It was now that his anger reached a peak. "I had a feeling that it was going to be something like this. That's why I got so furious and came to sleep near her," he said to himself. Full of rage he observed them. The group headed straight for his sister's grave. When they reached it, the wolf started throwing the rocks to both sides. When he had removed all the rocks, he started digging.

The boy now picked up his bow and one of his arrows. Carefully, he placed the arrow on the bow to shoot the wolf. Then a thought occurred to him, "What on earth do they intend to do with my sister that they are unearthing her body?" This went through his head and so he decided not to shoot the wolf. "I'll have to find out somehow."

Now that the wolf was getting close to her, the men took over. After a short while, they pulled the girl out. Then they carefully wrapped her up in something. Finally someone loaded her body on his back and they started in the direction they had come from. The one that carried her went first. The others followed, and this time the wolf walked behind them.

When they had disappeared along the foot of the mesa, the boy started running after them along the mesa edge. He followed them secretly as they went due north past the east side of Oraibi along the base of the mesa. Upon reaching the north base, they went up to the top. From there they headed east, and evidently somewhere northeast of Oraibi, there was a kiva. That was their destination. And indeed, soon they disappeared into it.

Then the boy came to the place where they had entered. He had never seen that kiva before. Lots of people were in it; men and boys, and a few women, too. When he peeked in they were just placing his sister north of the fireplace. And while he watched, they covered his sister with a wedding robe. After that they smoked over her. Then they chanted some kind of

81

tawlalwa. Pantsatskyaqw, pu' yaw pay siwa'at hihin poniniyku. Pantsak-kyangw pu' pay yaw pas a'ni poniniyku. Yaw pam oovi awsa taytaqw, pu' yaw nawlökna. Pantit pu' yaw taynuma. Pay yaw sumataq mooti as qa hakiy tuwat, pu' yaw kur pas suyan unangwtiqe pu' yaw naavakhuruuta, sinmuy hapi tuwaaqe'.

Paasat pu' yaw hak angqw aw nakwsu, hak yaw wuuti, pu' yaw aw pangqawu, "Um qa pakmumuyni, pay son um hintini. Um oovi okq, nu' ung aw naawusnani," yaw aw kita.

Noq i' paava'at yaw pay put wuutit maamatsi hakniqö'. Pam yaw pumuy kya'am. Pam yaw oovi kur put siwayat naawusnani. Pu' yaw oovi angqw tuuwimo wiiki. Pep pu' yaw pam kya'at put naawustotoyna.

Oovi yaw pantsakqw, pu' i' tiyo yaw itsivuti. "Piw naat kur songqa hintsatsnani," yan yaw pam wuuwa. "Son pi nu' hakiy haqami qa hepqw nuy hak pa'angwani."

Yan yaw pam wuuwaqe, pu' yaw pam Pöqangwhoyatuy u'na. "Puma pay nuy songqa pa'angwani," kita yaw pam naaminit pu' pangqw oovi pumuy kiiyamuy aqw wari. Pay pi pangqw aw qa yaavo, niqw oovi pam yaw aw suptu. Pu' yaw pam aqw pakiqw, pay yaw soosoyam yeese, Pöqangw-hoyat niqw pu' so'am. Pu' yaw pay pam oovi qa sööwu hintsakt, pu' yaw pay amumi pangqawu, "Nu' as angqw umumi'i. Ura taavok isiwa aapiyniqw, tooki hakim put horoknayaqw, nu' pumuy amungkniiqe nu'ansana haqami wikyaqö'. Noq sumataq naat piw hintsatsnaniqw, oovi nu' angqw umumi taqa'nangwti. Noq sen pi son uma nuy pa'angwayani?" kita yaw pam amumi'.

Paasat pu' yaw so'am lavayti, "Pay pi itam son ung qa pa'angwayani. Pay itam oovi pisoqtotini. Pu' oovi um pay itamuusavo ahoy awni. Pay itam hiisap ungk son qa ep ökini," kita yaw awi'. Yan yaw pam pay lomana-votqe, pu' pangqw ahoy yamakt, pu' pangqw ahoy aw'i.

Paasat pu' yaw so'wuuti Pöqangwhoyatuy amumi pangqawu, "Uma umuutalwiipikiy horoknani. Pay uma putsa yawmani," kita yaw amumi'.

song during which his sister began to stir a little. This went on for some time, and then she really began to move quite noticeably. While his eyes were fixed on her, she uncovered herself. She looked around. It was apparent that at first she could not see anyone. But when her senses became clear, she burst into tears for she saw the people.

Someone went up to her. It was a woman who said, "Don't cry. Nothing will harm you. When you have stopped crying, I will comb your hair."

The brother recognized the woman as their aunt. That is why she was going to comb his sister's hair. She took her over to the stone bench and began fixing her hair.

While she was doing that the boy got angry. "Evidently they're still going to do something to her," he thought. "I've got to find somebody who can help me."

He remembered the Pöqangwhoyas. "I'm sure they will help me," he said to himself and ran to their house. Since it was not far from where he was, he reached it in no time. He entered and they were all at home, the two Pöqangwhoyas and their grandmother. Without many preliminaries he told them, "I came to you. You remember that my younger sister passed away yesterday. Now, last night some people dug her body up, and by following them, I discovered where they were taking her. Apparently they intend to do something more to her. Therefore I came to ask you for assistance. Will you help me?"

The old grandmother answered, "Of course we will help you. So let's get busy. You run back there ahead of us. We'll follow shortly after you." With this favorable response to his plea, he left and hurried back.

Then the old woman turned to the two Pöqangwhoyas and said, "Take your lightning sticks out. That's all you will carry along." She then poured

83

Paasat pu' yaw pam tuwat neengem kuyqe pu' yaw naavahomta. Naapa yaw tusnat muriwankyangw suuvo pölölanta. Pay yaw oovi su'awwukoq pölölaqe pu' yaw qe'ti. Paasat pu' yaw put angqw hiisakw tuku. Pu' yaw ephaqam put aw hintsaklawu. Pantit pu' yaw mokyaatat, pu' yaw pangqawu, "Ta'a, tumaa', pay itam pisoqtotini."

Pangqw pu' yaw puma tuwat nankwusa. Naat yaw oovi i' tiyo pu' kivami ahoy pituqw, pay yaw angk öki Pöqangwhooyam. Pu' yaw i' tiyo piw kivamiq kuyvaqw, pay yaw piw qöpqöt kwiningyaqw siwa'at wa'ökiwta.

Noq yaw oovi pam aqw taytaqw, yaw hak angqw aw nakwsu, noq pay yaw pam put suumamatsi. Pam yaw aw nakwsuqa Kwitaveq kivamongwi. Pam hapi yaw kur put siwayat tsopni. Kur yaw pam kivamongwi pay put maanat sunengem tunglay'taqe, oovi kivasngwamuy pan ayata put maanat mu'ayaniqat. Pam hapi yaw kur pay a'ni himuniiqe ooviyo'. Noq puma pepeq amum tangawtaqam pay an piw a'ni yaw hiitu'u, popwaqt hapi yaw puma'a.

Noq pam hapi kur put maanat pas susmooti aw hintsanniqe oovi pan naawakna. Paasat pu' yaw oovi maanat aw tamötswunuptuqe pu' yaw kwasayat oomi hölökna. Okiw yaw as maana qa naawakna, niikyangw kur pi yaw pam hintini.

Paasat pu' yaw oovi wuutaqa atsmi wupniniqw, pu' yaw Pöqangwhoyatuy so'am kivamiq hiita maatavi, yaw kur tootovita. Put hapi kur pam tusnay angqw yuku. Pu' yaw pay kivaapeq tangawtaqam kur nanapta tootovi pakikqö', niiqe yaw pangqaqwa, "Haakiy, sumataq hak pakiy." Pu' yaw puma pepeq put angk savinumya. Pu' yaw pay antsa niinaya.

Paasat pu' yaw wuutaqa angqw piw ahoy maanat aw'i. Paasat pu' yaw piw atsmi wuuvi nit pu' yaw pangqawu, "Hala', hongyat tsiikya." Kitat pu' yaw oovi maanat aqw pananiqw, pu' yaw so'wuuti piw sukw pookoy maatavi. Su'aw yaw oovi wuutaqa yomikqw, yaw atpikyaqe maanat himu suurokna. Pay yaw okiw wuutaqa tutskwamihaqami muusiy söökwikna.

Paasat hapi yaw kur so'wuuti sawyat kivamiq maatavi. Pam hapi kur

some water for herself and sprinkled it over her body. She rolled the dirt on her body and molded it into a ball until it was a good size. Then she cut a small piece off and began working with it. After she had done that she put it in a bag and said, "All right, let's go; we should hurry."

Now they started out. The boy had just gotten back to the kiva when the three Pöqangwhoyas arrived behind him. When he looked into the kiva, his sister was lying on the north side of the fireplace.

He was still watching when someone started toward her. He recognized him at once. It was the kiva chief from Kwitavi, the Excrement Place. It appeared that he was going to have intercourse with his sister. So the kiva chief had evidently desired the girl for himself and had, therefore, asked his kiva partners to wound her with the poisoned dart. He was of course a person with supernatural power, and those that were assembled there with him were also endowed with supernatural faculties. They were all sorcerers and witches.

It was obviously the sorcerer's intention to be the first to rape the girl. He knelt down by the girl and lifted up her dress. The poor girl did not want it, but could do nothing.

When the old man got ready to climb on top of her, the grandmother of the Pöqangwhoyas let something loose into the kiva. It was a fly that she had molded out of her own dirt. Thereupon the people in the kiva noticed that a fly had come in and said, "Wait a minute, it looks as if something has come in." They struck at it and killed it.

Then the old man went back to the girl again. He climbed back on her and yelled, "Now let me tear her hymen!" He was just at the point of penetrating her when the old woman released another animal. The very moment that the chief pushed forward, something snatched the girl from underneath him. So the poor old wizard poked his erect penis into the ground.

That time the old woman had let a bat loose into the kiva. It had grab-

wuutaqat atpikyaqe maanat suurokna. Pay i' sawya piw kur tusnat angqw yukiwta. Yan yaw puma pangqw maanat horoknaya. Yan pay yaw popwaqt maanat qa aw hintsatsna.

Paasat pu' yaw so'wuuti Pöqangwhoyatuy amumi pangqawu, "Ta'a, umani. Pay pi uma naap hin yukunani. Pay pi nuunukpantu, niikyangw pay pi son hin piw qa napwatotani," kita yaw pam amumi'.

Paasat pu' yaw Pöqangwhoyat kivamiq tuwat talwiipikiy maatavi. Paysoq yaw tu'mumuyku, suyan taalawva. Pu' yaw epeq tangawtaqam tsa'a'ayku. Paasat pu' pumuy talwiipiki'am pepeq tangawtaqamuy paysoq yaw tutkita. Pepehaq yaw puma popwaqt tutki'iwkyaakyangw hoyoyo-tinumya. Peetuy yaw maayamuy ayo' tutkita, pu' petuy hokyayamuy pu' kukyamuy. Pay yaw pas naap hiita hakiy angqw ayo' tukungwu. Pu' yaw puma pepehaq may'numya. Pay yaw hak hiita aw tongokye', pay put naami tsokyangwu. Peetu yaw taataqt momoymuy qaasiyamuy qaasiy'yungwa, pu' momoyam taqahokyay'yungwa. Yan yaw puma pepehaq napwatota, qa sosniwa yaw hiitu'.

Paasat pu' ima naasiwam niqw pu' Pöqangwhooyam pangqaqw ahoy Oraymiya. Oovi yaw puma Oraymi haykyalayaqw, pu' yaw so'wuuti naasiwamuy amumi lavayti, "Pay pi soosoyam sinom nanapta i' uusiwa mokqö'. Noq kur um hin it qa maataknanik, oovi yaapiy naalös taalat ephaqam um hiituy tiivanani, niikyangw um imuy Angaktsinmuy ep tiivanani. Niqw i' uusiwa hapi ep nuutumni, nuutum man'iwmani. Pu' ason tiitso'q, pu' um paas yuwsinani, niikyangw it uusiway um pay qa enang yuwsinani. Pu' um paas yuwsinat pu' um hoonani. Pantit pu' um it uusiway ayo' langaknani. Pantit pu' pay um wikkyangw nimani. Paasat pu' pay sinom songqa pan wuuwayani kur pay pam qa mokqö'. Yan hapi um it sinmuy amumi maataknani."

Yanhaqam yaw pumuy aw tutapta. Paasat pu' yaw tiyo pangqawu, "Antsa'ay, pay nu' songqa pantini," kitaqw pu' yaw puma naanahoyya. Ima naasiwam nimaqw, pu' Pöqangwhooyam tuwat ninma.

bed the girl from underneath the old man. The bat, too, had been made out of the dirt that she had rolled off her body. And this is how they rescued the girl. The sorcerers had not been able to harm her.

Thereupon the old woman said to the two Pöqangwhoyas, "They are all yours now. You can do to them whatever pleases you. But since they are evil, they will find a way to restore themselves."

Now the Pöqangwhoyas let their lightning fly into the kiva. There was an explosion like muffled thunder and it became bright as day. The people inside began to cry. They were torn to pieces by the lightning. The sorcerers and witches were crawling around, cut up in various ways. Some had their arms severed and some their legs. The lightning had hacked off parts from their bodies at random. Now they were all groping around. Whenever one bumped into something, he simply stuck it back on himself. Some men fitted women's thighs to their bodies, some women had men's legs attached; this is how they came out of that situation as ugly-looking creatures.

Thereupon brother and sister as well as the three Pöqangwhoyas returned to Oraibi. When they were getting close to the village, the old woman said, "All the people have heard by now that your sister is dead. You can't possibly show her. Therefore, I suggest that you put on a dance four days from now. Arrange for the Longhair Kachinas to dance. The crucial part is that your sister participates. She can go along as one of the female kachinas. After the dance is over, you will present a prayer feather to every dancer, as is proper. You will not include your sister, however. When you send the kachinas off, you must pull your sister aside and lead her home. The people will believe then, that she did not really die. In this way you can, of course, show your sister to the people again."

These were her instructions. The boy said, "Fine, I will certainly do that." Then they went their own ways. The brother went home and the Pöqangwhoyas, too, went home.

Yaw puma pituqw, yaw yumat haalayti. Pay yaw as mootiniqw qa tuptsiwa, noq pay yaw kur pas pam'i. Paapiy pu' yaw oovi puma naalös taalat ngöytota.

Pu' yaw i' tiyo kivay ep kivasngyamuy amumi pangqawu, "Itam as yaapiy naalös taalat ephaqam hiituy akw tatapkiqwyani."

"Ta'ay," yaw aw kitota. Pay yaw aw su'unangwtatve. "Hiituy itamyani?" yaw aw kitota.

"Pay nu' Angaktsinmuy wuuwantay," yaw pam amumi kita.

Paasat pu' yaw oovi puma naalös taalat aqw kwangwtotoya. Pu' yaw antsa aqw pitu, nalöstalat aqwa'. Qa hak yaw navotiy'ta puma ökininiqw. Pay yaw oovi su'awtapkiwtaqw, yaw kivangahaqaqw yaw hiitu hingqaw-wisa. Pu' yaw kur pay sinom nanaptaqe, yaw kiisonmi yuyutya pang-qawkyaakyangw, "Angqw katsinamya," kitikyaakyangw.

Pu' yaw oovi puma kiisonmi ökiiqe pu' pep tiiva. Noq yaw antsa maana nuutuma. Pu' yaw oovi puma pep tiivaqe yukuyaqw, pu' yaw i' tiyo amumi nakwsu. Paas yaw kur amungem yuwsi. Pam yaw oovi paasat pu' pumuy pahohuyta, niikyangw siway pay yaw qee'. Paas yaw oovi pam yukut pu' yaw katsinmuy hoona. Pantit pu' yaw pam angqw ayo' siway langakna. Oovi yaw katsinam soosoyam ninmaqw, pu' yaw pam tuwat pangqw siway wikkyangw nima.

Pu' yaw pay antsa sinom pangqaqwa, "Kur pam yanhaqam it hiita tunatyawtaqe oovi mokqay atsata. Pay kur as pam qa mooki." Yan yaw sinom wuuwaya.

Yanhaqam yaw pam ahoy siway naami pitsina. Noq pu' yaw pam ep mihikqw pu' Pöqangwhoyatuy amungem tuwat hiita hinti. Tatsit yaw amungem yuku, pu' awtat piw. Pu' yaw soyamuy engem piw pam paas yuwsi. Pu' yaw pam put amumi kima. Yaw pam ep pituqw yaw aw haalaytoti, "Askwali, itam su'an yukuya."

88

When the children arrived, their parents were overjoyed. At first they could not believe that it was really their daughter. But from that time on they gave all their attention to the deadline of the fourth day.

The boy spoke to his kiva partners, "Four days from today I would like to put on an evening plaza dance with kachinas."

"All right," they said. They supported him right away. "What kind should we impersonate?" they asked.

"Well, I had Longhair Kachinas in mind," he replied.

Now they began looking forward to the fourth day. Finally the day came. No one suspected their appearance. It was full evening when the kachinas emerged from the kiva with their peculiar calls. The people heard them and hurried to the plaza. "The kachinas are coming!" they shouted.

When the dancers reached the plaza, they began to dance. And the girl actually participated. When the kachinas were through with their dancing, the boy went up to them. He had prepared everything most meticulously. He distributed the prayer feathers among them, but did not give one to his sister. When he had done all this very carefully, he sent the kachinas off. Then he pulled his sister aside. And so, while all the kachinas were going home, he in turn led his sister home.

Now, indeed, the people said, "So this is why she had planned to pretend to be dead. Evidently she never really died." This is what the people were thinking.

In this manner the boy succeeded in getting his sister back. That same night he prepared something for the two Pöqangwhoya brothers. He made a shinny ball for them, and for their grandmother he carefully arranged the appropriate prayer feathers. Then he took these things over to them. When he arrived there, they said, "Let's be thankful that we succeeded."

"Hep owi, pas nu' haalaytiqe oovi yep nu' umungem it yanva." Kitat pu' yaw pam amumi put oya. Yaw haalaytoti. Yantit pu' yaw pam pangqaqw ahoy nima.

Aapiy pay yaw qa wuuyavotiqw, pay yaw popwaqt hin nönga. Pu' yaw pay aapiy puma popwaqt, pay yaw himuwa haqam hihin töngökt pay mokngwu. Pay yaw puma pas sulawti.

Yanhaqam yaw puma pumuy amumi naa'o'ya, popwaqtuy awi'. Paapiy pu' yaw puma piw ahoy soosoyam yeese. Pay yuk pölö.

"Yes, I too am very glad about that, so I brought these things for you," he said, and handed them their gifts. They were happy. He then returned home.

It was not long after that the sorcerers and witches somehow got out of their kiva. But from that time on, whenever one of them tripped even just a little over something, he immediately died. All of them perished.

In this way the Pöqangwhoyas took revenge on the witches and sorcerers. From then on life went on again as before. And here the story ends.

Pöqangwhoyat Mantuy Owata

How the Pöqangwhoyas
Turned Two Girls into Stone

Aliksa'i. Yaw Pöqangwwawarpive yeesiwa. Noq yaw pep Pöqangwhoyat kiy'ta. Pay yaw puma panis soy'ta. Wuuyoqwa yaw Pöqangwhoya, pu' tsaywa yaw Palöngawhoya. Yan yaw puma maatsiwa. Pay pi yaw puma pas qa hophoyat, nukpanhoyat. Pu' yaw puma pay sutsep piw tatatsngwu. Pay putsa yaw puma pas suyan apit.

Noq yaw hisat pumuy so'am amumi pangqawu, "Uma hapi qa hisat yukyiq teevengeni, pepeq hapi nukpana kiy'ta. Noq oovi paapu uma inumi tuuqayte', paapu qa hisat pansoqni." Pay yaw pam pumuy meewaqe songyawnen yaw pam kur pumuy ayata.

Noq oovi yaw antsa puma hisat piw tatatsi, niiqe pu' yaw naami pangqawu, "Pas itam as kur nanavö'ni. Itam kur yaapiy teevenge tatatstikyangw warikni. Hak pi mooti ahoy pituni," kita yaw naami'. Pu' yaw pay antsa puma piw sun unangwti. "Itam ayoq teevenge hakiy paasayat qöniktoni."

Aliksa'i. They were living at Pöqangwwawarpi. The Pöqangwhoya boys had their house there, and the only family they had was their grandmother. The older one was named Pöqangwhoya and the younger, Palöngawhoya. Those were their names. They were not well behaved and were always up to some mischief. In addition, they were constantly playing shinny, and that's the only thing they were really good for.

One day their grandmother said to them, "Be sure never to go west from here, because an evil person lives there. If you obey me, you will never visit that area." But by warning them she was, of course, more or less inviting them to go there.

And indeed, one day, when they were playing shinny again, they said to each other, "Let's compete with each other. We'll run westward from here, hitting our shinny ball, and see who gets there first." Sure enough,

Paasat pu' yaw oovi puma naqlap wunuptu. Paasat pu' yaw Pöqangwhoya pangqawu, "Ason nu' naalöq aqw pootoylaqw, pu' itam warikni," yaw
kita.

"Ta'ay," yaw tupko'at aw kita. Pu' yaw oovi Pöqangwhoya pootoylanta, "Suukya', lööyö', paayo', naalöyö'."

Kitaqw pu' yaw puma tatatstikyangw wari. Pas yaw puma sun hoyta.
Teevenge yaw puma'. Panmakyangw pu' yaw puma pasmiq haykyala. Naat
yaw sun hoyta. Panmakyangw pu' yaw puma pasmi paki. Pang pu' yaw
puma uysonaq teevenge'e. Yaw oovi puma qalavoq naat qa yamakt, yaw
puma hakiy aw pitu. Piw yaw hak maana. Pu' yaw pay pumuy amumi
hingqawu, "Ya uma hintsaki?" yaw amumi kita.

Noq pay pi yaw maananiqw, oovi pay yaw puma aw huruutikyangw
pu' yaw aw pangqawu, "Itam nanavö'ay. Hak pi mooti ahoy itaakiy aqw
tatatstikyangw pituni."

Paasat pu' yaw maana amumi piw lavayti, "Ya uma hin'ur tatatstuwiy'ta?" yaw amumi kita.

"Owi, noq hinti?"

"Pay pi itam as kur yep soosoyam tatatsyani. Nu' piw sukw maanat
sungway'ta, noq umuy nakwhaqw, itam kur soosoyam tatatsyani," yaw
amumi kita.

Noq pay pi yaw puma pas tatatshoyatniiqe, pay yaw puma sunakwha.
Paasat pu' yaw oovi maana pumuy taqatskiy aqw tuutsamta. "Itam mooti
nöönösat pu' asonyani."

Pu' yaw oovi puma angqw put maanat angk taqatskimiqa. Antsa yaw
puma aqw ökiqw, piw yaw suukya hak maana epeq qatu. Yaw pumuy paas
tavi. Pu' yaw amumi pangqawu, "Pay itam nitkyay'ta, oovi itam ason mooti
nöönösat pu' ason tatatsyani." Kitaaqe pu' yaw nitkyay tsawikna. Pu' yaw
puma pephaqam soosoyam noonova.

Pu' yaw puma öö'öya. Paasat pu' yaw mant pangqawu, "Ta'a, itam
kur tatatsyani. Uma naamaniqw, pu' itam piw tuwat naamani. Hakim pi
hakimuy pö'ani."

they both agreed. "There in the west we will turn around at somebody's field."

Both of them got into position next to each other and Pöqangwhoya said, "I'll count up to four and then we'll run."

"All right," his younger brother replied. So Pöqangwhoya started to count. "One, two, three, four."

Now they ran off playing shinny as they went. They moved along at the same speed toward the west and eventually came to a field, still side by side. Upon reaching the field, they continued west through the corn plants and had not crossed the edge of the field yet when they met someone. They were quite surprised to see a girl, and even more so when she asked them, "What are you two doing?"

Since it was a girl, the two brothers stopped running and told her, "We are competing with each other to see who will return first to our house playing shinny."

The girl then asked them, "Are you good shinny players?"

"Yes, why?"

"Well, we could all of us play. I have a girl friend here, and if it's all right with you, we could all play shinny together."

As the two Pöqangwhoyas were fanatical shinny players, they agreed without delay. So the girl invited them to eat at the field shed. "Let's eat first," she said.

They followed her to the shelter, and, sure enough, when they arrived, another girl was there. She greeted them politely and said, "We have a packed lunch with us. Let's eat first and then we'll play." With these words she unwrapped the food and all of them had lunch.

When they had eaten enough, the girls said, "Well then, let's get going. You play together and we, too, will be a team. We'll see who wins."

"Ta'ay," yaw puma amumi kita.

Paasat pu yaw oovi mant taqatskiy oongaqw tatsimrukhoy horokna. Pay yaw kur piw puma put himuy'ta. Paasat pu' yaw puma angqw paasat sunasamiya. Pu' yaw puma aw öki. "Pay kya yephaqamni," yaw suukyawa maana kita. Pep pu' yaw oovi puma tatsiy amya. Pu' yaw sutsvaqw aw maana wunuptu, pu' sutsvaqw yaw Pöqangwhoya. Paasat pu' yaw suukyawa maana amungem pootoylanta. "Ason hapi nuy naalöq aqw pootoylaqw, pu' uma aqw hangwanvani," yaw amumi kita.

Paasat pu' yaw oovi antsa naalöq aqw pootoylaqw, pu' yaw puma nan'ivaqw tatsit aw saviva. Hisatniqw pu' yaw Pöqangwhoya horokna. Pu' yaw puma pephaqam tatatsya. Pas yaw mant a'ni. Pas yaw puma sun wuktota. Pas yaw puma kwangwa'ewlalwa. Pantsatskyaqw pay yaw mant pumuy pö'a.

Paasat pu' yaw puma piwya. Paasat pu' yaw Pöqangwhoyatwat pumuy pö'a. Paasat pu' yaw mant pangqawu, "Itam piw suusyani, niikyangw itam pu' hapi pas itaaqatsiy ooviyani," yaw amumi kita. Noq pay pi yaw pas lomamantniqw, oovi pay yaw piw puma sunakwha. Pu' pay pi yaw son pumuy pö'aniqw ooviyo'.

Paasat pu' yaw oovi piw puma angqw paasat sunasamiya. Pu' yaw puma aw ökiqw, pu' yaw suukyawa maana kweeway angqaqw hiita horokna nit pu' yaw amumi pangqawu, "Hakim hapi hakimuy pö'e', itakw niinamantani." Yaw kur poyot pam horokna. Pu' yaw pep sunasave put tsööqökna.

Paasat pu' yaw Pöqangwhoyat pangqawu, "Antsa'ay," yaw kita. Paasat pu' yaw puma oovi piw tatatsya. Pas yaw puma sunya. Paasat yaw pas Pöqangwhoyat qa atsay'ta. Pay yaw pas hinte', pas puma peep tatsit kiyat aqw panaqw, pu' pay piw yaw maanatwat tuwatningwu. Pantsak-kyangw pu' yaw Pöqangwhoyat piw himuyamuy aqw haykyalniy'maqw, paasat pu' yaw mant mongaqw kwasay höliknat pu' kweeway aqw tsurukna. Pas pi yaw qötsaqaasitu, piw wukoqaasit. Yanti yaw pumaniqw,

96

"All right," Pöqangwhoya and Palöngawhoya replied.

The girls now took their shinny clubs down from the ceiling of the shed. Then all of them headed towards the center of the field and when they got there, one of the girls said, "I guess this is the place." They buried their buckskin ball in the sand. One girl positioned herself on one side of it and Pöqangwhoya stood on the other. The second girl was going to count for them. "When I've counted up to four, you strike at the ball," she advised them.

She counted to four and immediately the two hit at the ball from both sides. Eventually Pöqangwhoya managed to get it free and they started playing. The girls were really good. Indeed, both teams were evenly matched and they enjoyed themselves very much. Finally the girls won.

Then the game started all over again. This time the two Pöqangwhoyas were the winners. Now the girls proposed, "We'll do it once more, but this time we will play for our lives." Because they were such pretty girls, the two boys quickly agreed. They were sure they would not lose.

They all went to the center of the field, and when they arrived there, one of the girls pulled something out of her belt. She said, "Whichever side wins is to use this to kill the others." She had pulled out a knife and now thrust it into the ground right in the center of the field.

The two brothers answered, "Very well," and the game was on again. Both sides played equally well. The Pöqangwhoya boys really exerted themselves. Once in a while they came close to scoring and then the girls almost scored, too. But when the boys were getting ready to score again, the girls simply lifted up their dresses and tucked them into their belts. Were their thighs white! And nice big ones as well! From this moment on the boys kept their eyes glued on the girls' thighs and stopped paying attention to the

pu' yaw pay puma pumuy qaasiyamuy aw taykyangwniiqe, pay yaw puma qa an wukta. Pay yaw mantuy qaasi'am moopeqti. Yan pay yaw puma nuvö'iwkyangwniiqe pay puma pö'i.

Paasat pu' yaw mant pumuy pö'aaqe pu' amumi pangqawu, "Ta'a, pay pi itam nuwupi umuy pö'a, noq oovi uma pewni." Kitat pu' yaw angqw paasat naasami, haqam poyo tsööqökiwtaqw, panso'.

Pu' yaw ima nawus amungki. Paasat pu' yaw ima naamisa'a. Pöqangwhoya yaw tupkoy aw itsivuti. "Um pas naapas qaasiyamuy awsa taykyangw, niqw oovi itam pö'i."

"Pay pi um piiwu. Um pas tis teevep aw taykyangwniqw, oovi utsviy pi itam pö'i."

Pu' yaw puma aw öki. Paasat pu' yaw ima nawus amumi pangqawu, "Ta'ay, pay pi nuwupi uma itamuy pö'a. Pay pi oovi uma itamuy niinani."

Paasat pu' yaw mant pangqawu, "Pay itam qa pas umuy niinani," yaw amumi kita, "noq oovi uma haqawa mooti pewni."

Pu' yaw pay Pöqangwhoya tupkoy aw hoona, "Yupa, um mootini," yaw aw kita.

"So'ni, umni, um pi wuuyoqa," yaw aw kita.

"Oovi'oy, um pi inuupe tsayniiqe oovi mootini."

Pu' yaw nawus Palöngawhoya aw'i. Panis yaw aw pituqw, pu' yaw maana put ngu'a. Panis yaw ngu'at, pu' yaw sutsvaqw maayat tupkyaqe ayo' tuku. Pantit pu' yaw piw ayangqwat an tupkyaqe ayo' maayat tuku. Pantit pu' yaw aw pangqawu, "Yantani," yaw aw kita.

Paasat pu' yaw Palöngawhoya angqw ayo' löövaqw ngasta may'kyangw nakwsu. Paasat pu' yaw Pöqangwhoya tuwat aw'i. Paasat pu' yaw putwat hokyayat löövaqw ayo' tuku, qastupkyaqe. "Yantani," pu' yaw mant kita, "pay pi nuwupi uma pö'i." Kitat pu' yaw aapiyo'.

Puma yaw pephaqam naami taynuma. Paasat pu' yaw suukyawa pangqawu, "Ya itam sen hintini? Nu' pi löövaqw ngasta may'ta."

game. The girls' thighs seemed more important. And because of their lust, they lost the game.

Now that they had won, the girls said, "Well then, it can't be helped. We have won. Come here." And they went to the place where the knife had been pushed into the ground.

The two boys had to follow them whether they wanted to or not and they started blaming each other. Pöqangwhoya was furious at his younger brother. "Why did you have to watch their thighs all the time? That's the reason we lost."

"Well, so did you. You were staring at them all the time, so thanks to you we were beaten."

Then they reached the center of the field and the two had to resign themselves to their fate. "All right, there is nothing that we can do about it. You are the winners, go ahead and kill us."

But the girls replied, "We do not really intend to kill you. One of you come here first."

Pöqangwhoya sent off his younger brother. "Go on, you can be first," he told him.

"Oh no, you go. You are older," he protested.

"Well, that's just why you should go first. You're younger than I am."

So Palöngawhoya had to give in and go. The moment he came up to the girl, she grabbed him. And no sooner had she gotten a hold of him than she severed one of his arms right at the shoulder. Then she cut off his other arm at the same place. "That will do," she said.

Palöngawhoya stepped aside with both his arms gone. It was now Pöqangwhoya's turn. The girls cut both his legs off just where they joined the body. "Now, that'll be it," they said. "After all, we beat you." With these words they went their way.

The two brothers just looked at each other until one of them finally broke the silence. "What are we going to do? I have no more arms," he said.

99

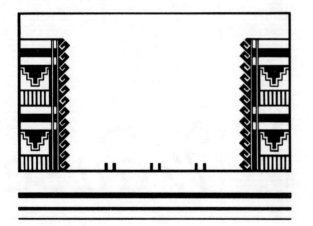

"Niikyangw um pay ngas'ew hokyay'ta, nu' pi pas ngasta'a," yaw aw paava'at kita.

"Hep owi, niikyangw um pay ngas'ew löövaqw may'ta, nu' pi pas ngasta'a," yaw tuwat aw kita. "Ya itam sen hin nimani?"

Paasat pu' yaw paava'at pangqawu, "Nu' pi pay löövaqw may'ta, niiqe nu' oovi sutsvaqw uumay nit pu' ihokyay nu' tawimokkyangw, pu' sutsvaqw uupitkunay nu' nguy'mani, pu' um pay nuy lölökintani. Um pi pay löövaqw hokyay'ta."

Paasat pu' yaw oovi Palöngawhoya paavay aw lööqmuy may hokyay akw hoyokna. Pantit pu' yaw hokyayat piw aw hoyokna. Paasat pu' yaw Pöqangwhoya put soosok sutsvaqw tawimokyaata. Pantit pu' yaw sutsvaqw may akw tupkoy pitkunayat ngu'a. Pantit pu' yaw tupkoy aw pangqawu, "Ta'ay, tumaa', pay itam son hin qa pituni."

Paasat pu' yaw Palöngawhoya pangqaqw paavay lölökinta. Panmakyangw pu' yaw puma tupo pitu. Pang pu' yaw o'wat ang pam paavay lölökinta. A'ni yaw paava'at tupkoy aw itsivu'iwma. "Is anay, um pas naanap hiniy."

"Pay pi nu' kur hinniqe'e."

Pangqaqw yaw puma naaqööqöytima. Panmakyangw pu' yaw puma pitu. Pu' yaw puma kiy aqw mooti hokyay nit pu' may maspa. Paasat pu' yaw puma aqw angk pay nawus nu'an poosi.

Pu' yaw kur so'am navota, pu' yaw amumi pangqawu, "Is uti, kur pi pas uma qa navotngwu. Ura nu' umuy paas meewa, ura uma qa hisat teevengeniqat, noq pay kur uma piw epeq'a. Pay uma oovi haak pantani, noq nu' kur haqami hiita hepni." Kitat pu' yaw yamakma. Paasat pu' yaw puma naatupkom pephaqam naami yanta. Hisatniqw pu' yaw so'am ahoy pitu, hiita yaw mokkyangw. Paasat pu' yaw ephaqam put aw hintsaki. Hisatniqw pu' yaw kur kya pi yukuuqe, pu' Palöngawhoyat yaw mooti wangwayi. "Um pewni," yaw aw kita.

Pu' yaw pam angqw soy aw'i. Noq kur yaw pam yöngöt mokva, niiqe

"But at least you have your legs. Mine are gone," the older brother retorted.

"Yes, that's true, but at least you have both your arms, while mine are missing," he in turn replied. "I wonder how we're going to get home."

Thereupon his older brother suggested, "I have both of my arms and hands so I'll carry your arms and my legs in one arm and you can drag me along while I hold on to your kilt with the other. After all, you still have both of your legs."

So with his foot Palöngawhoya pushed his own arms to his older brother. Pöqangwhoya loaded everything into one of his arms and then he grabbed his younger brother's kilt with his other hand. When he had done that he said, "All right, let's go; somehow we'll get home."

So Palöngawhoya dragged his older brother along. Eventually they reached the foot of the mesa, where he had to drag Pöqangwhoya over some rocks. The older brother was furious. "Ouch, you couldn't care less where you are going!"

"I can't help it," the other replied.

From then on they kept scolding each other. Finally they arrived home. First, they threw the legs and arms into the house. Then they had no choice but to fall in after them.

Their grandmother evidently heard them and said, "Oh dear, you simply never listen. Don't you remember I warned you never to go west? But no, you had to go. So just stay there for the time being while I go look for something." Then she was gone and the two brothers were by themselves. Eventually their grandmother came back with a bundle. She did something with it and when she was finished she called Palöngawhoya first. "Come here," she said.

He went to his grandmother and noticed she had brought some cactus.

101

pu' yaw kur pam put kwanamna. Pu' yaw oovi pam put yöngöt akw pu' maayat ahoy aw piitakna. Nan'ivaqw yaw panti. "Yantani," yaw aw kita. "Pay um haak paapu qa pas uumay akw hintsakqw, pay songqa ahoy aw huurtini," yaw aw kita. Yaw Palöngawhoya naanakwhaniy'taqe soy aw yokokolawu.

Paasat pu' yaw Pöqangwhoyat piw pay an yukuna. Hokyayat ahoy yöngöt akw aw piitakna. Paasat pu' yaw amumi pangqawu, "Pay uma haak paapu hikis taalat ang qa pas hintsakqw, pay songqa ahoy huurtotini," yaw amumi kita. Kitat pu' yaw pumuy wa'ökna.

Noq pay yaw piw qa wuuyavotiqw pay yaw piw Palöngawhoya paavay aw pangqawu, "Ya uuhokya hintay?" yaw aw kita.

"Pay qa hintay. Meh," kitat pu' yaw a'ni horarayku. "Noq uuma hintay?" yaw tuwat tupkoy aw kita.

"Pay qa hintay. Meh," kitat pu' yaw tuwat a'ni mapyayayku.

Pu' yaw kur pay so'am piw navota, pu' yaw amumi a'ni itsivuti. "Ura uma paapu haak sun yantani, naat son pas aw huurti." Noq pay yaw kur puma pas piw son navotni. Pu' yaw pay piw oovi qatuptu.

Yan pay yaw puma piw suqlaptu. Pu' yaw paasat qavongva. Pu' yaw puma piw pay naami pangqawu, "Itam kur piw aqwni, lomamantuy aqwaa', niikyangw itam itaahotngay pu' yawmani."

Pu' yaw pay puma piw sun unangwti. Pu' yaw oovi puma hotngay kwusut yamaktoq, pu' yaw so'am pumuy tuuvingta, "Uma haqami'?" yaw amumi kita.

"Pay itam maqtoy," yaw aw kita, "pay itam ahoy songqa suptuni." Kitat pu' yaw puma pangqw yama.

Paasat pu' yaw pay puma yuumosa teevenge pasmiqa. Pu' yaw puma aqw pitu. Pay yaw piw mant epeqa. Pu' yaw mant amumi pangqawu, "Uma piw pitu?"

"Owi," yaw puma amumi kita, "pay pi kya as itam piw nanavö'yaniqw oovi itam piw angqö."

She had split them and now used the pieces to attach his arms again. She did that on both sides. "This will do for now," she said. "Be sure not to do anything with your hands for the time being, and they will grow to your body again." Palöngawhoya agreed with everything and kept nodding yes to his grandmother.

Then she treated Pöqangwhoya in the same manner, attaching his legs back to his body by means of the cactus. When she had finished she told the boys, "Be sure now not to do anything for a few days and your limbs will be joined fast to your bodies again." With these words she put them to bed.

But it did not take long before Palöngawhoya asked his older brother, "How are your legs?"

"They are fine. Listen," he said and shook them really hard. "And how are your arms?" he in turn asked his younger brother.

"There's nothing wrong with them," he replied and then he shook his arms quite energetically.

Grandmother heard this and scolded them severely. "Don't you remember, you were to lie still for the time being? Your joints have not completely hardened yet." But they were not going to obey her and got up.

Thus their limbs were healed in no time. And then it was another day. They said to each other, "Let's go visit those pretty girls again. But this time, we'll take our bows and arrows along."

They both agreed, picked up their quivers and, as they were going out the door, their grandmother asked them, "Where are you going?"

"We're going hunting," they replied. "We'll be back soon." Then they left.

They headed straight to that same field. They arrived and found the two girls there again. The girls said, "So you're back again?"

"Yes," they answered, "we thought we might have another contest. That's why we came back."

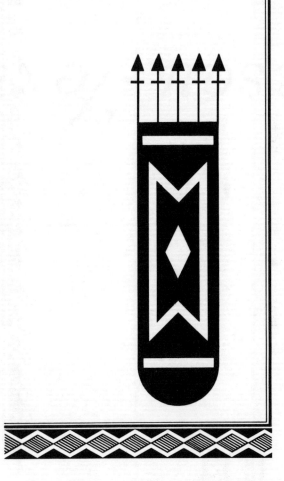

Pay yaw mant piw sunakwha.

"Niikyangw itam pu' itakwyani," yaw puma amumi kita. Pu' yaw amumi awtay maatakna. Pay yaw kur piw mant himuy'ta. Pu' yaw piw oovi taqatskiy oongaqw horokna.

Paasat pu' yaw puma piw pephaqam awtat akw nanavö'ya. Pay yaw pas sun maamapsim. Pay yaw pas sumataq qa hakimwat hakimuy pö'ani. Pay yaw oovi pas puma wuuyavo pantsatskyaqw, pay yaw pas qa hakimwat pö'a. Paasat pu' yaw Pöqangwhoyat pangqawu, "Pay pi qa hakimwat hakimuy pö'ay. Noq oovi itam kur hinwat pu' piwyani," yaw kita.

"Ta'a," yaw mant kita.

"Niikyangw pu' hapi hakim hakimuy pö'e', pu' pas suyan niinamantani."

Noq pay yaw mant sunakwha. Paasat pu' yaw oovi puma angqw paasat teevenge qalavoqya. "Yangqw hapi itam teevenge pookyayani. Hakim hapi susyavoq pookye', hakimuy pö'amantani."

Paasat pu' yaw oovi suukya maana mooti pookya, teevenge. Noq Palöngawhoya pi yaw sustala'vo. Pam yaw oovi angk tayta maanat pookyaqö'. Niiqe yaw pangqawlawu, "Angqe'e, angqe'e, angqe'e, aqw tsööqö," yaw kita. Paasat pu' yaw Pöqangwhoya tuwati. Teevenge yaw tuwat pookya. Pu' yaw Palöngawhoya piw angk tayta. Pu' yaw hisatniqw pu' pangqawu, "Aqw tsööqö."

Paasat pu' yaw mantuy aw pangqawu, "Pay itam umuy pö'a, pay itam susyavoq pookya."

"So'on pini," yaw mant kita.

"As'ay, uma qa tuptsiwqw, itam aqwyani."

Noq pay yaw mant qa tuptsiwa. Pangqw pu' yaw puma oovi teevenge. Hisatniqw pu' yaw puma mantuy hooyamuy aw öki. Paapiy pu' yaw puma piw teevengeya. Panwiskyaakyangw pu' yaw puma Kaktsintuyqat kwiningqöyve pumuy hooyamuy aw öki. Pas yaw paasat pu' mant tuptsiwa. "Ta'a,"

The two girls readily agreed.

"But let's use these now," the boys added, showing their bows. The girls, too, had bows of their own. They took them down from the ceiling of the shed.

Thereupon the four started competing with the bows. They were equally good sharpshooters. Apparently neither side was going to beat the other. The contest went on for a long time and still neither of the two teams had won. Thereupon Pöqangwhoya suggested, "No side has beaten the other, so let's continue in a different way."

"That's all right with us," the girls replied.

"But this time the loser will be killed," the Pöqangwhoyas added.

The girls agreed without hesitation. So they went to the west edge of the field. "From here we'll shoot west. The side that shoots further is the winner."

One of the girls shot first into the west. Palöngawhoya had the keenest eyesight and followed the arrow that the girl had shot. He was saying, "There it flies, there... there... now it has hit the ground." Then it was Pöqangwhoya's turn. He also shot west. Palöngawhoya again looked after the arrow. In a while he said, "It's in the ground."

Then they said to the girls, "We have beaten you, we shot further."

"Can't be," the two girls replied.

"Oh yes, if you don't believe it, let's go there."

But the girls would not believe it and so they went west. After some time they reached the girls' arrow. From there they continued on west and then, eventually, on the north side of Kaktsintuyqa, they came to the Pöqangwhoyas' arrow. Now the girls were convinced. "All right," they said, "you can treat us any way you wish. You have beaten us."

105

pay yaw kita, "pay pi uma itamuy naap hin yukuyani, pay pi uma itamuy pö'a."

"Pew tur umani," yaw amumi kita.

Pangqw pu' yaw puma Kaktsintuyqamiya. Pu' yaw puma oomiq yayva. Pepeq pu' yaw puma mantuy tumpoq wunuptsina. Pantit pu' yaw puma amumi töhahayku. Pay yaw paasat puma mant owatniwti.

Yan yaw puma pumuy aw naa'oya. Paniqw yaw oovi Kaktsintuyqat ooveq lööyöm tukwiwyat wunu. Puma hapi yaw mant pepeq wunuwta.

Pangqw pu' yaw puma nima. Naat kya yaw oovi puma haqam soy amum qatu. Pay yuk pölö.

106

"Come on then," the boys commanded.

Thereupon they all went to Kaktsintuyqa. They climbed up to the butte and there the brothers made the girls stand at the edge. Then they spat at them and instantly the girls were turned into stone.

In this way Pöqangwhoya and Palöngawhoya got their revenge. And that is the reason why there are two little buttes standing on top of Kaktsintuyqa. They are, of course, those petrified girls.

From there the boys went home. I suppose they are still living with their grandmother somewhere. And here the story ends.

Maasaw niqw Orayvit
Naatsawinaya

How Maasaw and
the People of Oraibi
Got Scared to Death Once

Aliksa'i. Yaw Orayve yeesiwa. Noq pu' yaw Orayviy aqlap, Mastupatsve, yaw Maasaw piw kiy'ta. Pay yaw pam panis soy'ta. Pam yaw sutsep mihikqw pep Orayve sinmuy tokvaqw, pu' Orayviy angqe pootangwu. Yan yaw pam pep Orayvituy tumalay'ta.

Noq yaw pam hisat piw pangqe Orayviy angqe pootiy'makyangw ahoy pitu. Yaw pam kiy aw pitut, yaw pam hiita navota. Pas yaw haqam suupan hiitu kwanonota. Pay yaw Orayve'ewakwhaqam. Pu' yaw pam angqw Oraymi hiisavo nakwsu. Nit pu' piw tuqayvasta. Noq pay yaw kur pas Orayve hakim hingqaqwa. Pay yaw pam panis yan navot, pu' yaw pay ahoy kiy aw'i. Pu' yaw pam pakiiqe pu' soy aa'awna, "Pas hapi Orayve-haqam hakim suupan haalayyay," yaw soy aw kita.

"Hep owi, pay nu' navotiy'ta. Puma pep mihikqw kivaape tootim,

Aliksa'i. People were living in Oraibi. Not far from the village, at Mastupatsa, was Maasaw's home, where he lived with his grandmother. Every night when the villagers went to bed, he inspected the area around Oraibi. In this way he guarded the Oraibians.

One day when he was returning from his inspection tour around the village, he heard something just as he reached his house. It sounded as if someone was having a good time, and the shouting and laughing seemed to be coming from Oraibi. So he went a little distance toward Oraibi and listened once more. Evidently some people were making a great deal of noise in Oraibi. As soon as he had realized this, he returned to his house. He entered and blurted out to his grandmother, "Some people in Oraibi really seem to be very happy."

"That's for sure, and I'm aware of it. Boys, girls, men, and women play

109

mamant, pu' taataqt, momoyam pep kivaape mihikqw sosotukwyangwu. Niiqe pas pu' nungwu pay qa iits tokwisngwu. Pay as mootiniqw suutokwisngwu, nit pay pu' pas qa iits tokwisngwu. Pay nu' oovi put navotiy'ta," yaw aw kita.

Paasat pu' yaw Maasaw lavayti, "Pas nu' as kur hisat nuutum awni. Hin pi hak sosotukwngwu."

Noq pu' yaw so'at aw pangqawu, "So'on pini, um qa panhaqam hintsakni. Puma hapi ung mamqasya, um oovi qa panhaqam hintsakni," kitaaqe pay yaw qa hin put nakwhana.

Pu' yaw pay aapiy i' Maasaw put wuuwankyangw mihikqw Orayviy angqe pootangwu. Pantsakkyangw pu' yaw pam hisat piw pituuqe, pu' soy aw pangqawu, "Pay nu' pas sutsep Orayminiqay wuuwankyangw angqe pootangwu. Noq nu' oovi qaavo piw ahoy pite,' pu' nu' kur awni," yaw kita.

"Pay pi nu' as ura ung meewa, noq pay pi puye'em um son tuuqayni.

---

sosotukwpi there in the kiva every night. It's getting so bad that they go to bed late. At first they used to go to bed right away, but now it's usually very late. So I'm well aware of what is going on."

Thereupon Maasaw replied, "I'd very much like to be there together with the others one of these days. I have no idea how to play *sosotukwpi*."

"That's out of the question," his grandmother replied. "You can't do that. They are afraid of you, so don't count on doing anything like that!" Her words made it clear that she would not give him permission to go under any circumstances.

From that day on Maasaw kept mulling this over as he made his nightly rounds at Oraibi. One day when he returned home, he said to his grandmother, "It's always on my mind to visit Oraibi when I'm inspecting the area there. So tomorrow, after I make the rounds, I will go there."

"Well, if you will recall, I forbade you to do that. On the other hand,

111

Noq pay pi oovi um antsa awni. Pay ason um suus awni. Niikyangw um hapi awnen, um uupösaalay akw huur naakwapmani. Um hapi qa naw-lökintani, puma hapi ung mamqasya. Um hapi oovi paapu inumi tuuqayte' qa naahöltoynani," kita yaw awniiqe pay yaw put nakwhana.

Pu' yaw Maasaw qavomi mihikmi kwangwtoya. Pu' yaw oovi qavong-vaqw mihikqw pu' yaw pam piw Orayviy angqe poota. Panis yaw oovi pam ahoy pitut, pösaalay kwusut, pu' yaw pam pangqw Oraymi'. Piw naat yaw so'at meewa, "Um hapi qa ephaqam naahöltoynani. Pay um panis amumi yorikt, pay um ahoy angqw nimani."

Pu' yaw pam oovi Oraymi pitu. Noq yaw antsa sup kivaape yaw kur sosotukwyangwu. Noq yaw kivats'ove tootim, taataqt wuuhaqniiqamya. Noq pay yaw oovi pam qa pas kivats'omi wupt, pay yaw pam haqaqw kiihut tuyqayat angqw wunuwkyangw tuuqayta. Pas pi yaw haalayya. Yaw kivaapehaq kwanokmanta.

Pay yaw oovi pam pangqw su'awsavo wunuwtaqw, pu' yaw kivats'o-veyaqam pay yaw himuwa kya pi öönate', pay nimangwu. Pantsakkyaa-kyangw pu' yaw pay hak pas suukya kivats'ove akwsingwa. Paasat pu' yaw pam pan wuuwa, "Nu' pi pas awnen pu' aqw kuyvani. Nen pu' nu' pas naap hin yorikni. Hintsatskyangwu piniiqe oovi pas haalayyangwu."

Kitaaqe pu' yaw pam angqw kivats'omi'. Pu' yaw pam put hakiy suukw akwsingwqat aqle' kivamiq tsooralti. Pay yaw pam oovi huur naakwap-kyangw, pay yaw pas poosiysa hihin kuytoyniy'ta. Pu' yaw pam pangqaqw pumuy tiimayi. Pas pi yaw kwangwa'ewlalwa.

Pu' yaw kur put amum oongaqwniiqa hisatniqw put aw yori. Noq pam yaw kur pas kwangwatimayqe, yaw kur pam pösaalay qa aw tunatyalti. Niiqe yaw kur pam qötöy hölökna, noq put yaw kur aqle' tsoorawtaqa tuwaaqe, pay yaw okiw sumoki. Pu' yaw pam pangqw nuutum hin unangway'ta. Pantsakkyangw pay yaw kur pam pösaalay posnat qa navota. Pantsakkyangw pu' yaw pay kur pam pas hin unangwtiqe, pay yaw pam kur pas kivamiq pakit qa navota.

I have a hunch that you don't intend to obey me. So why don't you go. But if you do go, be sure to cover yourself tightly with your blanket and don't let it slip off, for the people are very much afraid of you. For once, listen to me and don't reveal your face!"

Now at last he had her consent. Maasaw started looking forward to the following evening. And once more he made his inspection rounds. But as soon as he got home, he grabbed his blanket and headed towards Oraibi. Once again his granmother had warned him, "You must not show your face under any circumstances! Take just a quick look at them and then come back."

He arrived in Oraibi and, sure enough, in one kiva they were playing *sosotukwpi*. Since there were a lot of boys and girls on the kiva roof, he did not climb up on the roof but stood at the corner of a house and watched. The people were in a happy mood. There was shouting and laughter in the kiva.

After he had stood there for a long time, the people watching from the roof one by one got tired and departed. Eventually only one person remained on the top of the kiva. Thereupon Maasaw thought, "I'll go up there and peek in. Then I can see for myself what the game is like. I have no idea why they are carrying on so happily."

Saying this, he climbed up to the kiva. He lay flat on top of the roof right alongside the one remaining person. He kept his head tightly covered and let only his eyes show a little bit. Then he started watching the players below. They were enjoying themselves tremendously.

After a while his neighbor took a look at him. Now, Maasaw had been having such a good time watching the players that he stopped paying much attention to his blanket. He had uncovered his head and when the person lying next to him saw his face, the poor soul passed out right away. Maasaw was by now just as excited as the others down in the kiva. He was completely unaware that he had dropped his blanket. In the end he got so worked up

113

Yaw oovi pam pas aqw pakiqw, pu' yaw kur hak tuwa. Pu' yaw mimuywatuy aa'awna, "Himu pakiy," yaw kita. Noq pay yaw pas qa nanapta. Pu' yaw as pi'epningwu. Pas yaw hisatniqw pu' yaw kur nanapta. Paasat pu' yaw suuqe'toti. Pu' yaw kivaapeq kwiniwiq tupoq soosoyam yuutu.

Paasat pu' yaw Maasaw nuutum pansoq wari. Panis yaw oovi pam amumiq pituqw, pu' yaw piw taatöqwat yuutu. Pu' yaw pam piw nuutum aqw wari. Pu' yaw pay puma pepehaq naahoy pantsatskya. Pu'yaw kwiniwiq yuutukngwu. Pu' yaw pay piw pam nuutum aqw warikngwu. Puma hapi yaw kur as it angqw waytiwnumyaqw, pam nuutum waayangwu.

Pas pi yaw putniqw is uti. Pay yaw pam piw tsawnaqe, oovi nuutum pepeq naahoy waytiwnuma. Hisatniqw pu' yaw soosoyam so'a. Pay yaw pam paasat naala epeq wunuwta. Aqle' yaw sinom aasaqawta.

Paasat pu' yaw pam pangqw suyma. Pu' yaw pösaalay sukwsut pu' yaw pam pangqw kiy aw waaya. Paysoq yaw pam kiy aqw poosi. Pavan yaw hin unangway'kyangw, "Hihiya, uti, is uti," yaw kita.

"Ya hinti?" yaw so'at kita.

"Nu' Orayve'e. Nu' pep nanavö'yaqamuy amumiq pakiqw, pay hintotiqe kivaapeq naanahoy yuyutyaqw, pas nu' kyaanavota. Is uti, pay nu' son paapu hisat awni. Pay pi taataqtuy qötöyamuy ooveq himu qöötsa puvuyaltimangwuqa, pay pam pas nuy tsaawina. Pay put nu' hiita pas mamqasi. Pas is uti," kita yawi'.

Paasat pu' yaw so'at lavayti, "Ya um piw pay pas kivamiq paki?"

"Owi, pas kwangwa'ewyaqw, oovi nu' amumiq paki. Noq pay naat nu' hiisavo epeqniqw, pay hintotiqe naanahoy yuyutya, noq paasat pu' nu' put hiita tuwaaqe put nu' angqw waytiwnuma."

114

that he did not even notice that he had entered the kiva.

But someone had apparently heard him come in and announced to the others, "A stranger has come in!" However, the players paid no attention to him. Again and again the man tried to point it out to them. Finally they heard him. Their game stopped immediately and then all of them started running towards the northern wall base in the kiva.

Maasaw too ran there with them. He had hardly reached them when they started running back to the southern base. And again he ran with them. Thus they kept running back and forth. They headed for the northern part, but he ran there too. They tried to run away from him, but he kept running along beside them.

As he said later, it was awfully spooky. Because he, too, had become scared, he kept fleeing back and forth with the others. After a while all the players had fainted and he stood there all by himself. Next to him, people lay scattered on the floor.

He rushed out, snatched up his blanket and ran all the way home. He entered the house so fast that he more or less tumbled in. Excited and nearly out of his mind, he gasped, "How horrible, how dreadful!"

"What is it?" his grandmother asked.

"Well, I was in Oraibi, and I entered the kiva where they were playing and competing with each other. All of a sudden something happened and all the players started dashing back and forth in the kiva. It was dreadful for me! Let me tell you, I will never go back there. Something white hovered over the men's heads. It frightened me out of my wits. I really was scared stiff of that white thing, whatever it was. It was awful!"

Thereupon his grandmother spoke. "So you entered the kiva?"

"Yes, the people were having such a good time that I went in. And then, when I had been there only a few minutes, they all went crazy and started running back and forth. That's when I saw that white thing and started running from it, wherever it was."

"Qa'e," yaw aw so'at kita, "puma hapi ung mamqasyaqe, oovi uungaqw puma waytiwnumyaqw, um pepehaq pumuy tsatsawina. Pay um oovi paapu qa hisat awni. Put hapi um mamqasqay pangqawqw, pam hapi pumuy kwavöönakwa'amu. Son pi pam ung hintsanni," kita yaw put so'at awniiqe yaw put qööqöya.

Pu' yaw kivaapeq himuwa yaw hisatniqw yan unangwte', pu' pangqaqw kiy aw waayangwu. Yan yaw puma Orayve tootim, taataqt, pu' momoyam, mamant Maasawuy pitsinayaqe pas yaw puma naatsawinaya. Paapiy pu' yaw pay qa hisat puma kivaapehaqam mihikqw nanavö'ya.

Paapiy pu' yaw Maasaw pay ahoy piw Orayvit tuuwalangwu. Naat kya oovi pu' piw haqam songqe angqe pootiy'numa. Pay yuk pölö.

116

"It was quite the contrary," his grandmother interjected."They were afraid of you and so they took to their heels when you scared them. That's why you must never go there again. What you said scared you were only the white eagle feathers they wear in their hair. They can't do you any harm." With these explanations his grandmother chided him.

In the kiva, meanwhile, as soon as somebody gained consciousness, he just got up and ran away home. Thus those boys and girls, and men and women who tempted Maasaw to Oraibi got frightened to death. Never again did they gamble in the kiva at night.

From that day on Maasaw guarded Oraibi again. I suppose he is still making his inspection tour there somewhere. And here the story ends.

Takurmana niqw Sakwapu
Tiyot oovi Nanavö'a

Takurmana and Sakwapu
in Love with the Same Boy

Aliksa'i. Yaw Orayve yeesiwa. Noq yaw pep hakim maanat kiy'ta, niikyangw puma yaw naakwatsim. Pay yaw puma sutsep hiita naama hintsakngwu. Noq suukyawa yaw Takurmana, noq pu' suukyawa yaw Sakwapu. Pay yaw puma ephaqam naama kuytongwu, pu' yaw pay piw ephaqam sukwat kiiyat ep puma ngumantangwu. Pay yaw puma sutsep yan hintsaki, niikyangw yaw puma piw hakiy suukw tiyot naawakna. Pep pi yaw hak piw suhimutiyo kiy'ta. Noq yaw puma put naama naawaknaqe yaw puma put naanaqasi.

Noq yaw hisat Takurmana pan wuuwa, "Pas nu' as Sakwaput pay hintsanqw, itam qa put tiyot naanaqasni," yan yaw pam wuuwa. Niiqe pu' yaw pam hisat Sakwaput kiiyat aqw'a, wikoroy yaw pam yawkyango. Pu' yaw pam epeq pituuqe pu' Sakwaput ngemna, "Itam as naama kuytoni."

Pu' yaw pay kwaatsi'at sunakwha, "Antsa'a," yaw kita, "ason nu' iwikoroy horoknaqw pu' itamni."

Aliksa'i. People were living in Oraibi. Two girls were living there who were close friends. They always did things together. One was Takurmana and the other Sakwapu. Sometimes they went together for water and other times, they would grind corn at one of their houses. In this way they always kept busy. They also happened to love the same young man. He was handsome and lived in the village. Both girls were in love with him and both competed for him.

One day Takurmana had the following idea, "I should do something to Sakwapu and then there won't be two of us trying to win the same boy." So she went to Sakwapu's house as usual with her water canteen. When she arrived, she invited Sakwapu to go along with her for water. "Why don't we go together for water?"

Pu' yaw oovi pam wikoroy horoknaqw, pu' yaw puma Kookyangw-vamiq kuyto. Pu' yaw oovi puma pepeq kuyt pu' yaw puma angqw ahoyi. Puma yaw angqw ahoyniikyangw pu' haqami pisatvelmo pitu. Yaw oovi puma panso pituqw, pu' yaw Takuri pangqawu, "Itam as hiisavo yep naasungwnat pu' ason nimani," yaw kita. Pu' yaw oovi puma pep naasungwna. Pu' yaw pay puma pep naami yu'a'ata. Pu' yaw piw Takur-mana pangqawu, "Itam as hintsakni," yaw kita. "Um oovi atkyamiqniqw, nu' uumiq it muumani," yaw kita. Pangqawt pu' yaw kweeway angqaqw ngölat horokna.

Paasat pu' yaw kwaatsi'at pisatvelat atkyamiqa. Noq yaw Takurmana put aw pangqawu, "Nu' hapi it uumiq muumaqw, uumiq pituqw, um sung'ani," yaw aw kita.

Pu' yaw oovi Sakwapu pisatvelat atkyamiq pitu. Paasat pu' yaw put aqw ngölat muuma. Pu' yaw put aqw pituqw, pu' yaw pam put sung'a. Pas yaw a'ni himu putu. Panis yaw oovi pam put ngu'aqw pay yaw put munukna. Noq yaw pam munukqe pay yaw pam iisawniwti. Pu' yaw Takurmana aw tayati, "Yantani um'i," yaw kita. "Yante', pu' um son nuy tiyot naanaqasnani. Pu' pay nu' yaapiy put naala siwatway'tani." Kitat pu' yaw pam kuuyiy iikwiltat pu' pangqw nima.

Paasat pu' pam yaw kur hintini. Pu' yaw pam angqw kuuyiy aw'i. Pu' yaw as pam put iikwiltanikyangw pay yaw kur hinni. Pu' yaw pam pep kuuyiy aqlap qatuwkyangw pu' as hakiy nuutayta. Pay kya as yaw hak kuyte' put tuwaniqw oviyo'. Noq pay yaw pas qa hak kuyto. Noq nungwu yaw pay tapki. Paasat pu' yaw pam okiw qa haalayti. Pu' yaw oovi pam as pangqw kiimi'. Naat yaw pam oovi pu' qalangaqw aw pakiqw, pay yaw kur popkot put tutwaqe pay yaw put a'ni ngööngöya. Yan pay yaw pam kiimi qa paki.

Pu' yaw pam Orayviy angqe poniwma. Pu' yaw pam as piw tuwanta, noq pay yaw piw popkot put a'ni ngööngöya. Paasat pu' yaw pam kur

120

Her friend agreed, "All right, let me just get my canteen and then we can go."

They went down to Spider Spring. On the way home with their water, they passed a sandy slope and there Takurmana said, "Let's rest here for a little while and then go home." So they rested and were chatting with each other, when Takurmana suggested again, "We should be doing something. Why don't you go down to the bottom of the hill and I will roll this toward you." With that she extracted a wheel from her belt.

Thereupon her friend walked to the foot of the slope and Takurmana called her, "I'll roll this toward you and you grab it when it gets to you."

As soon as Sakwapu was all the way down, the wheel came rolling toward her. She caught it quickly enough, but it was extremely heavy and, as soon as she got hold of it, she was knocked over. The instant she hit the ground, she turned into a coyote. Takurmana laughed at her, "This is what you will be now. In this shape you won't be my rival for the young man anymore. From now on I'll have him alone as my lover." With these words she shouldered her canteen and headed home.

Sakwapu was at a loss. She went to her canteen and tried to place it on her back but was not able to. So she sat down by it and waited. Some woman who came to get water might find her. But no one came and in the meantime it got dark. The poor thing was miserable and started trotting toward the village. She had just crossed the village boundary when the dogs discovered her and furiously gave chase. Thus she was prevented from entering the village.

So she made a circle around Oraibi, but when she tried to enter, the dogs took after her again. Now she really did not know where to go. The

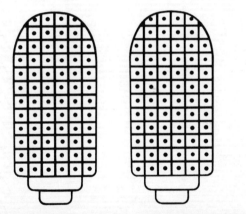

haqamini. Pu' yaw pam okiw wuuwanta, "Haqami sen nu'ni? Pay pi kur popkot son nuy kiimi panayani."

Yan yaw pam wuuwankyangw Orayviy kwiningye' teevenge. Pu' yaw pam taavangqöymiq haawi. Paapiy pu' yaw pam teevenge. Pay pi yaw pam navotiy'taqw, pang Orayviy teevenge' yaw sinom paasay'yungwa, niiqe pang yaw puma taqatskiy'yungwa. Pu' peetu pas ang piw kiy'yungwa. It yaw pam navotiy'taqe oovi pansoqwat yaw pam nakwsu. Pay pi kya as yaw pam haqam hakiy taqatskiyat ep hiita tuwe' put nösni. Pam yaw tsöngmoki.

Panmakyangw pu' yaw pam taqatskimi pitu. Pu' yaw pam pep hiita as sowaniqay hepnuma. Pantsakkyangw pu' yaw pam taqatskit atsveq lööq tu'tsit tuwa. Put yaw pam nöösa. Pantit pu' yaw pam wuuwanta, "Ya sen nu' hintini?" Nit pu' paasat yaw pam pan wuuwa, "Pay pi nu' suus kur piw tuwantani. Pay kya as pu' popkot qa nanaptani nu' kiimi pituqö'."

Yan yaw pam wuuwaqe pu' yaw pam pangqaqw piw ahoy Oraymiqa. Paasat pu' yaw pam piw aw oomi wuuvi. Pay yaw naat piw pam panis qalangaqw aw pakiqw, pay yaw piw kur popkot put hova'ikwyaqe pay yaw piw put ngööngöya. Paasat pu' yaw pam naami pangqawu, "Pay pi kur nu' son kiimi pakini. Pay pi nu' oovi nawus haqam hakiy pasve kiiyat ep kya as puwni." Paasat pu' yaw oovi pam pangqw teevenge. Haqam pu' yaw pam pasve kiihut aw pitu. Noq pay yaw qa aw uutsiwta. Pu' yaw pay qa hak piw epe'. Panso yaw pam paki. "Pay pi nu' haak yep puwni," yaw pam yan wuuwa. "Ason pi nu' qaavo pu' piw haqamini. Pay pi nu' kur haqamini," kitaaqe pu' yaw pam pep hiita piw sowaniqay hepnuma. Pu' yaw pay antsa pam piw hiita hiisakw tuwaaqe pu' put nöösa. Pantit pu' yaw pay pam wa'ökqe wuuwankyangw pu' yaw kur pam hisatniqw puwva.

Pay yaw oovi qavongvaqw taawat yamakiwtaqw pam taatayi. Pu' yaw pangqawu, "Pay pi kur nu' haqamini," yaw kita. Paasat pu' yaw pam pangqw Apooniviy su'aqw nakwsu. Pu' yaw oovi pam aqw pituuqe pu' yaw pam piw u'na. "Ura pi hakim pepehaq taavanghaq kanel'oyiy'ta. Pay pi nu'

poor creature was worrying, "Where on earth can I go? The dogs will never let me into the village."

With thoughts like this, she ran along the northern part of Oraibi in a westerly direction. She descended on the west side, and from there, continued on westward. She knew, of course, that people had their fields in the area west of Oraibi and also had some temporary shelters there. Some even had actual houses. Because she was aware of this, she headed in that direction. After all, she might find something to eat in a field shelter. She was hungry by now.

Eventually she came to a hut and searched around for something edible. At last she discovered two ears of roasted corn on top of the roof. She devoured them, but then her old worries returned. "What am I going to do?" she thought. Then she decided, "I'll make one more attempt. The dogs might not notice me when I sneak into the village."

So once more she headed back towards Oraibi. She climbed to the top of the mesa, but no sooner had she crossed over the village line than the dogs smelled her and started after her again. Thereupon she said to herself, "It's impossible for me to enter the village. So I might have to sleep in somebody's field house." She trotted westward again and, at somebody's field, she came upon a house. It was not closed and no one was there. So she went in. "I'll sleep here for the time being," she thought. "Tomorrow I can move somewhere else, although I have no idea where." She started searching for food again and, indeed, found several things to eat. Then she bedded herself down and, with all sorts of worries on her mind, finally fell asleep.

The next morning she woke up at sunrise. "Well, I'll go somewhere," she said and ran off in the direction of Apoonivi. When she arrived, she remembered, "Oh yes, two men keep their sheep there in the west. I'll probably be able to find something to eat at their place. And I'm sure I can

123

pansoqnen pepeq pay nu' son hiita qa nösniqay piw tuwani. Pu' pay nu' son pepeq piw qa puwni." Yan yaw pam wuuwaqe pu' yaw pam pangqw teevenge Yongyatsaymiqa. Pu' yaw pam oovi aqw haykyala, nit pay yaw pam haqam kiihut aw pitu. Pu' yaw pam aw taynuma, noq pay yaw qa hak ep'eway, pu' yaw pay qa himu haqam piw pooko'eway. Paasat pu' yaw pam aw'i.

Noq pam yaw kur pep Sikyaqöqlötuy kii'amu. Pam yaw kur pep pumuy makki'amu. Pu' yaw pam oovi aw paki. Pas pi yaw ep sikwi wuko'oyi. Pay yaw hihintuupewyungwa. Pu' yaw pam paasat sukw pavan kwasiwtaqat sowa. Pantit pu' yaw pay pam haak pepniqay wuuwa.

Noq Qööqöqlöt yaw ep su'its talavay pay pangqw maqto. Niiqe yaw puma pay oovi maqnumqe pay tapkiwmaqw, pu' yaw puma pangqawu, "Pay pi tapkiwmay," yaw kita, "pay pi itam ahoyniy." Pu' yaw oovi pay puma paasatniqwhaqam ahoy nima. Pu' yaw puma kiy aw ahoy pituqw, yaw kur suukya put tuwaaqe pu' yaw pangqawu, "Piw itaakiy ep iisaw pakiwta niiqe kur itaasikwiy angqw sowa. Itam niinani," yaw kita.

Puma yaw oovi paas tumostsokyaqw, pu' yaw suukyawa pangqawu, "Haaki. Haak um qa mu'ani."

Noq paasat pu' yaw i' iisaw okiw tsawnaqe yaw paklawu. Noq put yaw kur suukyawa tuwaaqe oovi sungway meewa haak qa mu'aniqat. "Pay um haak qa mu'ani, itam ngu'ani. Itam ngu'e', itaasoy aqw wikni. Pay pam sumataq himu'u. Oovi pas posvalay'ta." Kitaaqe pu' yaw puma put ngu'a. Pu' yaw oovi puma put ngu'aaqe pu' put soma.

Pay yaw kur puma ep suus maqto. Pu' yaw oovi qavongvaqw pu' puma soosok sikwiy mokyaata. Pantit pu' yaw suukyawa put iikwilta, pu' yaw suukyawa put iisawuywat iikwilta. Pangqw pu' yaw puma pankyangw nima. Hisatniqw pu' yaw puma Katsinwalay aw öki. Pep yaw kur pumuy so'am kiy'ta. Pu' yaw puma aqw pakiiqe pu' soy aw put maatakna. Pu' aa'awna hin puma put kiy ep tuwaaqe, pu' piw ngu'aaqe, pu' oovi put angqw wikqe, paas yaw soy aa'awna.

124

sleep there, too." Thinking this way, she ran on west to Yongyatsayvi. When she got closer, she came upon somebody's house. She examined it from all sides. Not a soul seemed to be there and no dogs were in sight. So she went up to it.

This house belonged to the Yellow Qöqlös. It was their hunting lodge. Upon entering, she found a large amount of meat that was only slightly roasted. So she devoured one piece that was better done than the others and decided to stay there for a time.

The two Qöqlös had gone hunting early that morning. They hunted until it was almost evening, then they said, "Well, it's getting evening, it's time to go back." So they started for home and when they reached their house one of them evidently spotted her and said, "Darn it, there's a coyote in the house again and it's eaten up some of our meat. Let's kill it."

He carefully placed an arrow on his bow when the other said, "Hold it, don't shoot right away!"

The poor coyote had gotten scared and started to cry. One of the Qöqlös had noticed the tears and that's why he told his partner to hold back. "Don't kill it," he said. "We'll capture it alive and take it to our grandmother. This seems to be an extraordinary creature because it has tears in its eyes." With these words they grabbed the coyote and tied it up.

That day had been their last hunting trip, and the following morning they bundled up all their meat. When they were done, one loaded the meat on his back while the other shouldered the coyote. In this way they started back home. At some time or other they reached Katsinwala where their grandmother lived. They entered and presented her with the animal. Then they narrated in detail how they had discovered the coyote at their hut and had caught it to bring to her.

125

Paasat pu' yaw so'am angqw aw'i. Panis yaw aw pitut, aw yorikt, pu' yaw pangqawu, "Okiwa, imöyhoya, ya hak ung yanhaqam hintsana?" kita yaw awi'.

Pay yaw paasat pam sukw Qööqöqlöt Oraymi hoona. "Um Oraymi kiiminen um angqw lööq tumo'alat yawmani," yaw sukw aw kita. "Pu' umwa piw tuwat yukyiq kwiniwiqwat ngömaapit yukutoni," kita yaw pumuy awniqw, pay yaw puma paasat yamakma.

Pantiqw pu' yaw i' so'wuuti aw tuupata. Su'aw yaw oovi tuupa'at mukiitiqw, yaw tumo'alat kwistoqa yaw pitu. Paasat pu' yaw pam siivut aqw tuupat kuuya. Pu' yaw aqw iisawuy pana. Pantit pu' yaw koopaveq nit pu' yaw hooviyat epeq nan'ivaqw tumo'alat akw ngu'a. Pantit pu' yaw siivut aqw naakwapna. Pankyangw pu' yaw pam nan'ivaqw tumo'alat toriipanta. Pantsakkyangw pu' yaw hisatniqw ang puukyat tsoopa. Pay yaw paasat ahoy pam maananiwti.

Paasat pu' yaw ngömaapit yukutoqa yaw pitu. Pu' yaw put so'wuuti aw kwiiva. Paasat pu' yaw put maanat aw pangqawu, "Ya hak ung okiw yanhaqam hintsana?" yaw aw kita.

"Hep owi, pay itam it Takurmanat amum yep Orayve suukw tiyot siwatway'taqe, itam put naanaqasqw, pay put oovi pam nuy yantsana. Pam hisat nuy kuyngemintaqw itam kuyto, noq itam angqw ahoyniqw, itam pisatvelpe naasungwnaqw, pep pam inumiq ngölat muumaqw, put nu' ngu'aaqe pay nu' i' himuniwti." Yan yaw pam so'wuutit aw naalalvaya.

Okiw yaw so'wuuti put ookwatuwiy'ta. "Pay pi tsangaw um qa hinti. Noq oovi nu' ung aw naawusnani." Pu' yaw pam oovi put paas naawusna.

Pantiqw pu' yaw ngömapkwivi'at kwala. Put yaw pu' pam siivut aqw piw kuuya. Pantit pu' yaw aapamiqhaqami pana. Pantit pu' yaw maanat aw pangqawu, "Um peqwni." Pu' yaw pam oovi angk aapamiqa. Pepeq pu' yaw pam put aqw naavahomna. Pantit pu' yaw put puhukwasaatoyna, pu'

126

Their grandmother went up to the coyote. No sooner had she gotten close to it and glanced at it than she exclaimed, "Oh my poor grandchild, who has done this to you?"

Thereupon she ordered one Qöqlö to go to Oraibi. "Run to the village and bring back two pieces of devil's claw. And you," she told the other, "can go get some juniper branches in the north." Those were her specific orders and then the two departed.

Now the old woman put water on the fire. Just when it got hot, the one who had left to get the devil's claw arrived. The old woman now poured the hot water into a bowl and dunked the coyote in it. Then, using the devil's claw, she grabbed the animal at both ends, at the top of the head and at the buttocks. She covered up her bowl and, when everything was ready, started twisting the devil's claw at each end. She finally succeeded in pulling off the skin. Now the animal was back in the shape of the girl.

In the meantime the other Qöqlö who had gone to pick the juniper branches returned. The old woman boiled them and then asked the girl, "You poor thing, who did this to you?"

"Well, Takurmana and I, we're both in love with the same boy in Oraibi and, since we both wanted him, she did this to me. One day she invited me to go for water with her. Upon returning we took a rest on a sandy slope and she rolled a wheel down to me. I caught it and was transformed into this." In this way Sakwapu told the old woman about her experience.

The old lady was full of sympathy. "Thank God, nothing has happened to you. I will set your hair now." So she carefully combed Sakwapu's hair.

In the meantime the juniper greens were boiling. She poured the liquid into a bowl which she carried into the backroom. Then she called the girl, "Come here." Sakwapu followed her into the backroom and the old woman bathed her there. When she had finished, she put a new dress on

127

piw puhu'atö'öt usiitoyna. "Yantani," yaw aw kita, "pay um haak yep itamum qatuni. Nu' kur haqami hakimuy wangwayni."

Kitat pu' yaw yamakma. Pu' yaw oovehaqam tsa'lawu, "Pangqe' kya uma inatkom yeese. Uma pew tsovawmani. Uma qa sööwuyani. Pay haalaykyaakyango," yan yaw tsa'lawu. Pu' yaw ahoy paki.

Pay yaw antsa qa wuuyavotiqw pay yaw hiitu ökiwta, yaw katsinamu. Pu' yaw kur soosoyam tsovalti. Paasat pu' yaw pangqaqwa. "Ta'ay, ya um hintoq pas itamuy kyeteynawakna?" yaw kitota.

"Hep owi," yaw so'wuuti kita, "ima taavok imöyhoyat it maanat wikvaqw, uma as it yaapiy naalös taalat ep ahoy kiiyat aw wikyaniqw, oovi nu' umuy naawakna," kita yaw amumi'.

"Antsa'ay, pay itam songqa pantotini." Paasat pu' yaw pay nöngakma.

Paasat pu' yaw i' so'wuuti maanat matamiq pana. Pu' yaw pam pephaqam pumuy amungem ngumanta. Pu' yaw oovi kur naalös taalat aqw pitu. Noq pu' yaw pay taawansap'iwmaqw, pu' yaw katsinam piw ahoy öki.

Paasat pu' yaw so'wuuti maanat aw tutapta, "Ima hapi ung ahoy Oraymi wikyani. Noq oovi ung hapi ep wikvayaqw, pu' pay sinom songqa nanaptani, pu' ungu puma piw. Paasat pu' ungu puma son ung qa aw wiktoni. Noq oovi ason ung aw wiktoq, pu' um unay aw pangqawni, lööq paahot yukuni, ungem nit pu' katsinmongwit engem. Nit pu' aapiy piw peehut nakwakwustani, put ason imuywatuy katsinmuy engem. Pu' aason pas yukiltiqw, pu' una ason katsinmongwit aw paahoyat tavini, nit pu' uumi piw sukwat, pu' ason aapiy mitwat nakwakwusit imuywatuy huytani. Ason pas pantit pu' ung wikni," yan yaw aw tutapta.

"Antsa'a," yaw pam aw kita.

Paasat pu' yaw oovi puma pangqw Oraymiya. Katsinam yaw naanangk wiisiwta. Pu' i' maana pay susnuutungk. Noq yaw puma Orayviy kwiningyaqw aw kuukuyvaqw, pay yaw kur pumuy sinom tutwa. Pu' yaw oovi puma tipkyamiq mootiya. Noq pay yaw antsa sinom put maanat

128

the girl and gave her a new cotton shawl to wear. "There you are now," she said to her. "You can stay here with us for the time being. I want to call someone in the meantime."

She left and called out from the roof, "My children and offspring living out there somewhere, come and gather here. Don't tarry and come happily!" After this announcement she came back in.

And, indeed, it did not take long before some creatures started to arrive. They were kachinas. When all of them had assembled, they asked her, "Well then, why did you need us so quickly?"

"Yes," the old woman replied, "the Qöqlös yesterday brought this grandchild of mine, this girl here, to me and I would like you to take her back home four days from now. That's why I wanted you."

"All right, we will certainly do that." And so they departed.

Now the old woman led the girl to the mealing bin and there Sakwapu ground corn for them. Then the fourth day came. It was getting toward noon when the kachinas showed up again.

Thereupon the old woman gave Sakwapu the following instructions, "The kachinas will now take you back to Oraibi. The people will hear them, of course. Your parents will surely come to get you and when they do, tell your father to make two prayer sticks, one for you and one for the kachina leader. He should add some prayer feathers for the other kachinas. When he is through, your father is to hand the leader his offering and give the other prayer stick to you. After that he is to distribute the remaining feathers to the other kachinas. Only then may he take you along with him."

"Very well," Sakwapu replied.

So then they started for Oraibi. The kachinas marched in a line and the girl followed at the rear. When they appeared north of the village, the people spotted them. The procession first headed toward the smaller dancing court. Now the people also saw the girl and mentioned it to each

tutwaqe naa'awinta. Paasat pu' puma tipkyangaqw pu' kiisonmiya.

Oovi yaw puma kiisonmi ökiqw, pu' yaw kur hak yumuyatuy aa'awna put katsinam wikvayaqat. Paasat pu' yaw oovi na'at aw'i, it maanat. Pu' yaw aw pangqawu, "Ya um pituy? Pas itam qa haalayi um kur haqaminiqö'. Noq oovi nu' ung wikni."

"Haaki," yaw pam nay aw kita, "um mooti lööq paahot yukuni. Pu' piw imuy katsinmuy amuusa' um nakwakwustani. Ason um put yukye', pu' piw angqwniqw, paasat pu' nu' ason umumumni."

"Antsa'ay," pu' yaw na'at kita. Paasat pu' yaw oovi pay pam tiy naat qa wikkyangw ahoy kiy aw'i. Pep pu' yaw pam put paahot nit pu' nakwakwusit yuyku.

Noq paasat yaw katsinam kiisonve tiiva. Noq sinom yaw wukotitimayya. Hikis pi yaw Takurmana nuutum tiimayi. Noq su'aw yaw oovi tiitso'q, yaw kur na'at nakwakwusyuku niiqe pu' yaw angqw amumi'. Paasat pu' yaw katsinmongwit mooti paahot maqa. Paasat pu' yaw tiy piw sukwat maqa. Pantit pu' yaw aapiy mimuywatuy piw soosokmuy huyta. Pantit pu' yaw amumi haalayti. Oovi yaw pam amumi haalaytit pu' pumuy ahoy hoona. Pantit pu' yaw pam pangqw tiy wikkyangw nima. Paasat pu' yaw puma piw ahoy haalayya.

Noq pay yaw qavongvaqw pay yaw Takurmana it kiiyat epeq piw suptu niiqe yaw put aw haalayti. Pu' yaw pay pam piw qa aw hin unangway'taqe, pay yaw piw aw tuwat haalayti.

other. From there they proceeded to the actual plaza area in the center of the village.

When they reached it, somebody told the girl's parents that the kachinas were bringing her with them. So her father walked up to her and said, "Well, you've come? We were quite unhappy when you disappeared. Let me take you along now."

"Not so fast," she replied. "You must first prepare two prayer sticks and then also make as many prayer feathers as there are kachinas. When you have done that, you can come back and I will go with you."

"All right," her father said, and went back home without taking his daughter along. There he fashioned the asked-for prayer offerings.

Now the kachinas started dancing and singing on the plaza. There was a large crowd of spectators, even Takurmana was watching. Just when the dancing was over, the girl's father finished the prayer feathers and went to them. First, he handed the leader of the kachinas a prayer stick, then he gave one to his child. Thereupon he distributed all the others. He thanked the kachinas and sent them back home. Now he took his daughter along with him, and her family was happy to have her again.

The following morning Takurmana called on her right away and greeted her happily. Sakwapu showed no ill-feeling toward her and expressed happiness at seeing her again.

Pu' yaw aapiy pantaqw, pu' yaw i' maana hisat tuwat Takurmanat kuyngemna. Pu' yaw oovi puma piw Kookyangwvamiq kuyto. Yaw puma epeq pitu, pu' yaw puma wikoroy aqw kuukuya. Noq it maanat pi yaw so'wuuti kuyapit maqa, niiqe yaw aw pangqawu, "Um hapi hisat tuwat Takurmanat kuyngemne', pu' um put akw uuwikoroy aqw kuukuyni. Pu' pay son hapi ung qa tuwani. Pu' son uumi qa tunglay'tani. Pu' um qa hin naawaknat aw tavini. Pu' pay son ason tuwat hin naami qa navotni."

Yan yaw put aw so'wuuti tutapta. Noq oovi yaw pam put kuyapit akw wikoroy aqw kuukuya. Pas yaw pam wikoroy aqw kuuyit wuutaqw, pas yaw kuyapiyat angqw wikorot aqw tangaqvey'vangwu. Pas yaw lomahintingwu. Noq yaw pam pantsakqw, yaw kur put Takurmana tuwa niiqe pu' yaw aw pangqawu, "Is uni. Ya um put haqam kuyapit? Pas um uuwikoroy aqw kuyqw pas ang tangaqvey'vangwu. Kur nu' aw taatayi," yaw aw kita.

Pu' yaw pay pam sunakwhaqe pu' yaw aw kuyapiy tavi. Pu' yaw Takurmana tuwat akw wikoroy aqw kuuya. Noq pay yaw pas antsa lomatangaqvey'vangwu. Paasat pu' yaw pam aw pangqawu, "Put pas angqw piw kuuyi kwangwu, kur akw hiikoo'," yaw aw kita.

Pu' yaw oovi Takurmana angqw kuyt pu' yaw hiiko. Naat yaw oovi pu' hikwt pay yaw angqe' wa'ökma. Pay yaw paasat pam lölöqangwniwti. Paasat pu' yaw pam tuwat aw pangqawu, "Yantani um'i. Um nuy okiwsana. Pay pi um tuwat yangqe' okiwhinnumni. Ung pi pay son himu powatani," kita yaw pam put awnit pu' pangqw nima.

Paasat pu' yaw i' lölöqangw tuwat pephaqam hoyoyotinuma. Pay pi yaw kur pam haqamini. Niiqe pay yaw pam pep hiihiituy tuumoynuma. Pay pi yaw lölöqangw qa a'ni wartangwu, niiqe pay yaw pam kyaananvotkyangw tunöstuway'numa. Pay yaw pam hiita huutukye', ngu'e', pu' yaw put sowangwu. Yanhaqam yaw pam pangqe' okiwhinnuma.

From that time on things were like that, until one day Sakwapu invited Takurmana to go to the spring with her for water. They went down to Spider Spring again. When they arrived there, they scooped water into their canteens. Now the old woman had given Sakwapu a cup and told her, "When you ask Takurmana to accompany you to the spring, use this cup to fill your canteen. Takurmana will see it and want it. Just let her have it without asking any questions. She will definitely discover something about herself later on."

Those had been the old lady's instructions, and Sakwapu, therefore, now used this cup to pour water into her jug. While she was doing this, an array of rainbow colors appeared between the cup and the vessel. It was very pretty. Takurmana saw it and exclaimed, "How neat! Where did you get that cup? When you pour water into your canteen all sorts of colors become visible. Let me look at it," she pleaded.

Sakwapu readily handed her the cup and now Takurmana, too, filled her container with it. The colors were glorious. Sakwapu added, "The water in the cup also tastes very good, you should try it."

So Takurmana scooped up some water and drank it. The instant she did so, she fell on the ground and was changed into a bull snake. Thereupon Sakwapu said, "This is what you will be now. You caused me a lot of misery. Now you can suffer in turn wherever you go, and no one will restore you!" With this she went home.

Now the snake began to crawl around. She did not know where to go and lived on all sorts of animals. A bull snake is not very fast and has a hard time finding food. It sucks its prey in after it has caught it and then devours it. In this manner Takurmana had to suffer.

Nit pu' yaw pam hisat kiimi' niiqe pam yaw oovi kiy aw'i. Noq yaw kur yu'at lölöqangwuy kiy ep tuwaaqe pu' koongyay aa'awnaqw, pu' yaw pam put niina. Naap yumat puma yaw oovi put niinat qa navota. Pu' yaw pam put tuuvama. Yan yaw put Takurmanat naap yumat niina.

Pu' pay pi yaw panhaqam himuwa a'ni himu mokq, pay put hikwsi'at as yepningwu, niikyangw pam pay yaw qa hisat nuutum hiita hintsakngwu hiita so'qam hintsatskyangwuniqw. Naat kya yaw oovi haqe' songqa hiinuma. Pay yuk pölö.

134

One day she headed toward the village and crawled into her house. When her mother discovered the snake in the house she told her husband and he killed it. Her own parents killed Takurmana without knowing it. They went to throw the snake out. In this way Takurmana was destroyed by her own parents.

When a person like this with supernatural powers dies, his soul is still here but it does not take part in what the other dead people do. It is probably still around here. And here the story ends.

135

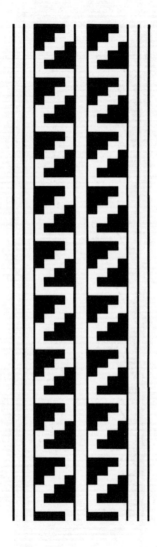

Namtökiwma

The Boy and the Demon Girl

Aliksa'i. Yaw Orayve yeesiwa. Yaw pep wukoyesiwa, noq yaw hak pep tiyo pay panis soy'ta. Pay yaw tuwat hak qa hingqawlawngwu. Pu' yaw pay nuutum kivay'ta, pay yaw niikyangw qa sutsep pepningwu. Pay yaw kiy ep pam tuwat pay hiita hintsakngwu, a'ni yaw pam tuulewkya. Pay yaw as pi sutsep pep hiita hintsatskyaqw, pay yaw pam hiita pas qa ningwu. Pay yaw qa nuutum hiita hintsakngwu.

Pu' yaw pay as so'at aw pangqawlawngwu, "Um paapu nuutum hiita hintsakmantani. Tootim, taataqt haalayyangwu. Pay um son pas sutsep yep inumi yantani. Pay nu' son hintini." Yan yaw put so'at aw as hingqaw-maqw, pay yaw pas piw qa pan unangwti. Pay yaw yan pam pep tuwat qatu.

Noq oovi pantaqw, yaw hisat tapkiqw maktsa'lawu. Yaw yukyiq Hotvelmoqwat yaw maqwisni. Noq oovi ep mihikqw yaw so'at piw aw

Aliksa'i. They were living in Oraibi. They were living in great numbers there, among them a boy who had only a grandmother. He was not very talkative and, although he shared a kiva with the others, he was not often there. He usually was doing something at home. Indeed, he was an excellent weaver. Although there were always people organizing things, he took no interest and as a rule did not participate in these things.

His grandmother kept saying to him, "Go and do something together with the others for once. Boys and men should have a good time. You can't always sit here with me like this. Don't worry, nothing will happen to me." Thus his grandmother was trying to tell him something, but again he did not change his attitude.

He continued in this manner until one evening a rabbit hunt was announced. They would go hunting in the Hotevilla direction. That night

pangqawu, "Paapu um qaavo nuutum maqtoni. Qaavo ura neyangma-
kiwni. Paapu um suushaqam nuutumnen angqe' nuutum haalayni. Qa
paapu um yephaqam inumi yantani."

Paasat pu' yaw tiyo lavayti, "Pay pi nu' ason aw hin wuuwe' sen
nuutumni," kita pam yaw soy awi'.

Pu' yaw antsa oovi talöngva. Yaw oovi puma tuumoytaqw, pay yaw
peetu maamaakyam nöönganta. Pu' yaw mamant piw. Pantsakkyaakyangw
pu' yaw sumataq soosoyam nönga, noq pay yaw pam piw qa nuutum yama.
Noq pay yaw so'at qa aw hingqawu. Oovi pay yaw se'elhaq maamaakyam
songqa aapiyyaqw, pu' yaw kur pam pan unangwti. Paasat pu' yaw
ephaqam yuuyuwsi. Pu' yaw kur yukuuqe pu' yaw tuwat nakwsu. Orayviy
kwiniwiq yaw pam nakwsu. Yaw pam qalavoq yamakqw, pay yaw qa hak
haqamo. Pay yaw kur se'elhaq soosoyam aapiyya. Pangqaqw pu' yaw pam
amungki.

Oovi yaw pam aw kwiningqöymi kuyvaqw, aw yaw hak mo'o'ota. Pu'
yaw pam oovi put hakiy angki. Noq yaw pam angk haykyalaqw, piw yaw
hak maana. Pam yaw kur hak tuwat qa iitsniiqe, pu' naat pansohaqami
tuwat pu' pitsiwiwta. Pu' yaw pam angk pitu. Pu' yaw pam aw pangqawu,
"Um pu' tuwat yangqe'?"

"Owi," yaw aw kita, "piw pi oovi umii'."

"Owi," yaw pam tuwat aw kita, "nu' kur qa iitsniqw, pay kur se'elhaq
aapiyya."

"Nu' piiwu," yaw maana kita. "Pay pi itam tur naamani."

"Ta'ay, pay pi antsa itam naamani."

Pay yaw pam sunakwha. Pas pi yaw hak lomamana. Pavan yaw angqw
taala. Paapiy pu' yaw oovi puma naama'a. Pu' yaw puma Hotvelmoq
maamaakyamuy amunk pitu. Nit pay yaw puma qa pas amumum
maqnuma. Pay puma yaw amungk hinnuma. Yaw puma oovi pepehaq
nuutum maqnuma. Noq yaw taawanasaptiqw, pay yaw paasat tiyo pay
qöya. Paasat pu' yaw maana pangqawu, "Pay pi itam tuwat tuumoytani.

138

his grandmother once again prompted him, "Why don't you join the others tomorrow? It will be a special hunt with girls and women going along with the boys and men. Take part, for once, and enjoy yourself with the others wherever you hunt. Don't stay here with me."

The boy replied, "I will give it some thought later. Maybe I'll go with them."

Then it was the morning of the hunt day. While the boy and his grandmother were having breakfast, the hunters were already starting to leave. And some girls, too. Pretty soon one might have thought that everybody was gone and that again he had failed to join them. When the hunters had been gone for quite some time, evidently he, too, got the urge to go. He dressed himself for the hunt and when he was ready, he also set out. He headed in the direction north of Oraibi. When he crossed the village boundary no one was in sight. They had all left a considerable time before. So he went after them.

When he got within view of the north side, he saw one person walking along. He followed the stranger and, when he got closer, he saw it was a girl. Evidently she, too, was late and had only gone part of the way. When he caught up with her he said as a greeting, "You are also on your way?"

"Yes," she replied, "and evidently you are too."

"Yes, I am late. The others left quite a while ago."

"I am late too," the girl said, "so let's go together."

"All right, let's indeed walk together."

He had not hesitated to agree. She was a beautiful girl and exceedingly charming. So they went along together. They reached the Hotevilla area soon after the hunters, but they did not hunt with them. Instead they kept their distance. By noontime the boy had already killed a good amount. So the girl suggested, "Why don't we eat our lunch? Afterwards we can follow the hunters again. They will probably return home from here," and

139

Ason itam nöst pu' piw amungkni. Pay pi songqa yangqw pu' ahoyyani."
Kitaaqe pu' yaw nitkyay tsawikna. Ali yaw somivikit kur moknuma, pu'
kuuyit piw. Pephaqam yaw puma put kwangwanösa. Paas yaw puma oovi
nöst pu' yaw piw nakwsu.

Noq pay yaw antsa paasat pu' maamaakyam pay ahoy kiimiqwat
hoyoyota. Pangqw yaw puma piw pumuy amungki. Noq paasat pu' i' tiyo
yaw piw peetuy qöya. Noq pu' yaw maana pangqawu, "Pay pi kya
yaasa'haqamni, pay putuuti," yaw kita.

"Antsa'ay," pam yaw aw kita, "pay itam yaapiy pu' nimiwmani."

Pangqaqw pu' yaw puma pay qa maqtimakyangw nimiwma. Pay pi
yaw paasat tapki. Yaw puma Qöma'wamiq kuyvaqw, pay yaw maamaakyam kur se'elhaq soosoyam ninma. Pangqw pu' yaw puma tuwat oovi pay
paasat nima. Panmakyangw pu' yaw puma haqam pam talavay maanat aw
pituqw, panso yaw puma pituqw, pu' yaw maana pangqawu, "Itam
pewni," yaw aw kita.

"Ya hintiqw oovi'oy?" yaw tiyo aw kita.

"Pay nu' yep kiy'ta," yaw kita maana, "oovi um pewni."

Pu' yaw angqw tumpo'. Pu' yaw pam angki. Noq yaw antsa kur
pephaqam kiva. Pep yaw kur i' maana kiy'ta. Pu' yaw puma oovi aqw paki.
Pu' yaw pam tuunimuy oovi piw aqw tangata. Paasat pu' yaw maana aw
pangqawu, "Pay pi tsangaw itam nuutum nukwangwnavota. Noq oovi nu'
ungem aw oyaqw, um nöst pu' ason tuwat nimani."

"Antsa'ay," yaw pam aw kita.

Pu' yaw oovi put engem tunösvongyaata. Pantiqw pu' yaw pam
tuumoyta. Pay yaw maana qa amum tuumoyta. Pu' yaw pam tuumoytaqe
pay yaw kur maanat qa aw tunatyawta. Noq paasat yaw pam maana tiyot
aatavang wunuptut yaw pep hintsaki. Hiita yaw tawlawu. Kitangwu yaw'i,
"Namtökiwma, namtökiwma, namtökiwma, namtökiwma, namtö." Kitat
pu' yaw namtötöyku. Pantikyangw yaw sutsvaqw poli'iniy tsawikna, noq
sukyaktsiyat yaw ang oovi siwu, höömi'at. Pantit pu' yaw angqw kwiniwiq.

she unpacked her lunch. She had delicious *somiviki* in her bundle and also water. They enjoyed their meal and, when they had stayed their hunger, they started out again.

And, indeed, the hunters were already moving back to the village. The couple followed them again and the boy killed a few more rabbits. Thereupon the girl said, "I guess this is about enough. My load is pretty heavy now."

"That's true," he replied. "Let's start on our way home."

So from then on they did not hunt anymore, but just continued walking home. It was late afternoon. When they got in sight of Qöma'wa, all the hunters had already left for home a while ago. They too headed home from there. Eventually they reached the spot where the boy had met the girl earlier that morning and it was then that the girl suggested, "Let's go this way."

"Why?" asked the boy.

"I live here," the girl replied, "so come with me."

She headed towards the edge of the mesa. He followed her and, true enough, there was a kiva—the place where that girl was at home. They entered and then he also brought in his quarry. The girl turned to him and said, "I am grateful we did so well on this hunt. I'll serve you some food now and after you've eaten you can go home."

"Very well," he replied.

She spread some food out for him and he ate. The girl did not join him and while he was eating he did not pay any attention to her. She had sat down somewhat west of him and was busy doing something there. She was singing some kind of a jingle. It went like this: "Turning, turning, turning, turning, turned around!" With that she turned around several times. While she was singing, she loosened her butterfly hair-whorl on one side so that her hair fell over her shoulder. Then she moved north from that place and

141

Pu' yaw pepeq piw anti. Paasat pu' yaw piw sukw poli'iniy tsawikna. Pay yaw pas hihin piw hin sonilti. Pantit pu' yaw angqw hoopo', pu' pep yaw piiwu.

Pantiqw pu' yaw pam aw piw yori. Paasat pay yaw qa lomamana, pay yaw himu'. Paasat pay yaw pam hihin tsawna. Pas yaw pam paasat pu' hiita tuumoytaqay aqw pas yori. Pam pi yaw wuuwantaqe öngavat tuumoyta, noq yaw kur qa pam'i. Yaw kur pam tootoptuy tuumoyta. Pumuy yaw kur pam kwiiviy'ta. Paasat pu' yaw pam nayö'unangwti. Pu' yaw oovi pam yamakye' naayö'niqay wuuwaqe pu' wunuptu. Nit yaw pam tuuwimoq yori. Paasat yaw pepeq maana. Pas yaw qa soniwa, nuutsel'eway yaw himu'. Pu' yaw pay angqw put aw'i. Pu' yaw pay sumataq yaw put ngu'ani, noq pas pi yaw qa soniwqw, oovi yaw pam waaya. Pu' yaw pay piw angki. Pu' yaw pam pepehaq put ngöynuma. Pu' yaw pam hintsakkyangw saqmi pitu. Noq pay yaw piw saaqa huur hömpawit akw nöömiwta. Pay yaw kur pam hin yamakni.

Pu' yaw pam pepehaq put angqw waytiwnuma. Pantsakkyangw pu' yaw pam poyoy u'na. Pu' yaw pam put horoknaqe pu' piw angqw saqmi wari. Paasat pu' yaw pam poyoy akw atkyaqw oomiq hömpawit tukiy'ma-kyangw pu' yamakto. Pay yaw put qa ngu'aqw pam yama. Pangqw pu' yaw pam kiimiq waaya. Yaw pam ahoy yorikqw, pay yaw piw angqw angki. A'ni yaw piw himu warta. Pay yaw pas put sungkiy'ma. Pu' yaw pam wuuwanma haqami waayaniqayu. Pay yaw as pam kiy aw waayaniqay unangwtit, pay yaw qa panso'. Pay yaw oovi put pas wiikiy'maqw, pu' yaw pam leelentuy u'na. Puma pi yaw tangawta. Pu' yaw pam pansoq waaya, leelentuy aqwa'.

Naat yaw oovi leelenyaqw, pam amumiq paki. Pavan yaw hin unangway'kyangw pu' yaw amumi pangqawu, "Uma as nuy tupkyayani, nuy angqw himu ngöytaqw oovi'o. Oovi uma as nuy tupkyayani."

Paasat pu' yaw suukya aw pangqawu, "Pew umni." Pu' yaw pam angqw aw'i. "Peqw um pakini," yaw aw kita.

Pu' yaw put leenay aqw pana. Pantit pu' yaw piw nuutum leelena.

142

repeated the song. When she had finished, she untied her other hair-whorl. Her complexion, too, had changed for the worse. She then moved east and repeated the ritual.

Only now he looked at her again. She was no longer the beautiful girl he had been with; she was something else. He became a little frightened. He took a closer look at his food. He thought he had been eating cooked beans, but that was not true. He was eating flies that she had apparently cooked for him. He wanted to vomit. He thought he would have to vomit, so he got up to run out. He looked to the upper level of the kiva where the girl was. She was awful looking, a monstrous being, and she was coming towards him. Apparently she intended to catch him, but because she was so ugly he ran away from her. She pursued him and when he reached the ladder, he found that it was tightly wrapped with hairstring so that it was impossible to climb out of the kiva.

So he continued to run away from her and while this was going on, he suddenly remembered his knife. He pulled it out, ran to the ladder once more and by cutting the hairstring from bottom to top he escaped. He had gotten away without being caught. He ran toward the village. When he looked back he saw her coming after him. She was running extremely fast and was rapidly catching up with him. He wondered where he could go to get away from her. He felt like running home, but on second thought he decided not to. She was about to close in on him when he recalled the members of the flute society, who were assembled in their kiva. So he ran to them.

They were still playing their flutes when he rushed in. Upset and excited, he begged, "Hide me, please, there is a creature chasing me, so please, help me!"

One of the players answered, "Come and climb in here."

The man tucked him away in his flute and continued playing with the

143

Oovi yaw pantiqw, yaw oongahaqaqw hak hingqawu, "Ya qa yep ikong pitu?" yaw angqaqw hak kita.

"Qa'ey," yaw aqw kitota, "qa hak pituy."

"As hapi, pay pew kuk'at so'ta. Uma oovi pew horoknayani."

"Pi pay qa hak pituy," piw yaw aqw kitota.

"As hapi, pay pew kuk'at so'ta."

"Pakye' um naap hepni," aqw yaw kitota.

Pu' yaw antsa paki. Uti, yaw himu qa soniwa nuutsel'eway. Pam kya yaw himu tiikuywuuti. Paasat pu' yaw pepeq pam put hepnuma. Pay yaw qa tuwa. Noq i' suukya, ura put leenay aqw panaaqa, pay yaw pas hihin hin leelena. Noq pay yaw kur piw maana navotqe pu' yaw pay pumuy leenayamuy ang kukuytima. "Pay as uma tupkiy'kyaakyangw pas piw nuy qa aa'awnaya," kitikyangw yaw leenayamuy ang kukuytima.

Oovi yaw put leenayat aqw kuyvaniqw, pu' yaw pam tiyot iipoq poyokna. Pay yaw piw masmana sunvota. "Puye'emo," yaw kita, "pay as uma puye'em tupkiy'kyaakyangw pas nuy qa aa'awnaya."

Kitat pu' yaw suymakma. Pay yaw piw ahoy tiyot tuwa. Pangqw pu' yaw pam kiy aw waaya. Yaw hin unangway'kyangw kiy ep paki. Pu' yaw so'at suutuvingta, "Ya himu'u, imöyhoya?"

"Hep owi, nuy angqw himu ngöytaqw, oovi um as nuy tupkyani," yaw soy aw kita.

"Pay pi nu' kur ung haqami tupkyani. Noq oovi um pay qa yepnit yukyiq tatkyaqöymiq uutahamuy aqw waayani. Pay yepeq tatkyaqöyveq puma tangawta," kita yaw awi'.

Noq pay yaw i' tiyo qa maamatsi hakimuy pangqawqö'. Nit pu' pay pangqw suyma piiwu. Pangqw pu' yaw pam taatöq waaya. Yuumosa tumpoq yaw pami'. Pam yaw kanelkit su'atsngaqw aqw pituuqe pu' yaw pam aqw haawi. Pay pi yaw kur pam paasat hakiy aw taqa'nangwtiniqe pu' yaw pay tsivaatomuy amumi pangqawu, "Uma nuy tupkyayani, nuy angqw himu ngöyta."

144

others. After he had hidden him, a voice was heard from the roof. "Didn't my husband come here?"

"No," they answered, "no one has come here."

"But he must have, his tracks end right here. Bring him out to me!"

"But there is no one down here," they insisted.

"Yes, there is, his tracks end right here."

"Come in and look for yourself," they suggested.

So she climbed in. What an ugly and detestable looking creature she was! A Tiikuywuuti must be such a creature. She searched for him but could not find him. Then the flute player who had tucked the boy away in his flute played a little bit off-key. The girl heard that, of course, so she walked along the line of flutes, examining each in turn. "You have him hidden here. You just wouldn't tell me," she said as she stepped from flute to flute inspecting them.

When she was about to look into the man's flute, he blew the boy right out of the kiva. Naturally, the demon girl noticed it immediately. "I knew it," she said. "You had him hidden but you wouldn't tell me."

With that she stormed out and spotted the boy as he ran away from her toward his house. When he rushed in, panic-stricken, his grandmother quickly asked, "What is it, grandson?"

"There is a creature pursuing me, so hide me please!"

"I can't possibly hide you. Instead of staying here with me run to your uncles. They are all on the south side."

The boy did not understand whom she meant, but in an instant he was gone again and ran south. He reached the edge of the mesa right above the sheep pen. He climbed down into the enclosure and since he had no one to turn to for help, he said to the billy goats, "Please hide me, there is a terrible creature after me."

Noq piw yaw suukyawa aw lavayti, "Pay um pep pantani, pay son ung hintsanni," yaw aw kita.

Suupaasat yaw angqw oongaqw masmana kuyva, pu' yaw pangqawu, "Ya qa yepeq ikong pitu?"

Pu' yaw aw tsivaatom pangqaqwa, "As'ay, yepeq qatuy," yaw aw kitota. "Peqw um haawe' nen wikniy," yaw aw kitota.

"Uma tis peqw wupnayani," yaw kita.

"Pay um putninik peqw hawniy," aw yaw kitota.

Paasat pu' yaw maana pangqawu, "Is uti, taq kya uma..." pay yaw panis kita.

"So'on piniy," yaw aw kitota.

"As'awu, taq kya uma nuy tsopyani."

"So'on pi itam panhaqam hintsatskyani, peqw haawii'. Um peqw haawe' naap wikni."

Paasat pu' yaw as pay maana aqw hawnikyangw pay yaw piw qa suutaq'ewtangwu. Pantsakkyangw pu' yaw hisatniqw amumiq haawi. Pu' yaw angqw tiyot aw hiisavo nakwsuqw, pay yaw aakwayngyangaqw suukya tsivaato paysoq siikikt pu' sumavokta. Pu' yaw pay pam pep put tsopta. Pu' yaw pay tsivaatom aw homikma. Pas yaw puma put tsovininaya. Nungwu yaw puma put tutkitota. Pay yaw pas öö'öqa'atsa angqe' aasaqawta, noq naat yaw tsivaatom put ang yomimitinumya, maanat öö'öqayat anga'.

Yan yaw puma tiyot pa'angwaya. Paasat pu' yaw aw pangqaqwa, "Ta'ay, pay pi um nimani, pay pu' son himu uumi hintsakni."

Paasat pu' yaw oovi pam pangqw nima. Pu' yaw pam pituqw, yaw so'at haalayti. Pu' yaw pam soy aw soosok put tu'awiy'ta. Okiw yaw so'at ookwatuwiy'ta. "Noq pay pi tsangaw uutaham ungem aw naa'o'ya," yaw aw kita.

Paasat pu' yaw i' tiyo soy tuuvingta, "Ya pay um pumuy tsivaatomuy pangqawu, puma itahamniiqat?"

"Owi, pay pumuy nu' pangqawu."

To his surprise, one of them answered him, "Just stay where you are; that creature won't do you any harm."

That very moment the demon girl appeared at the top and asked, "Didn't my husband come here?"

The billy goats replied, "Yes, he is right here. Come on down and take him along with you."

"Why don't you bring him up to me instead," she suggested.

"If you really want him, you better come down here."

Then the girl said, "Yes, but I guess you..." and that was all she said.

"Oh no, we wouldn't," they replied.

"Well yes, you just want to rape me."

"No, no, we wouldn't do anything like that. So just come down and take him with you."

The girl was about to climb down but she hesitated again. After wavering for a while, she finally climbed down. She had already proceeded a little distance toward the boy when a billy goat snorted behind her, quickly embraced her and copulated with her there. All the other billy goats then pressed toward her and destroyed her by copulating with her. At the same time, they tore her into pieces. Only her bones were strewn around and the goats were still pushing with their penises even into them.

This is how they helped the boy. Then they said, "All right, you go on home now. She won't harm you anymore."

So then he went back home. When he arrived, his grandmother was glad and he told her everything that had taken place. How sorry she felt for him! "But I am thankful that your uncles took revenge on that creature for you," she said.

Whereupon the boy asked, "Did you actually say that those billy goats were my uncles?"

"Yes, that's what I said."

"Pay kur antsa'ay," yaw pam soy aw kita, "pay it nu' hin pas suyan navotni. Noq pay pi tsangaw pi oovi nuy pa'angwaya."

Yanhaqam yaw pam tsivaatomuy amutsviy qa masnömata. Pay yuk pölö.

"Well, I suppose it must be true," he replied. "I was just curious to know for sure. I am most grateful that they helped me."

Thus it was thanks to the billy goats that he did not end up with the demon girl for a wife. And here the story ends.

Tsorwukiqlö

Tsorwukiqlö and His Eagles

Aliksa'i. Yaw Orayve yeesiwa. Pay pi yaw hisat pep wukoyesiwngwu. Noq pu' yaw pep hakim naawuutim kiy'ta. Pay haqam pi ephaqam puma kiy'ta. Niikyangw yaw puma lööqmuy tiy'ta, naasiwamuy.

Noq pay pi sutsep taaqa pasvaningwu, pu' tis qa na'öntaqa, qa suup paasay'tangwu. Noq i' taaqa yaw panta, pam yaw qa suup paasay'taqe yaw pam oovi sutsep pasmi sasqa. Pay pi yaw as pam tiyotiy'taqe pay yaw as pam okiw put aw tunglay'ta amum pasvaniqat. Noq pay yaw kur pas pam son hisat put amum pasmihaqami hawni.

Pay pi hisat kya pi Hopitotim soosoyam, sen pay as qa pas soosoyam, kwaavokmuy'yungwu. Noq i' tiyo yaw lööqmuy kwapkoy'ta, niiqe pam yaw tuwat pas pumuysa api. Panis yaw pumuy talavay yesvat nöönösaqw, pay yaw piw hotngay iikwiltat pu' maqtongwu. Qa hin yaw nay amum pasminiqay wuuwantat, pu' yaw pam angqe' teevep maqnumngwu. Pu'

Aliksa'i. They were living in Oraibi. Long ago there was a large settlement with many people. And at that time a man and his wife were living there. I don't know exactly where their house was, but the couple had two children, a son and a younger daughter.

A man, of course, is always busy in his fields; especially if he is not the lazy kind, and owns fields in more than one place. This man was like that. He had several fields and he was always on his way to some field or other. Since he had a son, it was his heartfelt desire that the boy would farm with him. But evidently he would never go with his father down to the fields.

Now long ago all the Hopi boys, or maybe not all of them, supposedly kept eagles for pets. This boy had two such pets and they were all he cared for. Every morning, as soon as the family had gotten up and breakfasted, he shouldered his quiver and went hunting. It never occurred to him to

151

yaw pite' yuumosa kwapkomuy aw pitutongwu. Pay yaw pam pas pumuysa amumum hiinumniqay antangwu.

Noq yaw antsa hisat piw talavay puma yesvaqw, yaw na'am pangqawu, "Pas nu' as wuuwantaqw, itam suushaqam as soosoyam pasmiyani," yaw kita.

Noq pu' yaw nööma'at pay suupan unangwti, pu' ti'at maana. Noq pu' yaw pay naat piw tiyo'at qa pan unangwtiqe yaw pangqawu, "Pas kya nu' kur hin umumum awni, pas nu' pu' qa hiita ikwapkomuy amungem tunösmaskyay'taqe oovi'o. Nu' songqa pumuy amungem pu' haqami piw tunösheptoniqe, oovi pas kya nu' kur hin umumumni," yaw kita.

Pay yaw as na'at qa haalaytikyangw pay yaw qa aw hingqawu. Pay yaw panis aw pangqawu, "Pay pi kur antsa'ay, pay pi um antsa pumuy amungem haqami tunösheptoni."

Pu' yaw paasat maana tuwat lavayti. "Pay pi uma inuusavo awni, noq nu' tuwat mooti tumtsokni. Pu' nu' ason taawansave umumi nitkyay'-kyangwni. Pay uma oovi inuusavoni." Yan yaw pam tuwat nay pumuy amumi lavayti.

Pu' yaw na'at puma aw haalayti, "Antsa'ay, pay pi antsa um ason paasatniqw aw itamumini." Yan yaw aw lavaytit pu' yaw puma pangqw nakwsu. Noq pu' tuwat tiyo'am maqtoqe aapiy.

Paasat pu' yaw maana tuwat antsa tumay aqw qööha. Aqw yaw qööt pu' yaw aw tuupata. Pu' yaw pam tuupay aw maqaptsiy'ta. Pu' yaw hisatniqw antsa tuupa'at kwala. Pu' yaw pam aw wuuta. Paas yaw oovi pam paavaqwri. Pantit pu' yaw pam pik'oya.

Niiqe pay yaw naat oovi qa wuuhaq pam hölömnaqw, yaw angqaqw himu aw paki. Yaw pam aw sunamtö, noq yaw kur paavayat suukya kwapko'at natkuqe pam kur yaw put aw paki. Yaw oovi aw pakit son pi kya yaw pam qa paanaqmokiwtaqe, pu' yaw pay angqw put paqwriyat aw puuyalti. Niiqe yaw tsaqaptayat aqw qatuptuqe pay yaw put paqwriyat soosok wehekna. Pas yaw pam itsivuti. A'ni yaw pam kwaahut aw itsivuti.

follow his father to the fields. Instead, he hunted all day long. When he returned home, he went straight to his eagles, and that's where he spent most of his time.

Now one day, when the family had risen in the morning, their father said, "I was thinking that for once we could all go to the field."

His wife was for it and his daughter, too, but again his son had no such inclination and said, "I can't possibly go with you because I have no food left for my eagles. I need to go and find some food for them today, so I won't be able to go along with you."

His father grew sad, but did not respond. All he said was, "Well, that's all right, you go looking for your eagle food, then."

Thereupon the girl spoke, "You can go ahead of me. I'll bake some piki first and then later at noontime I'll bring you lunch. So you go ahead of me."

Her father and mother were delighted and thanked her. "All right then, you join us later." With this they started out. The boy in turn left on his hunting trip.

The girl now commenced building a fire under the piki stone. After she had built the fire, she put some water on and waited for it to boil. Then she poured the boiling water on the cornmeal dough, carefully mixed her batter and started spreading it on the heated stone.

She had not peeled off many sheets yet when something came in. She quickly turned around and found herself looking at one of her older brother's eagles that had cut itself loose and come in. Apparently it had flown in because it was thirsty. It landed right on the rim of the bowl and spilled all of her batter. That made her so angry that she bawled the bird out. Then she picked up a stick that was next to her and ran toward the

Pu' yaw pam naqle' murikot sukwsu. Pantit pu' yaw pam angqw kwaahut aw wari. Panis yaw oovi pam aw pitut pu' kwaahut a'ni yaw wuvaata. "Um himu qa hopi," aw kita, pu' yaw piw wuvaata. "Naapas umuy pookoy'taqa son umuy hikwnangwu. Umuysa apiniikyangw son umungem wuuyaq kuyngwu." Pu' yaw piw wuvaata. Paasat pay yaw kwaahu angqe' puhikma. Paasat pu' yaw pam put ep kwusut pu' iipoqhaqami tuuva.

Paasat pu' yaw pam piw nawus tuupata. Pu' piw antsa kwalakqw, pu' piw aw wuuta. Paas yaw oovi piw pam paavaqwrit pu' piw pik'oya. Pu' yaw antsa pam yuku, pikyuku. Paasat pu' yaw pam put paas mokyaatat pu' aapiy hiita piw enang kimaniqay. Paas suuvo mokyaatat pu' yaw pam pangqw tuwat yumuy amungk pasmi'. Pay pi yaw paasat pas pay taawana-saptini.

Pu' yaw pay aapiy qa wuuyavotiqw pu' yaw paava'at ahoy tuwat makvitu. Pu' yaw pam kwapkomuy aqw wuuvi, noq pay yaw suukya sulawu. Pu' yaw pam itsivuti, pu' yaw piw qa haalayti. "Is ohi, kur suukya ikwapko natkuqe waaya. Son pi nu' nawus qa heptoni," yan yaw pam wuuwa.

Niiqe oovi yaw pam pu' hawniniqw, piw yaw kwapko'at aw lavayti, "Haaki," yaw aw kita, "pay um son putwat uuvokoy tuwaniy," yaw aw kita. "Pay put se'el uusiwa wuvaataqe put niina. Noq oovi pay um qa pas haqami put heptoniqay wuuwantat, umuutumtsokkiy iipo kwistoni," yaw aw kita. "Um aw kwistot pu' um pay put pantaqat tavitoni. Pay um qa hiita angqw neengem hintini. Um put tavite', ahoy pite', pu' um piw angqw peqwni. Paasat pu' nu' uumi piw hinwat tutaptani."

"Ta'ay, pay pi nu' antsa put aw kwiste' tavitoni."

Paasat pu' yaw oovi pam pangqw hawt pu' angqw tumtsokkimi'. Yaw pam aw pituqw ephaqam yaw antsa kwaavok'at qaatsi. Pas yaw pam as itsivuti. Paasat yaw pam nawus put tavito. Pu' yaw pam put tavimaqe ahoy pitu. Paasat pu' yaw pam piw kits'omiq wuuvi. Yaw pam oovi aqw wupqw pu' yaw aw kwaavok'at pangqawu, "Um uukiy awniy," yaw aw kita. "Um

eagle. As soon as she reached it she struck it with all her might. "You badly behaved creature," she said and beat it again. "The one who keeps you two as pets can't even give you water. All he cares about is you, but he can't even give you enough water." Again she hit it, and this time the eagle fell on the ground. She picked it up and threw it out.

Now she had to prepare hot water all over again. When it boiled, she poured it on the dough and having carefully made her batter, she started making piki again. When she was finished, she wrapped it up carefully together with the other things she was going to take along. After everything was in one bundle, she followed her parents to the field. By that time it was just about noon.

Not long after this her elder brother returned from his hunting trip. He climbed up to his eagles and found that one was missing. He became annoyed and then quite sad. "Oh dear, one of my pets evidently bit itself loose and flew away. I will have to go and look for it." These were his thoughts.

He was just about to climb down from the roof when to his amazement the other eagle began to talk to him. "Wait a minute," he said, "you won't find that other pet of yours. This morning your sister beat him up and killed him. So instead of pondering where to search, just go get him outside your piki house. Then bury him as he is. Don't take any feathers for yourself. After you have buried him come back here to me. I will give you more advice then on what to do."

"All right, let me go bury him."

So the boy climbed down and headed toward the piki house. When he arrived, he found his eagle lying there. He was beside himself with rage. Now he had to go and bury the bird. When he had done that, he came back and climbed on the roof again. His eagle said to him, "Go to your house and dress up. Put your kilt on and all the other clothing that you want to wear. Then get your father's feather bag and take out one eagle breast

155

awnen pu' um yuwsini. Um uupitkunay ang pakini, pu' um soosok hiita yuwsiy'taqay um soosok yuwsini. Pantit pu' um unay pöhömokiyat hawne', pu' um angqw suukw kwavöhöt horoknani. Put um neengem kwavööna-kwatani. Put um yukut pu' um put nakwatani. Pu' um paasat piw lööqmuy tawapaprot horoknani, niikyangw put um pay haak qa hokyaasomtani, put um pay haak yawmani. Paas um yan yuwsit pu' um ason yukyiq taatöq tumpoqni. Nu' pepeq ung nuutaytani. Um hapi qa sööwuni. Pay itam kyaktayni. Um oovi nuy ngayni."

Pu' yaw pam oovi put ngaaha. Noq pu' yaw antsa puuyaltikyangw taatöqhaqami'. Yantiqw pu' yaw pam tuwat pangqw haawi. Pu' yaw pam kiy aw'i. Pu' yaw pam yuwsiy ipwa. Pantit pu' yaw pam yuuyuwsi. Yewasyukuuqe, pu' yaw pam neengem nakwakwusta. Pu yaw pam put nakwata. Paasat pu' yaw pam ang wuuwa, "Ya vul himu piwni?" yan yaw pam wuuwa. Nit pu' yaw pam u'na, "Owi, ura tawapapro piwni." Paasat pu' yaw pam oovi lööqmuy tawapaprot horokna. "Ura pay naat nu' it qa hokyaasomtani. Pay nu' ura haak it yawmaniqat tutapta," yaw pam naami kita.

"Pay kya yaasa'haqamo," yaw pam kitat pu' kiy angqw yama. Pu' yaw pam pangqw taatöqa'. Yaw pam tumpoq haykyalaqw, pay yaw antsa kwapko'at epeq tumpoq qatuwta. Pu' yaw pam oovi aqw pitu, pu' yaw kwaavok'at aw pangqawu, "Um pitu?" yaw aw kita.

"Owi."

"Ta'ay, pay qa sööwuni. Um uutawapaproy hokyaasomtani." Pu' yaw oovi pam paasat nan'ivaqw tawapaproy hokyaasomta. Yaw pam yukuqw, pu' yaw aw kwapko'at pangqawu, "Ta'ay, um pewni," yaw aw kita.

Pu' yaw pam angqw aw'i. Paasat pu' yaw kwapko'at naahoy masavu-yalti. "Ta'ay, um inutsva tsooraltiniy," yaw aw kita. "Pay nu' yaapiy ung naap wikniy," yaw aw kita.

Pu' yaw pam oovi antsa tsooralti. Pantiqw pu' yaw kwapko'at puuyalti. Yaw oovi puma atkyami puuyalti. Sutpikvaqe yaw puma puuyawmakyangw

156

plume. Make yourself a head feather and tie it to your hair. Also bring two strings with dance bells, but don't put them on your legs yet. Merely take them along for the time being. When you are dressed like that and have all your gear together, come to the south edge of the mesa. I will wait for you there. So don't tarry. We should hurry. And now untie me."

The boy untied his pet and, indeed, the eagle flew south. The boy, too, climbed down from the roof and went to his house. There he took his clothes out and started dressing. When he had finished, he fashioned the prayer feather for his head. Then he reflected, "What else was there?" And then he remembered. "Oh yes, the dance bells." So he took out two strings of dance bells. "Oh yes, and I was not supposed to wear them yet. The bird told me to bring them along," he said to himself.

"I guess that's it," he said, and stepped out of the house. He headed south from there and when he approached the mesa edge he actually found his pet squatting there close to the edge. When he was close, the eagle said to him, "So you have come?"

"Yes."

"All right then, let's not waste any time. You can tie your dance bells on now." The boy attached them to both legs and when he was through, his eagle continued, "Now, come here."

Again he obeyed and then the eagle spread out his wings. "Now, lie flat on my back," he ordered him. "From here on I'll carry you."

The boy mounted the eagle and lay flat on top of him. When he was ready, the bird lifted himself into the air. They dove downward and, after

pu' oove'iwma. Panmakyangw pu' yaw puma hihin ooveti. Paasat pu' yaw piw kwapko'at lavayti, "Nu' ung tatawkosnani," yaw aw kita. "Um oovi paas inumi tuuqaymani. Itam hapi naat yanmakyangw pu' itam unay paasayat aqwni. Noq ason itam pansoq pituqw, pu' um ason it tawmani. Pu' um ason tawme', sootapne', pu' um horaraykumantani. Noq pay son una puma paasat qa nanaptani," kita yaw awi'.

"Kur antsa'ay," pu' yaw aw tuwat kita.

Paasat pu' yaw oovi kwapko'at put aw tawma.

Haa'o ingu'u, ina'a!
Haa'o ingu'u, ina'a!
Tuuwanasave'e
Itaa'uyiy epe'e
Silaqvuyata tutuvena.
Aya'aa'ay tutuvena.
Tutuvena, tutuvena, tutuvena.

Pay yaw oovi naalös aw sootapnaqw, pay yaw taawiy'va. "Pay nu' taawiy'vay," yaw pam kwapkoy aw kita.

"Antsa'ay."

Paasat pu' yaw oovi puma suutevengewatti, Tuuwanasaviy su'aqwa'. Pu' yaw puma aqw haykyalniy'maqe suutsepngwat yaw puma hawto. Pas yaw oovi puma sutpikvaqe puuyawmakyangw nay paasayat aw pitu. Hoopaqw yaw puma aw pitu. Paasat pu' yaw kwaahu tiyot aw pangqawu, "Ta'ay, um tawmaniy." Pu' yaw oovi tiyo tawma.

Pu' yaw pay kur yu'at puma nanapta. "Meh, pas pay itaapava haqaqw tawma," yaw maana kita. Pu' yaw puma tuqayvaasiy'yungwa. Puma pi yaw paasat noonova. Naat yaw oovi puma tuqayvaasiy'yungqw, suhopaqw yaw amumi puma kuyva. Su'aw yaw oovi puma pumuy amutsvaniqw, yaw pam

gliding low over the ground, they slowly began climbing. When they had gained a little higher altitude, the eagle said to him, "I'll teach you a song. So listen carefully to me. This flight will take us directly to your father's field. When we get there, you will sing your song. And when you finish, I want you to shake your legs. Your father and the others will surely hear you then."

"Very well," the boy consented.

Thereupon his pet began to sing to him:

Listen, my mother, my father!
Listen, my mother, my father!
At Earth Center
On our cornfield
Its husks he marked.
Aya'aa'ay he marked.
He marked, he marked, he marked.

When he had finished the song four times the boy had learned it. "I know it now," he said to the eagle.

"Fine."

They turned due west and flew toward Tuuwanasavi, the place called Earth-Center. When they got closer they slowly descended. Sailing along close to the ground, they reached his father's field. They approached it from the east. The eagle now bade the boy to sing. The boy complied and started singing.

His family evidently heard him. "Listen, that's my older brother! He's coming from somewhere and he's singing," said the girl. They strained their ears to hear better. Just then they were having lunch. They were still listening attentively when they spotted the eagle and the boy coming from the east. Just as they were flying above his family, the boy

159

taawiy sootapnaqe pu' horarayku. Antsa yaw tawapapro'at kwangwaqala-
layku. "Nooqa', pay pi pas itaapava. Kwaahu'at iikwiwma."

Pu' yaw pam pep kwaahu pumuy amutsve qöqöni. Pu' yaw puma aqw
taayungwa. Suutsepngwat yaw oove'iwma. Panmakyangw pas yaw
oovehaqti. Pu' yaw yumat puma paapu pas hihin tuway'yungqe, pu' yaw
pas supatangwa'ökiwkyaakyangw aqw angk taayungwa. Pankyaakyangw
pu' yaw pay puma pas qa tutwa. Yaw puma qa haalaytoti. Paasat pu' yaw
maana lavayti, "Pay pi songqa inutsviy'o," yaw kita. "Nu se'el piktaqw,
suukya kur itaapavay kwapko'at natkuqe inumi pakiiqe, itsaqaptay
yoohaqe ipaqwriy soosok weheknaqw, nu' itsivutiqe nu' put wuvaataqe, pay
nu' pas kur niina. Noq pay pi oovi songqa paniqw pam itaapavay wiiki,"
yaw pam yumuy aw kita.

"Pay pi nuwipi." Yanhaqam yaw puma qa haalaytotit pay paasat
pangqw ninma.

Paasat pu' yaw puma pi pep tuwat qöqönkyangw wupto. Panmakyangw pu' yaw puma haqami kur pitu. Oomihaqami yaw hiisay pay qa
pas wuuyaq hötsi. Pang yaw puma oomi paki. Noq yaw kur pep piw pas
yepniiqat an tutskwa. Niikyangw qa hak yaw haqam qatu. Pep pu' yaw
puma oovi ang puuyawnuma. Hoqlö yaw qa taala. Pannumkyangw pu' yaw
puma haqami tuukwiy'yungqat aqwat. Panmakyangw pu' yaw puma
haqami pas suswupatukwit aqw qatuptu. Pu' yaw aw kwaavok'at pangqawu, "Itam yepeq hiisavo naasungwnani, um oovi hiisavo hawni."

Pu' yaw pam oovi angqw haawi. Yaw pam oovi angqw hawqw, pu' yaw
aw kwaavok'at pangqawu, "Ta'ay, pay pi um yepehaq yantani. Uusiwa
itamuy okiwsana, noq oovi pay pi um yepehaq tuwat yantani. Pay pi um
yangqw hin haawe', pu' sen haqam hin qatuni." Yaw aw kitat pu' waaya.

Pam yaw okiw angk taynuma. Pay yaw hikis atsve poniltit pu' yaw pay
kur haqami'. Pu' yaw pam okiw pepehaq qatu. A'ni yaw atkyamiqhaqami
tuupela. Kur pi yaw pam hin pangqw hawni. Pu' yaw pam pepehaq okiw
wuuwanlawu, "Ya sen nu' hin yangqw hawni, hal pay pi nu' son yangqw hin

160

ended his song and shook his legs. And sure enough, his dance bells made a pretty sound. "That's our brother, isn't it? His eagle is carrying him on its back."

The eagle began circling right above them while they were watching with their eyes strained toward the sky. The two were climbing and slowly soaring higher. Eventually they were way up and the boy's family was barely able to make them out any more. Finally they ended up flat on their backs and still kept looking after them. At last they could not see them anymore. They grew sad and it was then that the girl said, "All of this is probably because of me. I was making piki this morning when one of my brother's pets, who had evidently cut itself loose, flew in, broke my bowl and spilled all of my batter. I got mad and struck it so hard that I killed it. So that's probably the reason that the other one carried off my brother."

"Well, it can't be helped," was her parents' reply. They were so unhappy now that they returned home.

In the meantime the eagle and the boy were circling and climbing. In this way they finally reached a place where there was a small opening in the sky and they passed through it. There was evidently an earth there just as we know it here. But no living soul was anywhere in sight. There was a dark forest where they were flying along now. Eventually they came to an area with buttes. After a time, they landed on the highest one and the eagle said, "We'll rest here for some time, so climb down for a little while."

The boy dismounted and when he was off, his pet said to him, "Now you can stay up here. Your younger sister has caused us great pain. In return for that you will remain up here. If you manage to get down from this bluff, you may survive." With this the eagle flew away.

The poor boy stared after the bird, who circled a few times above him and then disappeared. Now the boy was stranded up there. All the way down was a sheer wall; there was no possibility of climbing down. Miserable as he was, he kept thinking, "I wonder how I'll manage to climb down from

161

hawni." Yaayan yaw pam okiw wuuwanta.

Naat yaw oovi pam yantaqw, yaw himu angqaqw aw wuuvi. Pu' yaw aqle' warikngwu. Suupan yaw put aw tututsiwa, pam qa haalayqö'. Noq pas yaw pi'ep aqle' warikngwu. Noq yaw kur pam koona. Pu' yaw put aqle' pantsaklawu. Nungwu yaw pam itsivuti. Pu' yaw pam paasat pan wuuwa, "Nu' put niine' ngas'ew put sowani," yan yaw pam wuuwa. Pu' yaw pam paasat naqlavohaqami hiita heeva akw koonat taatuvaniqay.

Pu' yaw antsa pam owat tuwa, niiqe pu' yaw oovi pam maqaptsiy'ta. "Ason pas inumi haypotiqw, pu' nu' taatuvani," yan yaw pam wuuwa.

Pay yaw antsa qa wuuyavotiqw angqw yaw piw aw hoyta. Oovi yaw aw haykyalaqw pu' yaw pam aw oway tuuvaniqe mavasta. Su'aw yaw pam oovi pantiqw, piw yaw aw lavayti, "Taaqay," yaw aw kita, "um qa pas hintsakniy. Nu' ung ookwatuwqe oovi angqöy," yaw aw kita. Pu' yaw pay pam put qa taatuva.

"Nu' ungem haqami hiita hepniy," yaw aw kita. "Pay nu' navotiy'ta um suyan paanaqmokiwtaqö'. Noq oovi nu' ungem haqami hiita kur hepni. Pay nu' ahoy suptuni." Kitat pu' yaw ahoy atkyamiqhaqami hawma.

Paasat pu' yaw tiyo piw pan wuuwa, "Son pi pam ahoy pituniqw, nu' qa niina. Pu' pi pay nu' kur hiita nösni," yan yaw pam wuuwa.

Noq pay yaw oovi qa wuuyavotiqw pay yaw piw angqaqw aw'i. Pu' yaw aw pituuqe pu' yaw aw pangqawu, "Yep'ey, yep nu' ungem kuuyiy'vay," yaw aw kitat pu' yaw aw hiita tavi. Yaw kur tuvatspu. Put yaw kur pam akw put engem kuuyiy'va.

Pu' yaw pam aw taynuma, pu' yaw pam pan wuuwa, "Son pi nu' it yaasaqhoyat öyniniqw, it angqaqw inungem yawma," yan yaw pam wuuwa.

Noq pu' yaw aw koona pangqawu, "Pay um sonqa öyni, um oovi hikwni," yaw aw kita. Pu' yaw oovi pam put hiiko, niiqe pay yaw antsa pam ööyi.

Paasat pu' yaw aw koona piw lavayti, "Pay um haak yepeqni," yaw aw kita, "nu' haqami ungem piw hakiy kur hepni. Noq pay songqa hisatniqw

here, or rather, I don't see how I can get down."

While he was mulling over this situation, a creature came climbing up to him and started running past him. It seemed to be making fun of him because he was so sad. It kept passing him at intervals and was evidently a chipmunk. It kept up this behavior right alongside him. Slowly the boy got angry and thought, "If I kill it, at least I'll have something to eat."

So he searched for something close by that he could use to hit the chipmunk. He found a rock and waited for the animal. "When it gets close to me, I'll throw this stone at it."

And sure enough, it did not take long before the chipmunk started moving in his direction again. When it was fairly close, he got into position to hurl his stone. Just when he did, to his great amazement the animal began to talk to him. "My dear man," he said, "don't do that! I came because I felt pity for you." So the boy dropped his stone.

"I'm going to look for something for you to drink," the chipmunk said. "I know that you must be thirsty. So let me see what I can do for you. I'll be right back." With these words he ran down the bluff again and out of sight.

The boy thought, "He won't come back and I didn't kill him. Now I don't have anything to eat."

But it did not take long before the chipmunk reappeared. "Here, I brought you something." He put it down at his feet. It was a nutshell. With it the chipmunk had brought him some water.

When the boy inspected it closer, he thought, "I won't quench my thirst with this tiny amount."

But the chipmunk said, "You can be sure you'll have enough. So drink." The boy drank it up and, indeed, he was able to quench his thirst.

Again the chipmunk spoke to him. "Stay here for the time being while I go get someone for you. He will come shortly." The animal was gone again and the boy remained on the bluff.

163

pituni." Yaw aw kitat pu' yaw piw haqami'. Paasat pu' yaw pam pepehaq piw nawus qatu.

Naat yaw pam oovi yantaqw, piw yaw aqlavo himu qatuptu. Pu' yaw angqe' tso'tinuma. Yaw kur tutsvo. Pu' yaw pam oway su'u'na. "Itwat nu' paapu niine' sowani," yan yaw pam wuuwa.

Pu' yaw oovi aw haypotiqw, pu' yaw pam piw aw oway mavasta, noq pay yaw piw aw lavayti, "Taaqay," yaw aw kita, "pay um qa pas hintsakniy. Nu' ung ookwatuwqe oovi angqöy. Um oovi qa pas hintsakniy. Pay nu' son ung qa hawnaniy," yaw aw kita. Paasat pu' yaw tutsvo hiita mötsitsiyku. Pu' kya pi yaw ngahuy paas mömtsaqe pu' yaw put tumpoq pavoya. Pantiqw pu' yaw tuukwit ang atkyamiqhaqami hiisayhoya tsi'a. "Yantani," yaw aw kita. "Pay nu' son pas wuuyavotiqw pay ahoy pituniy " yaw aw kita.

Paasat pu' yaw atkyamiqhaqami puuyalti. Pu' yaw pay pam piw qa tuptsiwa. "Son pi pam paasayhoya nuy yangqw hin hawnani," yan yaw pam wuuwa. Naat yaw oovi pam yantaqw, yaw angqaqw himu wuuvi. Yaw himu hiisayhoya, paalavölangpuhoya. Noq pay yaw as kur pam tutsvo. Pam yaw kur atkyangahaqaqw tuukwit ang tsi'akput ang masay, pöhöy tsurumin-kyangw wupto. Pas pi yaw oovi ngasta pöhöy'ta, piw ngasta masay'ta. Pas yaw qa himu ang pöhö'at. Pay yaw pas panis puukyay'ta.

Paasat pu' yaw aw pangqawu, "Ta'ay, um pewniy," yaw aw kita. "Um pewnen pu' um inutsva tsooraltini," yaw aw kita.

Pu' yaw pam tuwat aw pangqawu, "Son pi nu' utsva tsooralte' ung qa niinaniy," yaw pam aw kita.

"Pay nu' son hintiniy," yaw kita. "Um oovi qa pangqawlawt inutsva tsooraltini." Pu' yaw oovi pam put atsva tsooralti. Paasat pu' yaw angqaqw tutsvo pangqawu, atpipahaqaqw, "Um hapi huur uvimaniy," yaw aw kita. "Ason nu' pas pangqawqw, pu' uuvosiy puruknani," aw yaw kita.

Pu' yaw oovi pam uviiti. Noq pay yaw antsa put kyaati. Paasat pu' pam tutsvo yaw pangqaqw tuukwit atsngaqw atkyamiq masay ang tso'tima put iikwiwkyangw. Panmakyangw nawis'ew yaw kur puma haawi. Pu' yaw

164

Suddenly something landed next to him and started hopping around. It was a wren. Then he remembered his rock. "This time I'll make sure to kill it and eat it."

This is what he thought and when the wren got close, he aimed his rock at it. But the creature spoke to him. "My man," he said, "don't do that. I came because I had pity for you. I'll help you down from here." The wren started chewing something. It was some medicine, and when he had chewed it all up, he spat it out over the edge of the cliff. Immediately a small fissure developed all the way down. "That's it now," he said. "It won't be long and I'll be back."

He flew down and the boy again would not believe it. "That little thing can't get me down from here; there is no way." He was still thinking this when something came up again. It was a tiny little creature, something like a small red ball. It was evidently the wren. From way down below he had come up and stuck his wing and breast feathers into the crack along the butte. That's why he had no more feathers left, neither on his wings nor his body. Not one single feather was left on him. He had only his skin.

Then the wren said to the boy, "Well then, come here. You can lie flat on my back."

But the boy protested, "I would certainly squash you to death if I did that."

"Nothing will happen to me," the wren answered. "So stop talking and do as I tell you." So he lay flat on the bird and then he heard the wren say from underneath him, "Be sure to close your eyes tightly. I'll tell you when to open them again."

So the boy shut his eyes and, sure enough, the wren managed to lift him up. Then the bird climbed down from the top of the butte on his feathers while carrying the boy on his back. In this manner they eventually

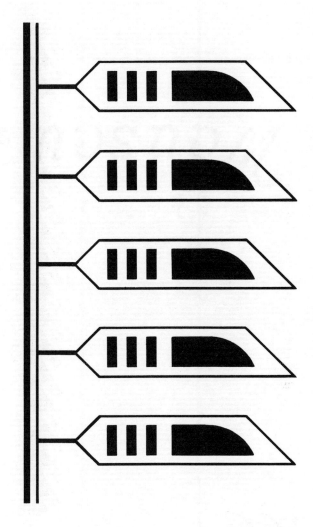

tutsvo pangqawu, "Ta'ay, uuvosiy puruknaa'," yaw aw kita. Pu' yaw pam oovi poosiy purukna. Pay yaw antsa pam tutskwave qatuwṭa. Pu' yaw pam tuukwit aw yori. Is tathihiya, yaw oomiqhaqami'.

Paasat pu' yaw tutsvo aw pangqawu, "Ta'ay, pay pi naat um son haqam hakiy aw qa piw pituniy," yaw aw kitat pu' yaw ahoy tuukwit awniiqe, pu' yaw masay ahoy naapa tsuruminmakyangw oomiq wupto.

Paasat pu' yaw pam tiyo tuwat nakwsu. Pay pi yaw kur pam haqamini. Pi yaw kur pam haqam. Pu' yaw pay pam haqami pi kur nakwsu. Pay yaw pam oovi su'awsavo nakwsut, pas yaw pam kwayngyavomoki. Pu' yaw pam naami pangqawu, "Ason nu' mooti siisit pu' piw aapiyni," naami yaw kita.

Pu' yaw pam oovi angqw himutskit awniiqe, pu' tsukuniltiqw, yaw himu haqaqw aw hingqawu, "Itse, yaavonitningwu," yaw himu aw kita.

Pu' yaw pam angqe' taynuma, noq yaw atpip tutskwamiqhaqami hiisayhoya hötsi, noq put qölöwtaqat aqlap yaw himu hiisayhoya qatu. Yaw kur kookyangw'u. Kur yaw pam aw hingqawu. Pu' yaw paasat piw aw lavayti, "Um ason siisit pu' peqw pakini," yaw aw kita. Pu' yaw pam wunuptut, pu' yaw angqw nawus hihin piw sutsvowat hoyo. Pu' yaw oovi pam siisit pu' ahoy aw'i.

Pu' yaw pam aw pituuqe aw taynuma, hötsiwat awi'. Pu' yaw pam aqw pangqawu, "Nu' kur hin uumiq pakini, hiisaqhoya hötsi," yaw pam aqw kita.

Pu' yaw angqaqw pangqawu, "Pay um uukuriy peqw rooroyaqw, songqa wuuyaqtini," yaw angqaqw kita. Pu' yaw pam oovi hötsiwyat atsve qatuptut pu' kuriy rooroya. Noq pay yaw antsa paasat aqw kivaytsilti.

"Ta'a, um pakini," yaw angqaqw kita. Pu' yaw pam oovi aqw paki. "Okiw himu imöyhoya," yaw aw kita, "okiw um pepehaq okiwhintaqw, oovi nu' pumuy uumiq hoona. Noq oovi um haak pephaqam qatuqw, nu' ungem aw oyaqw, um tuwat nösni. Son pi um okiw qa tsöngmokiwta." Kitat pu' yaw ephaqam hintsaki. Pu' yaw kur yukuuqe pu' aw pangqawu, "Ta'a, yep um tuumoytani."

reached the bottom and the wren said, "Now, open your eyes." He obeyed, and indeed, he was standing on the ground. Then he looked up the butte. What a tremendous height it was!

Now the wren said, "All right, you are bound to meet someone else." With that he hopped back to the butte and, while climbing up, started sticking his feathers back into his body.

The boy, too, started out, but didn't know which way to go. He had no idea where he was. He wandered in an unknown direction. He had been journeying for a long time, when he felt the urge to relieve himself. So he said to himself, "I'll go here first and then I'll continue."

So he walked over to a bush and, when he squatted down, he heard a voice say, "Shame on you, move a little farther on and then do it!"

He looked around. There it was, right below him, a little hole that led into the ground and next to it a tiny creature. It was a spider that had spoken to him. Again it admonished him, "You go to the bathroom first and then come in here." So he got up and moved to another place. There he relieved himself and then went back.

When he reached the hole, he took a closer look and said, "I can't possibly come in to you; this hole is much too small."

But the voice from inside replied, "Just wiggle your behind towards me and the hole will get larger." So he sat on top of the hole and jerked his behind with quick, short movements to and fro. And, sure enough, it opened up just like a kiva entrance.

"All right, come in," the voice called again. So he entered. "My poor grandson," she said to him, "did I feel sorry for you when you were up there on that butte in such a miserable state. That's why I sent the chipmunk and the wren to you. Now just sit down there for the time being and I'll bring you some food and then you can eat. You must be really hungry." She busied herself and when she was through she said, "All right, here is something for you to eat."

Pu' yaw pam aw qatuptu. Noq yaw hiisayhoya hurusuki ep qaatsi; pu' yaw piw tsiroqaasi, pu' yaw piw öngaspala. Pu' yaw pam paasat pan wuuwa, "Son pi nu' it öyni," yan yaw pam wuuwa. Pu' yaw pam ep hurusukit kwusu.

Naat yaw oovi pam pu' put moytaniqw, yaw aw so'at pangqawu, "Taaqaa," yaw aw kita, "pay um qa pas put soosok moytani, pay hin'ur-ningwu," yaw aw kita.

Pu' yaw pay pam put oovi qa soosok moytat, pu' yaw pay pam angqw hiisakwhoyat sokotkut pu' mo'amiq pana. Yaw pam put mo'amiq panaqw, pay yaw antsa mo'angaqw oopo. Pu' yaw pay pam oovi piw tsirot qaasiyat öngaspalat aqw moroknat, pu' angqw tsootsonakyangw pay hiisakwhoyat angqw kyatkuqw, pay yaw antsa piw hurusukit su'an mo'angaqw oopo. Paasat pu' yaw pam tuptsiwa, pay yaw kur pas antsa pam a'ni. Pay yaw oovi pam put qa soosok sowat, pay yaw pam ööyi.

Paasat pu' yaw so'at piw ahoy ang ayo' oya. Oovi yaw paas yukut pu' yaw angqw put aw'i, pu' yaw aw pangqawu, "Pay pi kur um yangqw haqaminiqe oovi pay um yep inumum qatuni," yaw aw kita. "Pay ason yanmakyangw son hisat nu' ung ahoy qa tavitoni, niikyangw son pas pay'u. Pay pi oovi um haak yep inumum qatuni."

"Antsa'ay," yaw pam aw kita, "pay pi nu' antsa haak yep umum qatuni. Pay pi nu' kur haqami pi nimani," kita yaw pam soy awi'.

Paasat pu' yaw so'at aw pangqawu, "Yep taavang tsöqavö, noq panso tsiroot hikwmanta. Pay pi um yep öönate', pu' pansonen, pep itamungem um tsirootuy huuhuwni, noq itam qa it yaasakwhoyat naama tuumoytani. It pi pay nu' pep hisat mokput tuwaaqe pangqw it yawma, noq yaasay peetiqw, oovi um itamungem pumuy huwqw, itam nasaniy'tani," yaw aw kita.

"Antsa'ay," yaw kita.

Pu' yaw so'at put tutuwna hin hak tsirot huwngwuniqw. Pay yaw pam suutuwiy'va. Pu' yaw oovi puma tapkiqw nöst pu' yaw pay puma puuwi.

168

He sat down. It was a tiny amount of *hurusuki* pudding and in addition a bird's thigh. There was also a little bit of salted water. He thought, "I'll never get full with that."

When he picked up the *hurusuki* and was about to put it in his mouth, his grandmother said, "My dear young man, you must not eat it all at once; that's quite a lot."

So he obeyed. He pinched off only a little piece and placed it in his mouth. He had hardly laid it on his tongue when it increased in size and, indeed, filled his mouth. Then he also dipped the bird's thigh into the saltwater and, sucking on it, bit off a little piece. And sure enough, in the same manner as with the *hurusuki*, it filled his mouth. Now he was finally convinced that it was really enough. He had not even finished everything when he was satiated.

His grandmother cleared the things away and, when she had done everything neatly, she went up to him and said, "There is no place you can go from here, so you can stay with me. After a period of time I'll take you back to your parents. But not right away. So stay here with me for the time being."

"Very well," he replied, "I shall certainly remain here with you. I have no idea how to get home."

Now his grandmother said, "West from here is an earth dam with a small lake. It's a place where the birds come to drink. If you get tired of being idle here, you can go there and trap some birds for us. Then we won't have to eat such tiny things. I found the meat that I have here. It was from a dead bird and I brought it home. This much is left, so if you trap some birds for us, we can eat to our heart's content."

"Fine," he replied.

Then his grandmother showed him how to trap birds. He got the hang of it right away. After supper they went to bed.

169

Qavongvaqw pu' yaw puma qatuptu. Pu' yaw so'at piw noovataqw, pu'
yaw puma nöösa. Paasat pu' yaw pam tiyo pan wuuwa, "Pay pi nu' kur
tsöqavöt hepni, haqam pi'. Pay kur pi taavanghaqamniiqat pangqawu."
Pu' yaw pam oovi pangqw put hepto tsöqavöt, niiqe pay yaw antsa pam
tuwa. Pu' yaw pam pephaqam tsirohuhuwa. Pas yaw antsa tsiroot paami
homta. Pay yaw pam taawansami wuuhaqniiqamuy qöya. Pu' yaw pam
pangqaqw pumuy tsirootuy wukokima soy ahoy awi'.

Yaw pam pituqw yaw so'at haalayti. "Askwali," yaw aw kita, "yan pi
nu' naawakna. Yaapiy pu' itam pas sikwit qa ruurumnakyangw tuumoytani. Nu' pay oovi tuupeni, noq itam tapkiqw pas naasanni." Kitat pu' yaw
yamakma. Kur yaw pam paasat tumqööto. Pu' yaw hisatniqw ahoy pakiiqe,
pu' yaw tsirootuy kimakyangw pu' piw yamakma. Pas yaw haalayi, pi'ep
yawningwu, "Askwali, pas kur itam tapkiqw naasanni."

Pu' yaw pay i' tiyo pas kwangwaqtu tapkimi maqaptsiy'kyangw. Pu'
yaw hisatniqw so'at pakiiqe pu' yaw aw pangqawu, "Imöyhoya," yaw aw
kita, "suukw nu' kur hiita ung qa aa'awna. Pep um tsöqavöve se'elniqw, put
kwiningya i' hiihiimu qa talqw, panso hapi um qa hisatni. Naamahin himu
ung pan unangwtapnaqw, um hapi qa hisat pansoni. Pep hapi nukpana
kiy'ta. Um hapi oovi qa hisat pansoni."

The next morning they got up again and, when his grandmother had cooked some food, they had breakfast. It was then that the boy thought, "Why don't I look for this dam and see where it is. She said it was somewhere in the west." So he went searching for it and, indeed, found it and started setting up snares. The birds were flocking to the water in great numbers. By noon he had killed many of them. So he returned home to his grandmother with a big load of birds.

When he arrived, his grandmother was happy. "Thank you," she said to him, "that's the way I wanted it. From now on we'll have plenty of meat to eat. I'll roast the birds and then we'll have a feast tonight." With these words she went out. She built a fire for her *pik'ami* pit oven. When she came back in after some time, she picked up the birds and left again. She was in a happy mood. Every so often, she would exclaim, "Thank you, tonight we'll really stuff ourselves."

So the boy sat there comfortably and waited for the evening. After a little while, when his grandmother came in, she said, "My grandson, there is one thing which I haven't told you yet. North of that dam where you were this morning, where the brush is really thick, is an area where you must never go. An evil and dangerous person lives there. So be sure never to go there."

"Pay nu' son hisat pansohaqaminiy," yaw pam soy aw kita.

"Pay putsa nu' kur ung qa aa'awna."

Paasat pu' yaw oovi puma pay qatu. Pu' yaw kur tapki, noq pu' yaw so'wuuti pangqawu, "Pay pi nu' itamungem aw hurusuktaqw, itam itaasikwitpey yaahe', pay pi itam tuumoytani," yaw kita. Pu' yaw ephaqam oovi so'wuuti hurusuklawu. Pu' yaw kur yukuuqe pu' yamakma. Tsaavoniqw pay yaw angqaqw wukosikwi'inkyangw paki. "Ta'a, pay pi itam tuumoytani. Tsangaw pay nu' paas yuku." Pu' yaw oovi puma tuumoyva. Pas yaw puma naasana. Peep yaw puma tsirotpey soosok sowa, pay yaw pas hikiy akwsingwa. Paasat piw naat yaw so'wuuti haalayti. "Pu hapi itam pas qa rurumnösa. Askwali."

Paapiy pu' yaw pay pam sutsep tsirootuy oo'oya. Yaw puma nasaniy'ta. Pay yaw oovi pam su'awsavo tsirootuy oo'oyq, pu' yaw hisat so'at aw pangqawu, "Ta'a, imöyhoya, um yaapiy pu' hihin wuuwukoqmuy maqnumni. Um pu' yuk hoopowat pumuy oovimantani, pangwat puma tuwat naavinta. Pay um panis su'its talavay taatayt awmantani. Pu' um ep pite', haqami tsomooyat aw wuuve', pu' ang yorikmantani. Pay paasat susmataqningwu. Um ang taataye', sumats haqam suukya qatuqw, atsve pamös'iwtangwu. Paasat pay um songqa suutuwamantani." Kur yaw pam paasat taataptuy nit pu sowiituy yu'a'ata.

"Antsa'ay," yaw pam soy aw kita, "pay nu' antsa qaavo pansowatni. Niikyangw pi nu' qa hiita tunipiy'ta hiita nu' akw pumuy qöyantaniqay."

"Kur antsa'a, pay nu' ungem hiita kur hepni." Kitat pu' yaw aapamiqhaqami pakima. Angqaqw yaw ahoy yamakkyangw yaw putskohot yawkyangw. "It um akw pumuy itamungem qöyantani."

"Antsa'ay," yaw pam aw kita. Paasat pu' yaw tiyo pas qavomi kwangwtoykyangw puuwi. Pas yaw sööwu qa taalawva. Nawis'ew yaw sumataq talhayingwti. Pu' yaw oovi pam qatuptu. Pay pi yaw pam pas kwangwtoyqe pay paasat aw hoopo hoyoyota. Pu' yaw pam ep pituuqe pu' haqami tsomooyat aqw wuuvi. Pepeq pu' yaw pam qatuwta. Pankyangw

172

"I won't," he promised his grandmother.

"Well, that was the only thing I hadn't told you about."

So they relaxed there until it got to be evening. Then the old woman said, "I'll make some *hurusuki* pudding for us. When we've taken the roast out of the pit, we can eat." So the old woman was busy making her pudding. When she was done, she went out. Soon she came back in carrying a big roast. "All right, we can eat now; I'm glad I'm all through." So they started eating. They really ate all they wanted. They ate up almost all of the roasted birds and had only a little left over. Once again, the old lady was very happy. "Now at least we are not so short of food. Thanks."

From then on, he kept bringing home birds. They had an abundance of food to eat. When he had been bringing home birds for quite a long time, his grandmother said to him one day, "Now, my grandson, from today on you can hunt animals that are a little bigger. You'll find them east of here. There are plenty there. As soon as you wake up in the morning, you can start. After you get there, you must climb up a little hill and take a good look around. It will be quite clear then where the animals are. You'll notice a little bit of fog right above the spot where one of them happens to be sitting. Thus you will easily find one." She was evidently talking about cottontails and jackrabbits.

"All right," he replied to his grandmother, "I will indeed go there tomorrow. But I don't have any weapon to kill those animals."

"That's true, let me find you something." With that she had disappeared in the back room. When she came back out, she brought a rabbit stick with her. "With this you can kill them for us."

"Very well," the boy answered. Then he went to bed looking forward to the next day. It seemed as though it never would be daylight. At last dawn approached. He got up and with great anticipation walked along in an easterly direction. When he arrived at his destination, he climbed on top of a hillock. He sat down there and started looking around. And, indeed, it

173

yaw pam angqe' taynuma, noq pay yaw antsa susmataq'a. Yaw naanaqle'
himutsotskit atsva yaw hingsay pamös'iwyungwa. Pam hapi yaw kur
taataptuy, sowiituy hikwsi'am pang panyungwa.

Pu' yaw oovi pam sushaypniiqat angqw aw'i. Antsa yaw pam aw
pituqw, angqaqw yaw taavo tso'omti. Naat yaw oovi pu' aapiy hiisavo
warikqw, pu' yaw pam put wungwva. Pu' yaw pay pam pep pumuy
pantsaknuma. Pay yaw ephaqam hiitawat qa wungwvangwu. Yaw pam
pephaqam kwangwa'ewta, nit pu' yaw pay wuuhaqta. "Pay pi kya
yaasa'haqamni," yaw pam yan wuuwa, "pay pi nu' ahoy hoytani."

Pu' yaw pam oovi tuunimuy iikwiltat pu' pangqaqw ahoy nima. Yaw
pam pituqw yaw so'at haalayti. "Askwali," yaw aw kita, "pu' pas itam piw
naat kur naasanni."

Pu' yaw antsa puma piw ep tapkiqw pu' yaw pas sowitpet hurusukiy
enang nöösa. Pas yaw puma naasana. Noq pu' yaw qavongvaqw pu' yaw
pam soy aw pangqawu, "Nu' pay pu' haak qa maqtoni, pay pi naat itam
a'ni sikwiy'ta. Ason itam pay put sowaniy'maqw, pu' nu' piw ason maqtoni."

Pu' pay yaw antsa so'at sunakwha, "Pay pi antsa um haak qa maqtot
angqe' waynumni," yaw aw kita. "Ason hak qa pas hisatniqw pay angqaqw
ahoy nimangwu," yaw aw kita.

Pu' yaw oovi pam pay pep haahaqe' waynuma. Pay pi yaw pam naat
qa hisat pepniiqe yaw kyaataynuma. Pas yaw tuwat alöngot soniwa. Pu'
yaw pam hisatniqw antsa ahoy nimiwmakyangw yaw pam soy kiiyat
taavangqw aw pituto. Noq pas yaw tsöqavöt aapiy teevenge sun tutskwa.
Pu' yaw pam pan wuuwa, "Pay pi nu' ephaqam qa hintsakye', angqw
pewnen, yep pi pay nanamunwamantani." Yan yaw pam wuuwa.

Pu' yaw pam pituuqe soy aw pangqawu, "Pas taavang tsöqavöt
teevenge sun tutskwaniqw, pay nu' ephaqam qa maqte', pay pansoman-
taniqay wuuway."

"Antsa'a," pu' yaw so'at aw kita, "niikyangw ura nu' ung meewa, ura
um qa tsöqavöt kwiniwi hisatniqat."

was quite obvious. Here and there he saw little patches of fog hanging above a bush. They were, of course, caused by the breathing of cottontails and jackrabbits.

He approached the patch closest to him and, when he reached it, a cottontail jumped up. It had run only a short distance when the boy struck it with his throwing stick. So that's how he spent his time. Only once in a while did he miss a rabbit. He really enjoyed himself and killed a great many. "I suppose this will be all for today," he thought. "I'll be going back now."

He shouldered his prey and went home. When he arrived, his grandmother was grateful. "Thank you," she said to him, "now we can eat all we want again."

And indeed, that very same evening they had rabbit roast with *hurusuki*. They really stuffed themselves. The following day the boy announced to his grandmother, "I won't go hunting today; after all we still have plenty of meat. I'll go again when most of it is eaten up."

His grandmother had no objections. "Yes, you can go for a walk instead. But don't come home too late."

So he visited all sorts of places around there. Since he had never before ventured into that particular area, he was amazed what there was to see. This region looked entirely different. And after some time he was on his way home and was approaching his grandmother's house from the west. Westward from the dammed-up lake the earth was completely flat and the thought occurred to him, "Once in a while, when I have nothing else to do, I'll come here to run."

Back home, he said to his grandmother, "Just west of the dam there is some level ground. I thought that I might go there sometime when I'm not hunting."

"Very well," his grandmother replied, "but remember that I forbade you ever to set foot in the area north of the dam."

175

Pu' yaw oovi pay puma pep yanhaqam pi pay qatu. Pu' yaw antsa i' tiyo hopkye' taataptuy kwangwa'ewlawu. Sutsep yaw sikwi'o'oya. Noq pu' yaw hisat puma mihikqw soy amum qatuqw, yaw tiyot aw so'at pangqawu, "Qaavoviipiy pu' um imuy pas wuuwukoqmuy oovi kwiniwiwat pu'ni," yaw aw kita. Pu' yaw piw aapamiqhaqami pakima. Paasat pu' yaw piw yamakkyangw hotngat yawkyangw. "Pay hapi son um qa itakwat pumuy-watuyni." Pu' yaw oovi put aw tavi. Pu' yaw pam piw antsa kwangwtoy-kyangw puuwi.

Qavongvaqw yaw pam piw su'its tayta. Naat yaw oovi taawa qa yamakqw, pay yaw pam piw nakwsu. Paasat pu' yaw pam kwiniwiqwat. Pu' yaw pam antsa aqw haqami pitu. Pu' yaw pam pepeq maqnuma. Pay yaw qa wuuyavotiqw yaw pam peetuy tuwa. Yaw pam amumi taynuma. Yaw kur pam sowi'ngwamuy pu' maqnuma. Paasat pu' yaw oovi pam sukwat namorta, suswukotaqat. Pu' yaw pam oovi tumostsokya. Pu' yaw pam pas mavastat pu' pookya. Paysoq yaw oomiq tso'omtit pay yaw angqe' wa'ökma. Pu' yaw pam angqw aw'i. Yaw pam aw pituuqe aw taynuma. Pas yaw kur pam su'unangwpa mu'a. Pu' yaw pam paasat pep put oovi ponomiq hötaaqe pu' put siihuyat angqw ipwa. Pantit pu' yaw pam pangqaqw put soy kiiyat aqw hihin kyaakyatima. Yaw pam kyaanavot put pitsina.

Pu' yaw antsa piw naat so'at aw haalayti, pu' yaw aw pangqawu, "I' pi pay pas suyan niitiwtangwu, niqw oovi itam it pay peehut sikwitani. Itam pante' pu' itam pay put laknani. Pu' ason pay pi itam peehut songqa sowani." Pu' yaw oovi puma put tutkita. Pu' yaw puma antsa peehut sikwita. Pu' yaw puma yukuuqe haalayti. "Pay pi i' naat niitiwta," yaw aw so'at kita. "Pay um haak yaapiy qa piw maqnumni."

Pu' yaw oovi pam paapiy pay qa maqnumngwu. Pay yaw pam waynumlawngwu, niiqe yaw pam hisat tsöqavömi hikwto. Pam yaw pepniikyangw pu' pan wuuwa, "Ya sen himu nukpana kwiningya kiy'taqw oovi itaaso nuy panso meewanta?" yaw pam yan wuuwa. "Pay pi nu' awnen,

176

In this way the days passed. The boy enjoyed himself hunting the rabbits in the east and frequently he would bring home some meat. One night when he was with his grandmother again, she said, "From tomorrow on you can go north to hunt the big animals." She disappeared into the adjacent room and, when she came out, she held a quiver in her hands. "These will be your hunting weapons now," and she handed him the arrows. Again he went to bed with great anticipation.

The next morning he was up early. The sun had not yet risen when he started out. His destination was in a northerly direction. When he reached the area, he hunted around there. It did not take long till he spotted some animals. He followed them with his eyes. He was hunting deer now. He selected one of them, the biggest buck, and then he placed an arrow on his bow. He aimed carefully and shot. The deer leaped into the air and then collapsed on the ground. The boy rushed toward it and, when he reached the animal, he examined it carefully. He had shot it right through the heart. He opened its stomach and took the entrails out. When he had done that, he lifted it up with some effort and carried it home. He worked hard at getting it there.

Again his grandmother was delighted and grateful to him. "This is clearly too much to eat now. We will therefore slice some of it into pieces and dry them. After that we can eat a little bit at a time." They cut the deer into pieces and made some of them into jerky. When they were through, she was glad. "This will last us for quite some time. I see no need for you to go hunting now."

So from that day on, instead of hunting, he went exploring. One day while having a drink of water at the dam, he thought, "What evil man is living north of here that my grandmother warned me not to go there? I suppose going there and looking in just once won't cause me any harm. Or

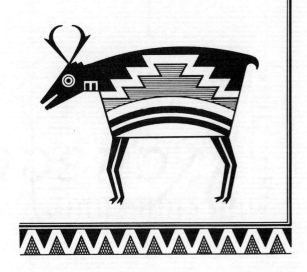

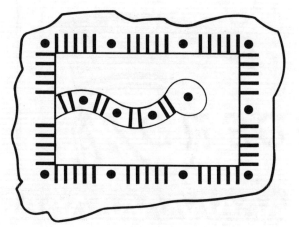

aqw suus kuyvaqw, suupan son pi hintini," yaw pam yan wuuwa. "Hal pay pi nu' qa pantini," yan yaw as pam piw wuuwa.

Nit pay yaw pam pas qa naa'angwutaqe pu' yaw pay pam pangqw aw'i. Antsa yaw pam aw haykyalaqw, hiihiimu yaw antsa huur hinta. Noq pu' yaw put pantaqat aasonveq yaw oomiq saaqa wunu. Pu' yaw pam hin hintsakkyangw aw paki. Pu' yaw pam paas kivats'omi wuuvi. Kiva pi yaw'i. Pu' yaw pam angqw hötsiwmi'. Pu' yaw pam aqw hihin kuyvaqw, pay yaw kur put tuwaaqe yaw angqaqw pangqawu, "Paki'iy, um hak waynumay."

Pas pi yaw hak su'pa. Qa hin pi yaw hak nukpana'eway. "Ta'ay, pakii'," pi'ep yaw angqaqw kitangwu.

Pu' yaw pay pam uunati. Pu' yaw pam aqw paki. Noq yaw hak taaqa, wupavuvuwpiy'ta yaw haki'. Yaw put aw haalayti. "Ta'ay, qatuu'," yaw aw kita. "Um piw hak waynuma. Pay um haak pep qatuqw, nu' kur peqw-haqami hiita hepniy," yaw aw kita, niiqe pu' yaw aapamiqhaqami pakima. Tsaavoniqw yaw angqaqw hiita yawkyangw yama. Pu' yaw pep kivay naasave put hiita yaw tavi. Nit pu' yaw aw pangqawu, "Ta'ay, um pangqw pew hoyoknii', itam totolosniy," yaw aw kita.

Noq pay pi yaw pam navotiy'taqw pam yaw kwangwa'ew. Pu' yaw pay pam oovi sunakwha. Paasat pu' yaw puma totoloslawu.

Noq pam pi yaw pep kiy'taqa Hasookata. Pam yaw pay pas putsa api, totolosniqay. Pu' yaw oovi puma pantsaklawu. Pay yaw mooti puma qa hiita oovi. Pu' yaw pay ephaqam tiyo pö'angwu. Pu' Hasookata piw tuwatningwu.

Pantsakkyangw pu' yaw Hasookata pangqawu, "Itam pu' as pas hiita oovini," yaw kita.

Noq pay yaw piw pam sunakwha. Pu' yaw puma oovi tootsiy mooti oovi'. Noq pay yaw Hasookata put pö'a. Paasat pu' yaw puma pitkunay oovi'. Pay yaw piw tiyo pö'i. Pantsakkyangw pay yaw Hasookata pas put ang soosok hiita himuyat pö'a. Paasat pu' yaw pangqawu, "Itam pu' suusni, niikyangw oovi itam pu' itaaqatsiy oovini. Hak hakiy pö'e' niinamantani."

maybe I shouldn't do it after all." These were the thoughts that flashed through his mind.

But since he could not resist his own curiosity, he started heading in that direction. And, true enough, when he got closer, the vegetation there was really thick. Right in the middle of it all was a ladder that stuck up into the sky. He had to maneuver his steps with some difficulty until he finally climbed up onto the roof. It was a kiva, of course. He moved onto the opening and peeked in. Evidently he had been spotted, because a voice called, "Come on in, stranger!"

The voice sounded friendly; in no way did it seem to be evil. Repeatedly he heard the voice say, "Come on, step right in."

Finally the boy was persuaded to enter. There was a man with long eyelashes there. He greeted the boy courteously. "There, have a seat," he said to him. "You must be a stranger in this area. Just make yourself comfortable; I'll go in here and look for something." He disappeared into the room next door and in a little while he came back with something in his hand. He placed it on the floor in the center of the kiva, and then he said, "Well, why don't you move closer to me. We'll play *totolospi*."

The boy knew, of course, that this dice game was a lot of fun. He agreed right away, and so they began playing *totolospi*.

The man who was living there was Hasookata. That was all he was interested in, the playing of *totolospi*. So they began gambling now. In the beginning they did not play for stakes. And sometimes the boy won and then again Hasookata won.

After a time, Hasookata said, "We should really play for something."

Again the boy consented without hesitation. To begin with, they played for his shoes. And Hasookata beat him. Then his kilt was at stake. Again the boy was defeated. Eventually, when he had won all the boy's belongings, Hasookata said, "Let's do it one last time, but this time we'll play for our lives. Whoever wins can kill the other."

179

Paasat pu' yaw pam qa haalayti. "Kur it itaaso son as qa nuy aw meewantaqw, nu' qa tuuqayqe oovi pay pi nu' nawus songqa nakwhani," yan yaw pam pu'sa wuuwa.

Pu' yaw oovi puma nanavö'a. Noq pay yaw antsa piw tiyo pö'iwma. Panmakyangw pay yaw pam pö'i. Paasat pu' yaw Hasookata pangqawu, "Ta'ay, pay pi nu' nuwupi ung pö'a. Noq um oovi pewni."

Pu' yaw puma angqw qöpqöt aqlavo'. Paasat pu' yaw Hasookata put soosok höömiyat ang aarila. Yaw put talqötöla. Pantit pu' yaw put maayat aakwayngyavoq soma. Pantit pu' yaw piw put hokyayat huur naami soma. Pantit pu' yaw put iipoq iikwiwta. Pu' yaw pam put kivaytsiway angqe tavi. Noq pam pi yaw ngasta yuwsiy'ta, piw ngasta höömiy'ta. Paasat pu' yaw aw pangqawu, "Pay pi nu' nuwupi ung pö'aaqe oovi nu' hapi ung kwitsmurtani," yaw aw kita.

Kitat pu' yaw ahoy kivay aqw paki. Paasat pu' yaw pam kiy kwiniwiq höta aapamiqa. Panis yaw pam pansoq hötaqw, angqaqw yaw nuvahukyangw yama. A'ni yaw angqaqw nuvahuhukya. Pas yaw tiyot su'aw yayma nuvahukyangw. Is iyo, yawi'. Qa wuuyavotiqw pay yaw pam tuusungwti. Pu' pam pi huur somiwtaqe kur yaw pam hin rohomtini. Pay yaw pam oovi nawus pangqe pankyangw nakwhaniy'ta. Pu' yaw tuwat Hasookata kivay epehaq tutsiwnanani, tuwat yaw haalayi.

Noq paasat yaw Tsorwukiqlöt so'at qa pitsinaqe yaw qa haalayi. Pu' yaw pangqawu, "Isti haaha', pay pi son pam qa Hasookatat awniiqe oovi pas qa pitu," yan yaw pam wuuwa. "Pay pi nu' as ura paas meewa qa hisat pansoniqat." Paasat pu' yaw oovi pam pangqw Hasookatat kiiyat aw'i. Antsa yaw pam ep pituqw, möyhoya'at yaw kivaytsiwat angqe qaatsi. Su'aw yaw nuvahukyangw pooyanta. "Puye'emo," yaw pam aw kita, "pay pi nu' ura ung meewaqw, kur um qa tuuqayi. Pay oovi um haak pangqe pantaqw, nu' ahoynen, angqw ungem hiita yawmani. Pay nu' ahoy suptuni."

180

Now the boy was no longer happy. "So this is what my grandmother tried to warn me against, but I didn't listen and that's why I have to say yes now." These were the thoughts that went through his head.

So then they started playing against each other once more. Sure enough, the boy was beginning to lose. Finally he was beaten. Hereupon Hasookata said, "All right, it can't be helped. I have defeated you, so come here to me."

They went near the fireplace and there Hasookata cut off all the boy's hair. He sheared him until he was bald. Then he bound the boy's hands behind his back, tied his legs tightly together and carried him out on his shoulder. He put him down right next to the kiva opening. The boy, of course, was completely naked and had lost all of his hair. Hasookata said to him, "There is no way out now. I was the winner and, therefore, I will put you to death by freezing."

With this he went back inside and opened the inner room that faced the north. As soon as he had flung open the door, a blizzard came storming out. It was snowing and blew ice cold air right out over the boy. It was bitter cold and soon the boy began to freeze. Since he was tightly bound, it was impossible for him to put up any resistance. Whether he liked it or not, he had to submit to the ordeal. Hasookata in turn gloated in his kiva and was satisfied.

In the meantime the old grandmother was without Tsorwukiqlö. He had failed to return and she was sad and said, "Oh dear, he probably went to Hasookata and that's why he did not come home. And I had strictly forbidden him ever to go there." So she went over to Hasookata's house. Sure enough, when she got there she found her grandson lying along the kiva opening with a blizzard blowing right at him. "I knew this would happen," she said to him. "Remember I warned you, but you wouldn't listen. So you'll have to remain here now for the time being while I go back home and get something for you. I'll return in no time."

Aw yaw kitat pu' yaw aapiyo'. Pay yaw antsa qa wuuyavotiqw pay ahoy pitu, niiqe yaw engem koyongvöhöt kwusiva. Pu' yaw sukwat put atpikyaqe pana, pu' yaw sukw atsva tsokya. Noq pay yaw antsa paasat pam kwangwamukiiti. Pay yaw paasat nuvahukyangw qa an suusungwa. Paasat pu' yaw so'at aw pangqawu, "Pay um haak pangqe pantani. Pay son pas wuuyavotiqw pay itam ahoy ökini," yaw aw kita, nit pu' yaw aapiyo'.

Pu' yaw pam so'wuuti ahoy kiy aw'i. Panis yaw oovi pam kiy ep pitut pu' yaw tsa'lawu, "Pangqe' kya uma inatkom yeese, uma qa sööwuyat angqw pew soosoyam tsovawmani," yanhaqam yaw tsa'lawu. Pu' yaw kiy aqw paki.

Pay yaw qa wuuyavotiqw pay yaw haqaqw hiitu hingqawwisa. Pu' yaw aw öki. Yaw kur pam katsinmuy wangwayi. Yaw wuko'öki. Paasat pu' yaw pam tuuvingta, "Ya pay uma soosoyam öki?"

She hurried off and, indeed, it wasn't long before she was back. With her she had brought two turkey down feathers. One of them she laid under the boy; the other she placed on top of him. Now he got nice and warm again. The cold of the blizzard was not as biting anymore. His grandmother said to him, "Stay here like this for the time being. It won't be long until I and some others will be back again."

So the old woman left and went home. As soon as she arrived, she made an announcement. "You children of mine that are living out there, I want all of you to gather here without delay." These were the words she used, and then she disappeared into her house again.

It did not take long and one could hear the noise of some beings approaching. When they arrived, it turned out that she had actually called the kachinas. They had shown up in great number. She asked them, "Are all of you here?"

Noq pay yaw soosoyam ökiiqat suukyawa pangqawu.

"Ta'a, pay itam tur qa sööwuyani, yep taavang i' Hasookata kur imöyhoyay kwitsmurniy'taqw, put nu' engem umuy naawakna. Itam oovi qa sööwuyat pay awyani," yaw pam katsinmuy aw kita.

Pangqw pu' yaw oovi puma awya. Pu' yaw puma aw öki. Pu' yaw angqaqw antsa Hasookata piw kuwawata, "Peqw huvamya'ay, uma hakim yaktay," yaw angqaqw kitangwu. Paasat pu' yaw puma oovi aqw yungta. Pu' yaw puma soosoyam aqw yungya. Pu' yaw Hasookata kiy yuumoq kwiniwiq su'uuta. Paasat pay yaw oovi qa nuvahuhukya. Paasat pu' yaw pumuy tuuvingta, "Ta'ay, pay pi uma songqa hiita oovi yaktay," yaw amumi kita.

Paasat pu' yaw Kooyemsi lavayti, "Owi," yaw aw kita, "um kur yephaqam itaatiw'ayay kwitsmurniy'taqw, oovi itam put oovi angqwyay."

"Kur antsa'ay," yaw amumi kita, "pay pi uma nuy pö'aye' pi wikyani," yaw amumi kitat pu' yaw piw aapamiqhaqami pakima.

Paasat pu' yaw piw totolospiy yawkyangw yama. "Ta'ay, ya hak mootini?" yaw amumi kita. Pu' yaw pay suukya katsina naatavi. Paasat pu' yaw Hasookata pangqawu, "Pay uma mooti Tsorwukiqlöt yuwsiyat oovi inumum nanavö'yani."

Pu' yaw pay katsinam naanakwha. Put yaw oovi puma mooti ooviya. Puma yaw oovi nanavö'q, pu' yaw katsinam tuwat tiiva. Pas pi yaw hin töötöqa. Pephaqam yaw puma put amum nanavö'ya. Pantsakkyaakyangw pay yaw puma Hasookatat pö'iy'wisa. Pay yaw sumataq puma pas tuwat qa hiita peetoynayani.

Kur nu' sukw qa pangqawu. Ura so'wuuti kiy ep tsa'lawu, noq ura katsinam ökiqw, muuyi yaw amumum ep pitu. Noq put yaw kur so'wuuti pay pep ayata, "Son Hasookata naat qa piw kwingyap'uyiy akw enang itamumi hepni. Oovi um pay itamuusavo panso kiiyat hoopo kwingyap'uyiyat awnen, um pay itamuusavo pep put ngayat soosok tutkitani. Pas kur hin qa put akw naat piw itamumi hepni." Paasat pu' yaw pam muuyi pangqw oovi antsa panso', niiqe pu' yaw pam pep put ngayat tutkitiva.

And one of them replied that everybody had come.

"Well then, let's not waste any more time. West from here that Hasookata is freezing my grandson to death. It is for his sake that I wanted you. So let's hurry to him without any further delay."

After these words to the kachinas, they went on their way. When they arrived, Hasookata received them cordially. "Please come in, you strangers." So they filed into his kiva and, when all of them were in, he quickly closed the northern opening way in the back of his house, so there was no longer a blizzard blowing. Thereupon he asked them, "Now then, I'm sure you have come for a specific purpose."

"Yes," a Kooyemsi replied, "you're freezing our nephew to death here and that's why we have come."

Very well," he said to them, "if you defeat me, you can, of course, take him along with you." With that, he went into a room next door.

Again he emerged with the *totolospi* board and the dice. "All right, who wants to play first?" he challenged. One kachina volunteered and after that Hasookata said, "To begin with, you can gamble for Tsorwukiqlö's clothes."

The kachinas agreed. These were going to be their first stakes. While they were playing, the kachinas started dancing. There was a spooky ring to their singing. So there the kachinas and Hasookata competed with each other now. Slowly the kachinas began to beat Hasookata. They apparently were not going to leave him anything.

There is one thing I have not mentioned in my story yet. After the old woman had made the announcement at her house and the kachinas began arriving, a mole came with them. He, too, had been given a particular order by the old woman. "Hasookata will definitely make an attempt to test us also with his oak shrubs. So you go ahead to that place where they grow, east of his house, and gnaw off all the roots. I'm quite convinced that he will challenge us with them." The mole had indeed gone there and had started biting off the roots.

185

Paasat pu' yaw antsa katsinam tuwat Hasookatat pas pay soosok hiita himuyat pö'ayani. Paasat pu' yaw Kwikwilyaqa pas yaw Hasookatat aw tuwat tututsiwa. Pavan yaw aw ngölöshoyay akw maasanta, pu' hihin aqle' tutsiwwunimantinuma. Ephaqam yaw pas qötöyat wuviviykinat pu' piwningwu.

Pantsakkyaakyangw pu' yaw puma put pö'aya. Noq pay yaw kur naat piw son pantani. Pu' yaw amumi pangqawu, "Itam suukw piw hiita akw namivootayaqw, pu' hak pö'aaqa hakiywat hin yukunamantani," yaw amumi kita.

Pu' yaw pay katsinam naanakwha. Paasat yaw kur puma natwanit akwyani. Paasat pu' yaw oovi puma kivaapeq nan'ip tuwamöyiknaya. Paasat pu' yaw Hasookata mootini. Pu' yaw oovi pam mooti tuwamöyikniy ang uuya. Hiihiita yaw ang uuya. Ang yaw uyqw, hiisavoniqw pay yaw uuyi'at kukuyaya. Pu' yaw suuwungwiwma. Humi'uyi a'ni yaw oomiq hoyta. Pu' kaway'uyi qa wuuyavotit pay yaw hotam'iwma, pu' aapiy hiihiimu suuwungwiwma. Pay yaw oovi humi'uyi naat qa kyeevelmoq pitut pay yaw wungwsoosok. Pu' yaw kaway'uyi naat pu' hingsakw himuy'vat, pay yaw piw wungwsoosok. Yan yaw pam yuku.

Paasat pu' yaw amumi pangqawu, "Ta'ay, uma tuwatyani. Kur uma nuy it ep pö'aye', pay pi uma nuy naap hinwat yukunayani."

Paasat pu' yaw oovi katsinam tuwatya. Pu' yaw puma tuwat tuwamöyikniy ang soosok hiita uu'uya. Pantotit pu' yaw puma piw tiiva. Pay yaw antsa piw qa wuuyavotiqw pay yaw uuyi'am tuwat kukuyaya. Su'aw yaw oovi pantiqw, yaw kivat tupkyaqe, tuuwivaqe, yaw oo'omawt nöönganta. Pu' yaw angqw uuyiyamuy su'atsmi hoyoyoykuya. Pantiqw pay yaw yooyoktiva. Yoknayat pu' ahoy yungya.

Paasat pu' yaw uuyi'am pas a'ni hoyoyoyku. Paasat pu' yaw sukw uuyit ep maahu tsokiwkyangw pu' leelentiva. Paasat pu' yaw kwangqat. Paasat pu' yaw tis pas uuyi a'ni hoyoyoykuya. Nungwu pay yaw humi'uyi peep kyeevelmoq pitsiwyungwa, pu' kaway'uyi yaw wupahotamtit pu' pay yaw

In the meantime, the kachinas had won almost all of Hasookata's belongings. Now it was Kwikwilyaqa that was making fun of Hasookata. He kept gesturing with his crook staff and danced around him in various funny ways. Once in a while he would actually hit Hasookata a few blows on the head.

In this manner the kachinas beat him in the game. That was, however, not going to be the end. So Hasookata proposed to them, "We'll measure ourselves with one more thing. And the winner of that contest can then do with the other whatever he pleases."

The kachinas accepted his challenge. They were going to compete with crops now. So, side by side, they spread sand out in the kiva. Hasookata was to begin planting on the scattered sand. He planted all sorts of things. When he was done, his plants started sprouting. They started growing immediately and were thriving quite rapidly. Before long, the watermelon plants were spreading out their vines. All the other things were growing fast as well. His corn plants had not reached the ceiling yet when they stopped growing. The watermelon plants had just gotten to be small melons when they, too, stopped growing. This is how Hasookata fared.

Thereupon he said to them, "All right, it's your turn now. If you defeat me in this challenge, you can treat me as you see fit."

So now it was the kachinas' turn. They, too, planted various things on the spread-out sand. When planting was over, they started dancing once again. Soon their plants started coming up. The minute they did, clouds emerged along the baseline of the wall and along the stone bench. They drifted right above the kachinas' plants and started raining. After they had released their rain, they moved back to where they had first come from.

Now the plants really were shooting up fast. On one corn plant a cicada sat and played her flute. The weather was pleasantly warm now and the plants grew even faster. The corn by this time nearly reached the ceiling and the melon plants had developed long runners and actual melons were

187

ang kawayvatnga maatsiltoti. Su'aw yaw oovi katsinam tiitso'q, pas yaw uuyi'am is tathihiya. Pay yaw puma Hasookatat pö'aya. Pay yaw pumuy uuyi'am sus'a'ni wungwa.

Paasat pu' yaw katsinam pangqaqwa, "Ta'ay, pay itam nuwupi ung pö'aya. Pay itam oovi Tsorwukiqlöt wikkyaakyangw ninmani."

"Qa'ey," yaw kita, "suukya peeti," yaw amumi kita. "Yep oove hopkye' ikwingyap'uyi. Pay pi uma put soosok tsaaqaye', pu' uma pas suyan nuy pö'ayani." Yan yaw piw naat rohomti.

Paasat pu' yaw oovi puma pangqw nönga katsinam. Pu' yaw puma angqw hoopoya, kwingyap'uyiyat awi'. Pu' yaw puma aw ökiiqe paysoq yaw puma langaminwisa. Pay yaw kur muuyi yukiy'ta. Soosok yaw kur pam ngayat tutkitaqw qa huur'iwyungwa. Pay yaw puma suyukuya.

Pantotit pu' yaw puma ahoy Hasookatat kivayat awya. Pu' yaw puma pangqaqwa, "Ta'ay, yantani kya'i. Pay itam soosok uu'uyiy siisikwtota. Pay oovi itam ung suus tiitaptotat, pu' itaatiyoy wikkyaakyangw ninmani." Pu' yaw pay sunakwha. Pu' yaw oovi puma tiiva.

Naat yaw oovi puma tiivaqw, pay yaw suvuvuyku. Su'aw yaw oovi puma oomiyaqw, pu' yaw pay kyee'ewta. Oovi yaw atkyaqyaniqw, pay yaw kivamiq munangwhoya tso'o. Paasat pu' yaw pay katsinam tiitso'qe pu' yaw nöönganta. Paasat pu' yaw pas a'nita. Pu' yaw paasat kivamiq pas hihin wuuyoq muunangw tso'okiwta. Su'aw yaw oovi katsinam soosoyam nöngaqw, paasat pu' yaw pas aqw wukotso'o. Pu' yaw katsinam paasat Hasookatat saqhönaya. Pu' yaw pay puma tiyot wikkyaakyangw ninma.

Paasat pu' yaw Hasookata kivay epeq naala pakiwta. Nungwu yaw kivayat epeq wukova'iwma. Pu' yaw paasat pam tuuwimo wuuvi. Noq pay yaw piw aqw pitu. Paasat pu' yaw pam tuupelngaqw lestavit iitsiwtaqat aqw

visible on them. By the time the kachinas stopped dancing, their plants had grown to enormous size and Hasookata was defeated again. Their plants had outgrown his.

The kachinas said, "All right, there is nothing you can do, we have won. We'll be going home now and take Tsorwukiqlö with us."

"No," he protested. "One thing still remains. Just above and east of here are my oak plants. If you manage to chop all of them down, you will clearly have conquered me." In this way he made another desperate attempt at resistance.

So the kachinas filed out of the kiva and went east to the oak shrubs. There they simply pulled them out of the ground. The mole had evidently done all the work. He had gnawed off all the roots so that they were completely loose. The kachinas were through in no time.

After this accomplishment, they returned to Hasookata's house. There they said, "Now then, this should be about it. We have pulled out all your oaks. So we'll entertain you once more and then we'll go home and take the boy along." He agreed and they started dancing.

They had barely begun to dance, when it started sprinkling. The moment they started singing the middle section of the song, it began to rain much harder. When they were finally about to sing the last part, a little stream poured into the kiva. The kachinas finished dancing and left the kiva. The rain was really coming down now and a slightly bigger stream was pouring in. Just when the last kachina had climbed out, the water flooded in. The kachinas pulled the ladder up and left Hasookata stranded. Hereupon they took the boy with them and departed for home.

Hasookata was all alone in the kiva now. Slowly the water rose in his kiva. He stood on the stone bench, but the water reached that too. So he climbed up to a beam that stuck out from the wall. There he sat and

wuuvi. Pepeq yaw pam tsokiwkyangw kuuyit aw tunatyawta. Pay yaw piw aqw pituto, oopokiwma yaw kivaapeq kuuyi. Panmakyangw pu' yaw pay aqw pitu. Paasat pu' yaw pay kur pam haqami waayani. Paasat pu' yaw pam paklawu, niiqe yanhaqam yaw pam paklawu, "Pay nu' mooki, Kwingyaw'u." Kitat pu' yaw poovoyangwu. Yaw poovoyaqw, paysoq yaw kivangaqw oomiq kuuyi kwalalaykungwu. Pantsakkyangw pay yaw pam pa'öymoki.

Yan yaw puma put niinaya, Hasookatat. Paasat pu' tuwat yaw kookyangwso'wuuti mööyiy ahoy pitsinaqe haalayti. "Askwali, um ahoy pitu. Pay pi nu' as ura ung meewaqw, kur um qa tuuqayqe oovi panso- haqami'. Noq pay pi tsangaw um ahoy pitu. Um oovi pewniqw nu' uuhömiy ahoy aw antsanni." Ura pi pam pölaqtö. Ura put Hasookata talqöt'arila. Noq put yaw so'wuuti kur ahoy wuptaniqay pangqawu. Pu' yaw oovi aapamiqhaqami pakima. Pu' yaw angqaqw ahoy suukway yawkyangw yama. Paasat pu' yaw angqw put aw'i. Pu' yaw pam put höömiyat suukway akw langangatoyna. Noq pay yaw antsa qa wuuyavotiqw pay yaw ahoy pam wupa'angay'va. "Yantani," yaw aw kita.

Paapiy pu' yaw oovi puma piw qatu. Pu' yaw hisat so'at aw pangqawu, "Pay ungu puma maamangu'a," yaw aw kita. "Pay pu' pas qa nöönö- sangwu. Noq oovi um yaapiy pu' piw maqtomantani. Noq itam put pay tsaakwintani. Pay son pas wuuyavotiqw pay nu' ung ahoy tavitoni."

Pu' yaw oovi pam paapiy piw maqtongwu. Pantsakkyangw antsa yaw puma sikwit niiti. Pu' yaw hisat talavay piw so'at aw pangqawu, "Pu' hapi um teevenge maqtoni," yaw aw kita, "niikyangw um pu' pay imuy tsaatsak- muywatuy maqtoni, sowiituy nit taataptuy. Pu' pay um hapi suukw hiitawat niinani. Pu' um niine' pu' um paasat ahoy tsöqavömini. Pu' um haak pay paasat pep maqaptsiy'tani. Pu' hapi hakim son uumi qa pituni. Pu' uumi pituqw pay um amumi yu'a'atani. Pantsakkyangw pu' um tuuvingtani sen nösniqat. Pu' pay songqa nakwhani. Paasat pu' um qööniqay pangqawni. Paasat pu' pay son ung qa meewani. Pu' son uumi qa

watched the water anxiously. Once again it was closing in on him until eventually it covered him. There was no place left for him to go. He began to cry and it was like this that he wept, "I am dying, Cold-wind-from-the-north." He started blowing air under the water. Each time he exhaled, water bubbled up from the kiva. Thus he eventually drowned.

This is how the kachinas destroyed Hasookata. The old Spider Woman was happy to have her grandson returned to her. "I am grateful to have you back. Remember, I warned you, but you wouldn't listen and went all the same. So I'm thankful that you are back. Come here to me and I'll put your hair back on again." He was still without hair, for Hasookata had shorn him bald. So this is what his grandmother was referring to when she said she was going to make his hair long again. She disappeared into the backroom and returned with a weaving comb. When she used that to pull his hair down, it only took a little while until he had his long hair back. "That'll do now," she said.

From this time on they lived together. One day his grandmother said to him, "Your mother and the rest of the family are sad because they miss you. They don't even eat anymore. I'd like you to go hunting again. We will make some more jerky, and then pretty soon I'll take you back home."

So from that day on he went hunting. In this way they accumulated a lot of meat. Then one morning his grandmother said to him, "Today you will go hunting in a westerly direction. I want you to hunt those little ones again, you know, cottontails and jackrabbits. You need to kill just one, no matter what kind. Then go back to the earth dam. There you will wait until two human beings come to you. When they reach you, you can talk to them. Sooner or later you should ask them if they would like to eat something. They will certainly say yes. Then tell them that you are planning to build a fire. They will ask you not to do that and say, 'We

191

pangqawni, 'Itam pay put qa kwasiwtaqat nösngwu,' son uumi qa kitani. Paasat pu' pay um qa hin naawaknat pu' amumi uutuniy tuuvani. Pu' son paasat qa aw pisoqtini. Pantikyangw pu' pay puma hiituniiqay pas ahoy songqa pumaniwtini. Paasat oovi pas kwangwatumoyvaqw, pu' um amutpipoq taatayni. Pay puma paasat son uumi tunatyawtani. Pu' um oovi amutpipoq taataye', susqötsat pöhöy'taqat um uumurikhoy akw paasat wuvaatani. Pan hapi um tuwat aw naa'oyni. Pam hapi uukwapko ung yep taviiqa. Pantit pu' um angqw ahoy nimani."

Yan yaw put so'at aw tutapta. Paasat pu' yaw oovi pam qavongvaqw antsa teevenge maqto. Pay yaw pam suusowinina. Pu' yaw pam ahoy tsöqavömi'. Pu' yaw pam pep oovi maqaptsiy'ta. Pay yaw antsa qa wuuyavotiqw pay yaw hakim haqaqw hingqawma. Panmakyangw yaw put aw hakim pitu. Yaw hakim mantu. Yaw hakim lomamant.

Pu' yaw pam amumi lavayti, "Uma piw hakim yangqe' waynumay. Huvam qatu'uy," yaw amumi kita. Pu' yaw pay pam pep pumuy aw yu'a'ata. Nit pu' hisatniqw pangqawu, "Itam kya as nöönösaniy," yaw amumi kita, "niikyangw ason nu' ituniy aw itamungem tuupeqw, pu' itam nöönösani. Nu' oovi qööni," yaw pam kita.

Noq pay yaw antsa paasat mant pangqawu, "Itam pay put qa kwasiwtaqatningwu," yaw aw kita.

"Kur antsa'ay," yaw pam amumi kita. Pu' yaw pam amumi tuuniy tuuva. Pu' yaw antsa aw naama tso'omti. Pantikyangw pay yaw puma maanat kwaahutniwti. Pu' yaw puma pep put tuuniyat oovi pisoq'iwta. Pu' yaw oovi pas qa atsat kwangwatumoyvaqw, pu' yaw pam amutpipoq yori. Pu' yaw pam paasat susqötsavöhöy'taqat put qötöyat wuvaata. Yaw pam put sunina.

Pu' yaw mi'wa kwaahu pangqawu, "Puye'emo," yaw kitat pu' waaya.

Yan yaw pam tuwat kwapkoy aw naa'oyt pu' pangqw nima. Yaw pam pituuqe, soy aa'awna hintiqay. Yaw so'at haalayti. "Askwali, um aw naa'oya. Pay pi tuwat pephaqam pantani. Pay pi ung okiwsana."

usually eat that raw.' Do whatever they prefer and throw your prey to them. They will rush toward it and upon reaching it, they will be transformed back into the creatures that they were before. When they start enjoying their food, look at their undersides, for they will not pay any attention to you. Then you must club the one that has the whitest down feathers. Thus you will revenge yourself. For that will be your eagle pet that left you here. After that you can come home again."

These were the old lady's instructions. So the following day the boy went hunting in the west. He quickly killed a cottontail and then headed back to the earth dam. There he waited and, indeed, it was not long before he heard two voices coming his way. When eventually they came upon him, they turned out to be two very pretty girls.

He greeted them, "So you two are also going for a walk here? Sit down." They chatted together until he said, "Why don't we eat something? I'll roast this prey of mine for us and then we can eat. So let me build a fire."

The girls replied, "We never eat cottontail cooked."

"That's all right with me," he said and threw his prey to them. They both jumped on it and thus the two girls were changed back into eagles. They were now busy on his prey and, when they began devouring it with pleasure, he looked under them. Then he struck the one that had the whitest down feathers on the head. He killed it at once.

The other eagle screamed, "Oh dear, I knew it." With that it flew away.

In this way the boy got even with his eagle pet and went home. When he arrived, he told his grandmother what he had achieved. She was glad to hear that. "Thank you, you have revenged yourself. That eagle can rot there now where it is. It really caused you a lot of misery."

193

Qavongvaqw pu' yaw so'at piw angqaqw aw'i. Niiqe pu' yaw aw pangqawu, "Pay nu' kya yaapiy naalös taalat ephaqam ung ahoy tavitoni," yaw aw kita. "Pay pu' ungu puma pas qa yesvangwu. Paas puma ung sölmokiwyungwa. Noq pay pas son wuuyavototiniqw, oovi nu' pay ung ephaqam tavitoni," kita yaw put awi'. Yaw pam kwangwtapna. Suupan as yaw pam son hisat paapu yumuy amumi yorikniqay wuuwantangwu.

Pu' yaw oovi pam paapiy pansoq maqaptsiy'kyangw soy engem maqnumngwu. Su'aw yaw oovi pam soy engemwat piw sikwit niitiqw, yaw aqw pitu, so'at ahoy tavitoniqat aqwa'. Pu' yaw oovi aw talöngvaqat ep yaw pam kwangwtoya. Pu' yaw puma paasathaqam oovi nakwsu. Pay pi yaw putniqw kur haqami'. Panmakyangw pu' yaw puma haqami kur pitu. Yaw pep atkyamiqhaqami hötsi.

Pu' yaw so'at aw pangqawu, "Ta'a, pew hapi itam hoyta. Ason um hiisavo naasungwnat pu'ni." Pu' yaw pam oovi sikwimokiy tutskwami puusukna. Put pi yaw pam iikwiwta, sikwit. Pu' yaw oovi pam naasungwna.

Pu' yaw so'at aw pangqawu, "Ta'a, um pewni," yaw aw kita. Pu' yaw pam oovi sikwimokiy iikwiltat pu' angqw soy aw'i. Paasat pu' yaw so'at aw pangqawu, "Um hapi hawte' huur uvimani. Um hapi haak uuvosiy qa puruknani. Ason um pas uukukuy tutskwami tongokqw, paasat pu' um uuvosiy puruknani," yan yaw aw tutapta.

"Antsa'ay," yaw aw pam kita.

Paasat pu' yaw so'wuuti put hiita akw wiwakna. "Ta'a, yupa, imöyhoya, pay ung ungu puma nuutayyungwa."

Paasat pu' yaw pam hötsit aqw paki. Pu' yaw pam pangqaqw hawto. Kur yaw put so'at kookyangwso'wuuti wishöviy akw hawnani. Pu' yaw oovi so'wuuti hötsit atsva naahoy kwanawtaqw, yaw kur put löwangaqw put wishövi'at yamakto. Paniqw yaw kur pam tiyo uvimaniqat naawakna. Pu' antsa yaw panmakyangw nawis'ew yaw put kuk'at tutskwami tongo. Paasat pu' yaw pam poosiy purukna. Pu' yaw pam put akw wiwtaqay yaw put tsoopa. Paasat pu' yaw pam put maatavi. Maatapt pu' yaw pam oomiq

194

The next day his grandmother came to him again and said, "In approximately four days from now I'll take you back. Your parents don't even get up anymore. They really long for you and will not last much longer. I will therefore take you back on that date." He was overjoyed. It seems he had never expected to see his parents again.

While waiting for the day, he went hunting for his grandmother. When she had plenty of meat again, the time came for his departure. He was anxious to go home now. So that day they started out. As he later said, he did not know where. Eventually they reached a place with a hole leading down.

His grandmother said, "All right, this is our destination. Let's first rest a little while." He threw the bag of meat that he had been carrying on the ground and rested.

Then his grandmother said, "All right, come here now." So he shouldered his bag again and went over to her. "On the way I want you to keep your eyes tightly closed. You are not to open them. Only after you have touched the earth with your feet can you look again." These were her instructions.

"Very well," he replied.

Hereupon the old woman tied something around him. "Go on now, my grandson. Your parents are waiting for you."

He went into the hole and began his descent. His grandmother, who was, of course, Spider Woman, was going to let him down by means of her thread. Therefore the old woman sat over the hole with her legs apart and with the thread coming out of her vulva. That was the reason that she wanted the boy to shut his eyes. Finally his feet touched the ground again and he opened his eyes. He took off what she had tied around him and let it go. Then he looked up. There his grandmother was, sitting with spread-out

yori. Angqw yaw so'at kwanawta. Noq yaw kur pam put löwayat angqw wishövi yamakiwtaqw, oovi qa naawakna pam taymaniqat. Yan yaw pam yorikt pu' pangqw nakwsu. Yaw kur pam nay paasayat su'ep haawi. Pu' yaw oovi pam pangqw nima.

Noq piw yaw kur hak paasat pasmi'. Niiqe yaw put tuwa. Noq pay pi Orayve sinom yaw soosoyam navotiy'yungwa, pam tiyo Tsorwukiqlö kur haqaminiqw. Niqw oovi paniqw pam yaw hak pasminiiqa naat put qa aasawvat yaw kur put maamatsi. Pay yaw pam paasat pep poniltit pu' yaw ahoy kiimiqhaqami warikma.

Pu' yaw pam pangqw ahoy kiimiq warikqe yaw yuumosa Tsorwukiqlöt yumuyatuy kiiyamuy aw'i. Yaw amumi uukwi pami'. Noq naat yaw antsa Tsorwukiqlöt yu'at puma wa'ökiwyungwa, soosoyam yu'at, na'at, pu' siwa'at. Yaw hiitu qa sosniwa. Yaw wukoqtöwyungwa. Puma hapi Tsorwukiqlöt sölso'qe pay yaw pas qa naawustota. Pas pi yaw oovi pataqtöwyungwa. Panyungqamuy yaw pam amumi uukwi. Pavan yaw hin unangway'numa. Pu' yaw amumi pangqawu, "Uma yesvaniy, angqw umuuti Tsorwukiqlö hoytay," yaw amumi kita.

Noq yaw qa hin tuutuptsiwa. Niiqe yaw pangqaqwa, "Son piniy, pam pay hisat haqami'," kitotaqe, pay yaw qa hin yesvaniqay unangwtoti.

Paasat pu' yaw ep tuu'awvaqa ahoy suymakma. Pu' yaw piw ahoy atkyamiqhaqami warikiwta. Hiisavoniqw pay yaw piw ahoy wuuvi. Pu' yaw piw amumi pangqawu, "Uma yesvaniy, angqw umuuti Tsorwukiqlö hoytay. Pas pay tupo pituniy," yaw amumi kita.

Pu' pay yaw piw an lavaytoti, "Son piniy, pay pi pam kur hak hisat haqami'," kitotaqe, pay yaw piw qa yesva.

Pu' yaw pam piw yamakma. Paasat pay yaw Tsorwukiqlö tumpaqw wuuvi. Pu' yaw piw pam ahoy aw'i. "Uma yesvaniy," yaw amumi kita, "pay pu' pas tumpaqw'öy," yaw amumi kita. Pay yaw piw qa tuutuptsiwa.

Pu' yaw piw pam suymakma. Nit pu' yaw angqaqw pangqawu, "Pay pu' pas yangqw pew'i. Oovi uma yesvaniy," yaw amumi kita. Noq pay yaw

legs, and because the thread was coming out of her vulva she had not wanted him to look. So now that he had cast a final glance up there, he started out. He had landed right on his father's field. He started on his way home.

And by coincidence somebody else was on his way to the field at that time. He spotted the boy. In Oraibi all the people were, of course, familiar with the story of Tsorwukiqlö's disappearance. For this reason the person going to the field recognized the boy before he had come face to face with him. He turned around and ran back to the village.

He ran straight back to Tsorwukiqlö's parents' house. He quickly entered. And, indeed, Tsorwukiqlö's parents and sister were lying there. They were awful to look at. Their heads were swollen and because they were stricken with longing for Tsorwukiqlö, they had stopped combing their hair. So it was all tangled up. This was the sight they presented, when the man entered. He was all excited and said to them, "Get up, your son Tsorwukiqlö is on his way home."

But they did not believe him at all and replied, "That can't be; he disappeared long ago." They had no desire to get up.

The man who had brought them the news quickly left and ran back down the mesa. After a while he came up again and said to them, "Get up, your child Tsorwukiqlö is on his way; he's about to reach the foot of the mesa."

But their response was the same. "That can't be; he disappeared long ago." Again they made no effort to rise.

Once more the man ran out and there Tsorwukiqlö was just reaching the edge of the mesa. Again he returned to them. "Get up," he urged them. "He's at the edge now." But they did not accept his words.

Once more he darted out quickly and then they heard him say, "He's right here, so get up." Again they failed to rise. Then he said to them, "He has arrived."

197

piw qa yesva. Paasat pu' yaw amumi pangqawu, "Pay pituy," yaw amumi kita.

Naat yaw oovi pu' kitaqw, yaw amumi ti'am paki. Pas yaw paasat pu' puma tuutuptsiwqe pu' yaw suyesva. Pu' yaw puma paasat pephaqam haalaytsaykita. A'ni yaw hiitu sosniwa.

Yanhaqam yaw puma ahoy tiy pitsinaya. Paasat pu' yaw puma naawusya. Qavongvaqw pay yaw puma qa hinyungwa. Pay yaw pam ahoy pituqw, pay yaw puma suqlaptoti. Pay yaw kur puma put akw tuutuyaya, Tsorwukiqlöt sölso'qe'.

Pu' yaw pam paasat yuy aw pangqawu, "Yep nu' it mokva. Noq um put soosok aw kwipt pu' um soosokmuy sinmuy tuutsamtani. Noq itam soosoyam put suup nöönösani," yaw pam put yuy aw kita, pu' siway aw piw.

Pu' yaw oovi puma antsa put soosok sikwit nöqkwiva. Qavongvaqw talavay pu' yaw na'at tsa'lawu, "Soosoyam yaw Tsorwukiqlöt kiiyat aqw nöswisniy," yan yaw tsa'lawu. Pu' yaw oovi antsa soosoyam sinom epeq nösmayaqe, yaw Tsorwukiqlöt haalaytoti, haqaqw ahoy pituqw. Yan yaw pam pephaqam soosokmuy sinmuy nopna.

Noq oovi naat kya yaw Orayve sinom put ööyiwyungwa. Pay yuk pölö.

198

No sooner had he uttered these words than their child stepped in. Now they were convinced and quickly got on their feet. They were crying with joy, but they looked terrible from their ordeal.

This is how they got their child back. They combed their hair and the next morning they were fine again. They recovered quickly, once he had arrived. They had been sick with desire and longing for Tsorwukiqlö.

Then he said to his mother and his sister, "Here, I brought this meat with me. You can cook all of it and then invite everybody to come and eat. We will all eat it together."

So then they made all the meat into stew. The following morning his father made the public announcement. "You all come to Tsorwukiqlö's house to eat." When all the villagers had come, they were happy that Tsorwukiqlö had returned home. He fed all of them there.

The Oraibi people are still satiated from that meal. And here the story ends.

Glossary

This glossary of background information on the general culture of the Hopi is added here to aid the reader in understanding their tales. It has been prepared by consulting frequently the reference works of Stephen, Voth, Curtis, Titiev, Beaglehole, Colton, Tyler, and Wright. A selected bibliography of titles by these people is also included. At the same time, the author's own contact with Hopi culture, the time he spent with Hopi people learning their language, and his effort of collecting their tales, have provided the general orientation for selecting, for ordering, and for presenting this additional information.

ALPHABET of the Hopi language. The notation which is used for the transcription of these tales that were collected exclusively in the Hopi language, is suited for reading and writing classes in Hopi, should reading and writing become a standard feature of Hopi education. A total of twenty-one symbols is sufficient to render all of the functional sounds which occur in the dialect of the Third Mesa villages. Nineteen of these are drawn from the English alphabet (a e g h i k l m n o p q r s t u v w y), one is borrowed from German orthography (the umlauted ö). The apostrophe is used to represent the glottal stop, one of the Hopi consonants. Stress and falling tone—the latter occurring in conjunction with long vowels, diphthongs, and certain vowel-nasal sequences—are not marked in the text. The following inventory lists all the functional sound units, with the exception of those characterized by falling tone, which exist in the Third Mesa dialect area and illustrates their use in sample words.

1. Vowel sounds:

(a) short vowels

a	pas	'very'
e	pep	'there'
i	sihu	'flower'
o	momi	'forward'
ö	qötö	'head'
u	tuwa	'he found it, saw it'

(b) long vowels

aa	paas	'carefully; completely'
ee	peep	'almost'
ii	siihu	'intestines'
oo	moomi	'he is pigeon-toed'
öö	qöötö	'suds'
uu	tuuwa	'sand'

2. Diphthongs:

(a) with y-glide

ay	tsay	'small, young'
ey	eykita	'he groans'
iy	hangwniy	'his ditch' (objective case)
oy	ahoy	'back to'
öy	öyna	'he gave him enough to eat'
uy	uyma	'he has been planting'

(b) with w-glide

aw	awta	'bow'
ew	pew	'here (to me)'
iw	piw	'again'
ow		nonexisting
öw	ngölöwta	'it is crooked'
uw	puwmoki	'he got sleepy'

3. Consonantal sounds:

(a) stops

p	paahu	'water, spring'
t	tupko	'younger brother'

201

ky	kyaaro	'parrot'
k	koho	'wood, stick'
kw	kwala	'it boiled'
q	qööha	'he built a fire'
qw	angqw	'from him; from there'
'	pu'	'now, today'

(b) nasals

m	malatsi	'finger'
n	naama	'both'
ngy	yungyapu	'wicker plaque'
ng	ngöla	'wheel'
ngw	kookyangw	'spider'

(c) affricate

| ts | tsuku | 'clown' |

(d) fricatives

v	ivasa	'my field'
r	roya	'it turned'
s	sakuna	'squirrel'
h	ho'apu	'carrying basket'

(e) lateral

| l | laho | 'bucket' |

4. Glides:

(a) preceding a vowel

| w | waynuma | 'he is walking about' |
| y | yas | 'last year' |

(b) following a vowel
see diphthongs

202

ANGAKTSINA is the Long-haired Kachina, named after his long hair (*anga*). The loose strands of hair which hang down the back of this kachina's impersonator are an important part of his costume. His pleasing appearance and beautiful songs make him one of the most popular Hopi dancing kachinas.

In addition to Angaktsina, the regular Long-haired Kachina, other related varieties exist. The *Palasowitsmiy'yungqam,* for example, are distinguished from the regular black-bearded type by their red beards. The halfmasks of *Tasap'angaktsinam* feature additional rain-cloud designs. Their red kilts and silver belts are typical Navajo trappings. *Qatots'angaktsinam* distinguish themselves by dancing without the customary Hopi footwear. *Talwip'angaktsinam* can be identified by the lightning symbols which protrude from their heads. Finally, the *Pusukin'angaktsinam* differ from all these types by their peculiar dance step as well as by having a drummer accompany their singing.

DART GAME. Exclusively played by boys, the Hopi dart game is known as *mötöplalwa.* It requires a cornhusk wheel or hoop (*ngöla*) that is rolled by a participant of one team. The players of the other side try to hit it with their darts in such a way that the missile will stick in the ring. The darts are fashioned of corncobs (*mötövu*) which are feathered on one end and to which a sharpened wood point is attached at the other.

Like most Hopi games on record, this one, too, is no longer practiced. Actions reminiscent of the dart game can, embedded in a religious context, still be witnessed occasionally during the fall, when members of the Owaqöl, Maraw, and Lakon women's societies throw corncob feather darts at netted wheels, at bundles of vines, or at cloud symbols drawn with cornmeal on the ground.

DEMON GIRL. The Hopi term *masmana*, which is rendered here by 'demon girl', is linguistically related to Maasaw. While thus evoking connotations of death, a *masmana* possesses none of the good aspects that Maasaw embodies. In her first life a witch that was caught at her craft, she is endowed with certain supernatural powers that allow her to come back to life. She always lives outside the community and appears to men as a sexually attractive seductress. Her intentions and actions are all evil.

HASOOKATA is the archetypal gamester and gambler-cheater who embodies everything that is evil and insidious. A monstrous creature, he is occasionally likened to the giant figure of So'yoko. It is said he steals from people and that he traps them into gambling with him for their lives. The unsuspecting victim loses all his clothes and belongings and is finally tortured to death by being exposed to the freezing north wind which Hasookata somehow seems to control. The fact that shortly before his death he turns to Kwingyaw, the god of cold weather from the north, suggests a certain affinity between the two personages.

HOPI is a word which is almost impossible to match with an English equivalent. It implies a gamut of positive character traits and qualities, such as moral uprightness, unobtrusive behavior, a poised disposition, nonaggressive conduct, modesty, and many others. One connotation from its core meaning of 'good in every way', has led to the now popular interpretation of the tribal name *Hopiit* as 'The Peaceful Ones'.

The Hopi Indians, who live in villages on several mesa spurs in northeastern Arizona, are the westernmost survivors of a planter culture which for over fifteen hundred years has dominated the southwestern United States. Geographically removed from the mainstream of Anglo-American civilization and technology, this group of Pueblo clans constitutes one of the tribes that still live on their original homeland. The Hopi people have succeeded in preserving their cultural heritage remarkably well.

HURUSUKI is a special Hopi dish, frequently described as 'cornmeal pudding'. It is made by mixing coarsely ground cornmeal with boiling water and constantly stirring. The dough mush that is formed is served when it thickens to a consistency which allows small pieces to be pinched off.

KACHINA (correct pronunciation, *katsina*) is one of the mainstays of Hopi culture. No other Hopi tribal institution has been more pervasive than the kachina cult. As every Hopi is initiated into it, it can be regarded as a spiritual tie which unites all Hopi people, regardless of geographical, linguistic, or political variations among the otherwise autonomous villages.

All attempts to unlock the etymological meaning of this word have thus far failed. To be sure, explanations do exist, but they are incompatible with the linguistic givens of the Hopi language. One such attempt suggests that *katsina* is a compound consisting of the elements *qatsi* 'life' and *na* 'father'. Although the interpretation of kachinas as "fathers of life" sounds appealing, this hypothesis breaks down at the phonological differences between the first consonants in *qatsi* and *katsina*. A word *katsinna* 'kachina father' does exist. However, it refers to the human godfather of someone who is initiated into the Kachina cult. That word is a compound of *katsin-* and *-na*. In this regard it may be interesting to note, that only genuine Hopi words allow a velar *q*-sound to precede the vowel *a*. Foreign words such as Spanish loans (e.g., *kaneelo* 'sheep', *kareeta* 'wagon') or names borrowed from other Southwestern Indian tongues (e.g., the Tewa name, Kawikoli, the supposedly Acoma name, Kahayle) precede the *a* with a palatal *k*. This linguistic fact may be an indication that the Hopi kachina cult is not indigenous. It may have been derived from a foreign religious context.

Kachina is a term that embraces a number of distinct concepts. It applies first of all to the costumed impersonator who, by donning a mask, becomes Kachina—that is, the essence of the associated spirit. He is imbued with the powers which are peculiar to the kachina whom he embodies. He can draw on these powers, for the harmony of the world and for the good of humankind

203

generally, and for rain on Hopi fields, sufficient crops and fertility in particular.

The transcendent beings who are impersonated are also Kachina. They represent with their multitude a cross section of reality as it now is, or formerly has been, encountered by the Hopi. They encompass flora and fauna, the world of objects and of cosmic forces, and they contain the essences of deceased individuals or of entire neighboring tribes. Membership in this body of spirits is not permanent, however. The kachina pantheon is in constant flux, just as life and the land itself. Old faces keep disappearing, and new ones join the ranks of those who happen to still be around.

The kachinas, impersonated by Hopi men in open air plaza performances or in underground ceremonial kiva chambers, are believed to be present in the Hopi villages from December through July, from the time when the Qööqöqlöm open the season till the Niman ceremony when they return again to their otherworldly homes. While the dance masks are held sacred, the kachinas themselves are not worshipped. They are considered to be personal friends who intercede on behalf of the Hopi and who assure the essential blessings for a prosperous existence.

KIVA is a Hopi term for an architectural structure that can easily be regarded as a focal point for Hopi culture, both esoterically and exoterically. Wholly or partially built into the ground, it is easily recognized by the poles of the entrance ladder which project from the hatchway on the flat rooftop. The kiva complex may be seen as representing the four worlds of the Hopi. From the fourth world, which is the present surface world, one first descends to an elevated kiva section (*tuuwimoq*) which during the night-dances is reserved for women and for uninitiated children. A step below this raised area extends the floor of the kiva chamber proper. Built into this floor is usually the *sipaapuni*, a small hole that symbolizes an entrance from the underworld. The kiva, as a whole, is a masonry womb and so constitutes for the Hopi a

204

constant reminder not only of their emergence and birth from the earth but also of their eventual return to the realm of earth after death.

Although now primarily reserved for ceremonial purposes, the kiva formerly served the additional function of a privileged clubhouse for initiated men and boys. The fact that in many Hopi stories and legends the hero or the antagonist lives in a kiva may be a hint that the stories still preserve some recollection of the ancient Pueblo mode of living in semisubterranean pithouses. When houses were finally constructed completely above ground, the pithouse with its halo of tradition was never entirely abandoned. It took on the function of a ceremonial chamber underground.

KOOYEMSI is the Hopi version of a popular kachina who was introduced from Zuni. He can readily be identified by his reddish-brown sack mask, to which several elongated and knoblike protuberances are attached, by his black kilt, and by the special rattle and the feather which he carries. Although his English name is 'Mudhead', a hematite mineral paint (*suta*) is ordinarily used for coloring the mask. Clay or mud, however, is applied as body paint. Kooyemsi is no longer the full-time clown he is often portrayed to be. He may act funny, for instance when he dares the Tseeveyo ogre to whip him, but many of his responsibilities are of a more serious nature. So for instance, when he appears alone, he accompanies the songs of dancing kachinas with his gigantic drum (*pusukinta*). He can also blend with the personalities of other kachinas. This is reflected in such hybrid names as *Koyemoshote, Koyemos'angaktsina* or *Koyemos'aya* in which characteristics of such different kachinas as Hoote, Angaktsina, and Aykatsina are merged with those of the Kooyemsi. During the weeks after the Powamuy ceremony, it is usually a pair of these kachinas (*Kooyemsit*) which, by going from kiva to kiva, announces the beginning of the night-dances. When they appear as a group, *Kooyemsim* or *Kookoyemsim* may, as a chorus, accompany certain fast dancing kachinas (*tawvong-yay'yungwa*); or they may provide their own show, such as the *Koyemsihoya* puppet drama (literally 'Little Kooyemsi'). At other times, during the night-dances or on a summer evening, some Mudheads may challenge the girls and womenfolk of the village to a guessing game (*nanavö'ya*). When active as clowns, they were usually referred to as *Koyemostsutskut*.

KWIKWILYAQA (literally 'Striped Nose') is one of the many kachinas who is never seen in a line dance. While his Hopi name refers to the prominent tubular nose with black and white rings, the Anglo term 'Imitator' alludes to his clownish behavior. He distinguishes himself by his relentless mimicry of every gesture of the victim he chooses and confronts. Kwikwilyaqa depends therefore on interaction with other personages, such as with the unmasked *tsutskut* 'clowns' or the masked *piptuqam* 'caricaturing buffoons' who entertain audiences during intervals at kachina dances. In addition to the nose, the case mask of Kwikwilyaqa features a pair of striped stick eyes, together with horizontal bunches of juniper bark to crown his head. Further characteristic attributes are a rattle and a cane. The rest of the costume is not specified.

KWINGYAW, whom Hasookata addresses at the moment of his dying, is thought of by the Hopi as a person who lives way up in the north where it is forever cold. As *Kwingyawmongwi* (literally 'Chief of Cold') he is the god responsible for freezing weather, chilling north winds, and blinding snowstorms.

MAASAW is one of the most complex and multifaceted personages in the Hopi pantheon. Tyler's study of the god in his *Pueblo Gods and Myths* gives a good account of the various roles that have been attributed to this god.

From the time he was first encountered by ancestors of the Hopi when they emerged from the underworld, he has been regarded as the original owner and keeper of this world. He is known as a god of fire and death, has been seen as a fertility spirit, and has been called Lord of *Maski*—of the underworld. He has been characterized in various stories and legends as both a handsome and a terrifying, ugly man. He has functioned as god of boundaries, of property, and of travelers.

More recently, in the aftermath of the collision between Hopi culture and white Anglo culture, the image of the god has undergone some radical changes. He is thought of today as the Great Spirit that will save and defend Hopi ways. He is expected to come and purify this world by destroying all its wickedness, and he will lead the way into a new fifth world in which only the true Hopi life pattern will prevail. The god thus has acquired the makings of a transcendent divinity, and he is firmly established as an omniscient and omnipresent supreme deity.

Most Hopi, when consulted about Maasaw's significance for them today, will admit that he is the great guardian who watches over their lives and destines their fate. They know that they themselves are only visitors on an earth which belongs to this god, and that one day he will claim again this land as his own. He was the first on this earth, and he will be the last after everybody else is gone. Thus Maasaw stands at the beginning and end of Hopi life.

MIXED HUNT is known as *neyangmakiwa* in Hopi. In contrast to the average communal rabbit hunt in which only men and boys participate, on this occasion unmarried girls accompany the hunters. The girls usually obtain the rabbits by either racing for them or by snatching them away from the boys. In return they pay the hunters back with special gifts of Hopi food. As may be expected, such a combined hunting outing provides ample opportunity for good-humored amusement and courtship.

ORAIBI is a Third Mesa village, approximately fifty miles north of the Little Colorado River in northeastern Arizona. Its proper Hopi form is *Orayvi*. To distinguish it from New Oraibi (*Kiqöts-*

movi), one of the satellite villages founded after the political schism of Oraibi in 1906, it is frequently labelled Old Oraibi today. Still a flourishing town around the turn of the century, with close to a thousand inhabitants, its disintegration since that tragic split has been continuous. While Hotevilla (*Hotvela*), another offshoot from the mother village of Oraibi, has become a stronghold of Hopi ceremonialism, Old Oraibi is nearly in ruins. While it is not as ancient as the Second Mesa village Shongopovi (*Songoopavi*), Old Oraibi vies with Acoma for the honor of being the oldest, continuously inhabited settlement in the United States.

PIK'AMI is a Hopi dish that involves a great deal of preparatory work. Finely ground cornmeal is mixed with boiling water and wheat sprouts (*ngaakuyvani*). A sweetener may also be stirred into the mixture. The thick batter is then poured into a jar and baked all night on hot embers in a special *pik'ami* ground pit. The vessel is sealed off with corn husks, the pit closed off with a layer of sand and clay. This explains the name of the dish, 'buried piki'.

A second fire is started on top of the oven and given sufficient fuel to burn all night. The paste-like pudding is ready to eat the following morning after it has been taken out of the pit.

PIKI, (properly pronounced *piiki*) once an almost daily item of the regular Hopi diet, is nowadays very much reserved for special festivities, such as weddings or ceremonial events. Like all foods from a different culture, translation attempts like 'waferbread' or 'paper-thin bread' will never do complete justice to this particular food.

The recipe for making piki requires first the mixing of finely ground cornmeal with boiling water. Ashes of saltbush (*suwvi*) have been left soaking in the water, so that not only the desired blue tinge is imparted, but also, as modern nutritional research has demonstrated, a number of vital food supplements, such as calcium, magnesium, manganese, iron, and zinc are added to ordinary cornmeal. A film of thin batter is then applied with the bare hand to the surface of the heated piki-stone, which is instantly baked to a crisp sheet that can be peeled off and stored on a tray. According to whether these sheets are rolled or folded the Hopi speak of rolled (*muupi*) or folded (*nömömvu*) piki.

PÖQANGWHOYA and PALÖNGAWHOYA are little demigod brothers that live at Pöqangwwawarpi, north of the old village of Oraibi. While they are often identified in literature as Little War Twins or Young Warrior Gods, the Hopi do not consider them twins but only brothers. Nor do their names imply anything about war. While the nominal *pööqangw* is used today in reference to a person who has great power and is capable of doing most anything, the verbal *paalöngawti* means that an echo occurred.

In referring to the two brothers, the Hopi language makes use of a dual form of either of the brother's names, thus *Pöqangwhoyat* or *Palöngawhoyat*. Since they are the grandchildren of the all-powerful Spider Woman, and since they live with her, linguistic reference is frequently made to the entire trio. This is done by pluralizing either *Pööqangw* or *Pöqangwhoya*, thus *Pöövöqangwt* or *Pöqangwhooyam*.

The mythological image of the two brothers comprises a wide spectrum of epithets which brands them as mischievous, ill-behaved pranksters and tricksters on the one hand, and gives them credit as culture heroes and helpful supernatural beings on the other. Courlander has adequately characterized this almost irreconcilable antithesis by recognizing the brothers as *"enfants terribles"* and at the same time also as "benefactors." Their actions range from playful teasing to dealing death.

The two brothers always go about together and devote most of their spare time to the old Hopi game of shinny. Their addiction to this game is so great, that in many tales their passion for it takes on hilarious if not ridiculous proportions.

Today the brothers carry out the difficult task of keeping the gigantic water serpent in check. Any let-up of their hold will result in convulsions, with which the animal will cause floods and earthquakes that could destroy this planet.

SHINNY is a Hopi stickball game. It is similar to field hockey and is known as *nahoytatatsya* among the Hopi. Once a seasonal game, it was played after the important Powamuy ceremony during the month of Powamuya (approximately February). It is extinct today. As a reminder of its former existence, uninitiated boys of Third Mesa villages still receive the straight or slightly curved ballstick (*tatsimrukho*) as a gift from the kachinas during the Bean Dance rite.

The stick is decorated with wide bands of encircling color and has attached to its end a ball (*tatsi*), which long ago was made of deerskin and stuffed with wool, but which nowadays has given way to painted cloth or canvas.

Goal areas (*tatsit kii'at*, literally 'the ball's house') were built in the fashion of little stone enclosures. The ball was then buried in the center of the playing field and two players representing the opposing teams tried to uncover the ball by vigorously striking into the sand with their clubs. Once the ball was dug out the hockey game was on, with each side intent on driving the ball into the opponent's goal. After a score the ball was buried again and the action would start all over.

SIKYAQÖQLÖ is the name of a Hopi kachina who makes his appearance during the Powamuy ceremony, in February. His case mask is painted yellow, a fact indicated in his name, 'Yellow Qöqlö'. Except for the spectacular event of Patsavu during which all new Wuwtsim initiates participate in the guise of Sikyaqöqlö, this kachina comes in pairs only. A characteristic feature of the two Sikyaqöqlö is that they talk incessantly. In this way they markedly differ from the Qööqöqlö kachinas who come during Soyalangw, the winter solstice ceremony late in December. The latter come in large groups and their masks are normally painted black. They never talk but combine instead their ritual function of opening the kivas with clownish antics that involve a great deal of gesturing, ridicule, and mimicry.

SOMIVIKI is a Hopi food for special occasions. A dough is first prepared by mixing blue cornmeal, boiling water, and sprouted wheat (*ngaakuyvani*) as a sweetener. As in the recipe for piki, ashes from the saltbush (*suwvi*) are added. These not only intensify the desired blue color but also make the dish more nourishing. The pliable dough is wrapped into corn husks, which are then tied up in two places with the string of narrow-leafed yucca. Before serving, the finished *somiviki* packet (literally 'tied piki') is cooked in boiling water.

SO'YOKO is a kachina who belongs to the pack of the terrifying *Sooso'yokt*. Besides the male monster, So'yoko or *So'yoktaqa*, these include his female counterpart *So'yokwuuti*, the girl *So'yokmana*, as well as their uncle *Sooso'yoktuy taaha'am*. So'yoko participates in an elaborately staged ogre drama with disciplinary actions toward the village children. He is a monstrous cannibal creature who threatens not only by means of his costume paraphernalia (black ogre mask, teeth-studded snout, dangling red tongue, bulging eyes, dishevelled skeins of hair, breechcloth, blood-stained knife, and huge burden basket), but also by way of ferocious utterances and wild and sudden gestures. He still appears in First and Second Mesa villages annually during the Bean Dance season in February.

SOSOTUKWPI is a guessing game that is no longer played among the Hopi. The fact that it frequently figures in Hopi tales attests to its former popularity.

Older Hopi still recall that the game on many occasions lasted all through the night and did not end before early dawn. Fewkes reports that during the month of Paamuya (approximately January) in 1900, it was played almost constantly, both in and out of the kivas. In one Hopi legend the inhabitants of the ancient village of Pivanhonkyapi become so addicted to the game that social chaos engulfs the community. When even the wife of the *kikmongwi* or village chief gets carried away with the gambling passion, her husband arranges for the destruction of the village through fire as a means of purification of the dissolute community.

Sosotukwpi is usually played in the kiva. The two teams which contest with each other normally represented age and/or sex divisions, but the number of participants was not limited. Prominent objects of the game are four wooden cups carved out of cottonwood (*paksivu*). With the guessing side covering up their heads, the challenging party hides a small object under one of the hollow cups. The challengers then begin their songs, accompanied by the beat of a drum, and a guesser knocks over the cup under which he suspects the hidden object.

An intricate scoring system keeps track of the number of attempts needed to uncover the object. If the guessing team succeeds in uncovering the object at the first attempt, the other side has to give up the cups, and the game resumes with the roles reversed.

SPIDER WOMAN (*Kookyangwwuuti*) or Spider Grandmother Woman (*Kookyangwso'wuuti*) is one of the familiar household gods of the Hopi. Her divine powers, her unlimited wisdom and all-encompassing knowledge have made her a culture heroine of Hopi tradition. She has prophetic access to the future and is familiar with all the languages of the world. Being a common spider she is ever-present and ever-ready to intervene, assist, counsel, guide, and save. While her commitment to the protection and welfare of people in need makes her a tutelary deity, her association with the earth in which she lives gives her the makings of an earth goddess.

The attractive image of this composite Spider Woman personage receives an additional dimension in her grandmotherly affections—in qualities which she exhibits not only to her two grandchildren, Pöqangwhoya and Palöngawhoya, but also to her Hopi protégés.

TIIKUYWUUTI figures as an ugly, terrifying, and powerful spirit-being in Hopi mythology. Her name, 'Child-protruding-woman', is explained in a migration legend where she is left behind by the traveling party because she is about to give birth. When someone returns to her, he finds her not only surrounded by a multitude of newly born game animals but about to bring forth another such young one. The Hopi verb *tiikuyta* 'a child is appearing, sticking out' refers to this parturient event.

Tiikuywuuti is thus the mother and owner of all the wild game animals. She is said to be grinding corn at night and is supposed to be related to Maasaw. Men are scared of her horrid appearance. She may grab a man, choke him, and cause him to have a nightmare.

Hunters make prayer sticks for her, and it is a Hopi belief that, if she copulates with a man, he will become a successful hunter who will always get his game.

TOTOLOSPI is a checkerlike board game that is still popular among the Hopi today. While in the olden days the board consisted of a sandstone slab on which alternate lines and dots were engraved, today some sort of wooden board will ordinarily be used. *Totolospi* is essentially a gambling game, played by either two or more participants, in which the gaming piece or animal (*pooko*) is moved in accordance with the number of points gained in the throwing of dice. The split halves of a reed (*paaqavi*) are used as dice. Depending on whether both hollow or round sides of the split cane dice turn up, the player moves five or ten marks. With one stick's convex side up and the other's concave side down, the player loses his turn. In case one player's piece reaches a space which is occupied by another, the one who was there first must move back to the center of the board and start all over again.

TSORWUKIQLÖ is a name which identifies the giver of the name as a member of the Bluebird Clan. Voth, who in his *Traditions of the Hopi* (pp. 159-167) has recorded a variant of the story of Tsorwukiqlö as it is presented in this collection, gives the name's meaning as "bunch of long bluebird wing feathers." Linguistically, *tsor-* is the compound form of *tsooro* 'bluebird'. The element *-wuki* also exists in the word *kwaawuki* 'eagle wing feather'. The suffix *-qlö,* a contracted version of *-qölö,* implies 'collectivity' or 'a mass of identical objects scattered over a given area'.

WITCH. *Powaqa* is the Hopi form for a concept that can be rendered by the approximate English equivalents of 'witch', 'sorcerer', and 'wizard'. *Powaqa* is an asexual term and can be applied to any person, regardless of age or sex.

The particular Hopi point of view of a sorcerer is one who is endowed with great powers which he derives from the heart of the tutelary animal with which he became associated during his initiation into the ranks of black magicians. Such a person is, therefore, regarded as *lööq unangway'taqa,* one who possesses two hearts, one human and one animal.

The belief that witchcraft can be brought to bear as a force on an individual or even on natural phenomena, such as weather or crops, is deeply rooted in Hopi society. It must be recognized as an important part of Hopi culture. Nevertheless, it is only among his own relatives that a witch or sorcerer can exert his evil influence to the point that it will have fatal consequences.

The fear of witchcraft is widespread and is reflected in the many didactic don'ts that allude to it. So for example, one is not supposed to sleep in someone else's house, because an evil-minded person might take advantage of his unconscious state and recruit him into the ranks of sorcerers. By the same token, one does not leave one's children sleeping unattended. If one has no other choice but to leave them alone, then at least a Hopi broom, placed next to them, will have to substitute for the mother and watch over them.

Two-hearted malefactors have always been part of the Hopi life pattern. Their evil influence and antisocial behavior plagued the Hopi back in the days when they were still living in the underworld. They caused disease, dissension, and death among them. The emergence into the present world actually was a desperate attempt to escape these destructive powers once and for all. This objective was thwarted, however, because one of the sorcerers succeeded with the others in finding his way into this world.

It is this obsession and constant dread of black magic which may account for the fact that many Hopi tales deal with witchcraft motifs. The sense of helplessness which a Hopi experiences in real life when confronted with acts of sorcery may be relieved by the punishment and holocaustic revenge which is usually dealt to sorcerers and witches in the folklore through the intercession of some supernatural being.

Bibliography

Albert, Roy, Tom Mootzska and Charlie Talawepi
 1968 *Coyote Tales.* Eighteen bilingual booklet sets. Flagstaff: Northern Arizona Supplementary Education Center.

Balentine, Bernice
 1956 "Stories from Hopi Land." Master's thesis. Flagstaff: Arizona State College.

Bascom, William R.
 1954 "Four Functions of Folklore." *Journal of American Folklore* 67:333-349.

Beaglehole, Ernest
 1936 *Hopi Hunting and Hunting Ritual.* Yale University Publications in Anthropology, no. 4, pp. 3-26.
 1937 *Notes on Hopi Economic Life.* Yale University Publications in Anthropology, no. 15, pp. 1-88.

Brody, J.J.
 1977 *Mimbres Painted Pottery.* Santa Fe: School of American Research (Southwest Indian Arts series).

Colton, Harold S.
 1959 *Hopi Kachina Dolls with a Key to Their Identification.* rev. ed., Albuquerque: University of New Mexico Press.

Colton, Harold S. and Edmund Nequatewa
 1932 "The Ladder Dance. Two Traditions of an Extinct Hopi Ceremonial." *Museum of Northern Arizona Notes,* no. 2, pp. 5-12.

Cosgrove, H.S. and C.B. Cosgrove
 1932 *The Swarts Ruin: A Typical Mimbres Site in South-western New Mexico.* Papers of the Peabody Museum of American Archaeology and Ethnology 15, no. 1.

Courlander, Harold
 1970 *People of the Short Blue Corn. Tales and Legends of the Hopi Indians.* New York: Harcourt Brace Jovanovich, Inc.
 1972 *The Fourth World of the Hopis.* Greenwich, Conn.: Fawcett Publications, Inc.

Culin, Stewart
 1907 "Games of the North American Indians." *Annual Report Bureau of American Ethnology* 24.

Curtis, Edward S.
 1922 *The Hopi.* Vol. 12 of *The North American Indian,* reprint New York and London: Johnson Reprint Corporation, 1970.

Cushing, Frank Hamilton
 1923 "Origin Myth from Oraibi." *Journal of American Folklore* 36:163-170.

Davis, Lawrence
 1972 "Three Hopi Tales." *Arizona Friends of Folklore* 2(2):23-31.

De Huff, Elizabeth W.
 1931 "The Witch." *El Palacio* 31:37-39.

Douglass, Don
 1972 *Hopi Legends.* Prescott, Az.: ATR Enterprises.

Dundes, Alan
 1965 *The Study of Folklore.* New York: Prentice-Hall.

211

Earle, Edwin and Edward A. Kennard
    1938   *Hopi Kachinas.* New York: J.J. Augustin.

Fewkes, Jesse Walter
    1895   "Archeological Expedition to Arizona in 1895." *Annual Report Bureau of American Ethnology* 17:519-741.
    1895   "The Destruction of the Tusayan Monsters." *Journal of American Folklore* 8:132-137.
    1903   "Hopi Kachinas Drawn by Native Artists." *Annual Report Bureau of American Ethnology* 21:3-126.
    1914   *Archeology of the Lower Mimbres Valley, New Mexico.* Smithsonian Miscellaneous Collections 63, no. 10.
    1916   "Animal Figures on Pottery of Mimbres." *American Anthropologist* 18: 535-545.
    1919   "Designs on Prehistoric Hopi Pottery." *Annual Report Bureau of American Ethnology* 33:207-284.
    1923   *Designs on Prehistoric Pottery from the Mimbres Valley, New Mexico.* Smithsonian Miscellaneous Collections 74, no. 6.
    1924   *Additional Designs on Prehistoric Mimbres Pottery.* Smithsonian Miscellaneous Collections 76, no. 8.

Gladwin, Harold St.
    1957   *A History of the Ancient Southwest.* Portland, Me.: Bond Wheelwright Co.

Hibben, Frank C.
    1975   *Kiva Art of the Anasazi.* Las Vegas: KC Publications.

James, Harry C.
    1940   *Haliksai! A Book of Hopi Legends of the Grand Canyon Country.* El Centro, Ca.: The Desert Magazine.

Kennard, Edward and Albert Yava
    1944   *Field Mouse Goes to War (Tusan Homichi Tuwvöta).* Washington: Education Division, Bureau of Indian Affairs.

Kidder, Alfred V.
    1962   *An Introduction to the Study of Southwestern Archaeology.* New Haven: Yale University Press.

Lockett, Hattie G.
    1933   *The Unwritten Literature of the Hopi.* University of Arizona Bulletin 4, no. 4. Social Science Bulletin no. 2.

Malotki, Ekkehart
    in   *Hopi-Raum. Eine sprachwissenschaftliche Analyse*
    press *der Raumvorstellungen in der Hopi-Sprache.* [A Linguistic Analysis of the Spatial Concepts in the Hopi Language.] Tübingen: TBL Verlag Gunter Narr.

Nequatewa, Edmund
    1932   "Yaponcha, the Wind God." *Plateau* 5(4):18-19.
    1932   The Kana-a Kachina of Sunset Crater." *Plateau* 5(4):19-23.
    1936   *Truth of a Hopi. Stories Relating to the Origin, Myths and Clan Histories of the Hopi.* Museum of Northern Arizona Bulletin 8. Flagstaff.
    1948   "Chaveyo: The First Kachina." *Plateau* 20(4):60-62.
    1955   "The Destruction of Elden Pueblo. A Hopi Story." *Plateau* 28(2):37-44.

Smith, Watson
    1952   *Kiva Mural Decorations at Awatovi and Kawaikaa.*

Papers of the Peabody Museum of American Archaeology and Ethnology 37.

1971 *Painted Ceramics of the Western Mound at Awatovi.* Papers of the Peabody Museum of American Archaeology and Ethnology 38, Awatovi Expedition, Report no. 8.

Snodgrass, O.T.
1977 *Realistic Art and Times of the Mimbres Indians.* El Paso: Privately printed.

Stephen, Alexander M.
1888 "Legend of the Snake Order of the Moquis, as Told by Outsiders." *Journal of American Folklore* 1:109-114.
1929 "Hopi Tales." Edited by Elsie Clews Parsons. *Journal of American Folklore* 42:1-72.
1936 *Hopi Journal.* Edited by Elsie Clews Parsons. Columbia University Contributions to Anthropology 23.

Titiev, Mischa
1939 "The Story of Kokopele." *American Anthropologist* 41(1):91-94.
1943 "Notes on Hopi Witchcraft." *Papers of the Michigan Academy of Science, Arts and Letters* 28:549-557.
1944 "Two Hopi Tales from Oraibi." *Michigan Academy of Science, Arts, and Letters* 29:425-437.
1944 *Old Oraibi.* Peabody Museum Papers 22, no. 1.
1948 "Two Hopi Myths and Rites." *Journal of American Folklore* 61:31-43.
1956 "Shamans, Witches, and Chiefs among the Hopi." *Tomorrow* 4(3):51-56.
1972 *The Hopi Indians of Old Oraibi.* Ann Arbor: The University of Michigan Press.

Tyler, Hamilton A.
1964 *Pueblo Gods and Myths.* Norman: University of Oklahoma Press.

Voth, Henry R.
1905 *The Traditions of the Hopi.* Field Columbian Museum, no. 96, Anthropological Series 8.
1912 "Four Hopi Tales." In: Brief Hopi Miscellaneous Papers. Field Columbian Museum, no. 157, Anthropological Series, 11(2):138-143.

Wallis, Wilson D.
1936 "Folk Tales from Shumopovi, Second Mesa." *Journal of American Folklore* 49:1-68.

Waterman, Richard A.
1949 "The Role of Obscenity in the Folk Tales of the 'Intellectual' Stratum of our Society." *Journal of American Folklore* 62:162-165.

Wright, Barton
1973 *Kachinas: A Hopi Artist's Documentary.* Flagstaff: Northland Press.
1977 *The Complete Guide to Collecting Kachina Dolls.* Flagstaff: Northland Press.

Wright, Beverly
1973 "Navajo and Hopi Tales." *Arizona Friends of Folklore* 3(3):23-38.

Paper: Wausau laid text; Teton laid cover
Composition: Baskerville by Lufa-type, Flagstaff, Arizona
    Centaur Display handset by McKenzie & Harris, San Francisco, California
Lithography: Classic Printers, Prescott, Arizona
Design: Sandra Mahan
Production: Rick Stetter, G.D. McClellan, Earl Hatfield
Editorial: Steve Gustafson, Rita Arnold